Francis Park

THE
ENEMY
OF EUROPE

1981
Liberty Bell Publications

Translated by

THOMAS FRANCIS

*from the German translation of Yockey's
lost original.*

First Paperback Printing
November 1981
Reprinted with corrections
November 1985
Republished
August 2003

ISBN 0-942094-00-2

Copyright © 1981

by Thomas Francis

Liberty Bell Publications
P.O. Box 890
York,SC 29745
libertybellpublications.com

Printed in the United States of America

TO THE MEMORY OF
THE FOUNDER OF THE FRANCIS PARKER YOCKEY
SOCIETY

LOUIS T. BYERS

AN ARYAN OF THE ARYANS
WHO ALSO FOUGHT A GOOD FIGHT TO ITS TRAGIC
END
22 OCTOBER 1981

Hitherto unpublished photograph taken at about the time he finished
IMPERIUM in 1948 and began work on its sequel,
The Enemy of Europe

FRANCIS PARKER YOCKEY

Francis Parker Yockey (1917-1960) on his way to the prison in which he would be found dead, reportedly a suicide.

CONTENTS

These thoughts were intended to form part of my book IMPERIUM, but for personal reasons that was not possible. They owe their present incarnation to the fact that many of those to whom that work was really addressed were unable to draw offhand the necessary conclusions. In this treatise, as in IMPERIUM, there is nothing personal, and thus, here as there, I refrain from entering the debate over political *tactics*. Such matters are better discussed orally.

Organic Laws constitute the vernacular of Politics. With IMPERIUM, my aim was to present those laws so that everybody who somehow identified his personal destiny, as it were, with the Destiny of Europe could draw his own conclusions from the basic principles and select his own tactics. Some people misunderstood this possibility to such an extent that they regarded the presentation of these Organic Laws as just another contribution to the usual politico-theoretical discussion. Therefore the Organic Laws are more fully elaborated here in that they are applied to the world situation of the moment, to help provide the worthiest minds with a clearer insight into it and to unmask the Enemy of Europe.

Politics, History, Life, Destiny heed no system. Yet if Europeans would take an active part in the world power-struggle, now, more than ever before, they must put their politics on an intellectual basis, for no physical force whatever is available to them. They must outwit the enemy at every turn, outplay him, until, years later, they will eventually be in a position to dictate conditions and compel fulfilment of them. The Organic Laws are presented here in the form of an intellectual exercise from which may be evolved a method of evaluating events, possibilities, decisions. A grammar that proves inadequate can be revised, but every branch of thought advances only when it has a grammar at its disposal.

This treatise was written from beginning to end in the year 1948. Only two passages, on Japan and on Russia, have undergone revision. The latter of the two, as can be readily perceived, was modified when in the past year, 1952, Russia gave its politics a new orientation. Both passages contain not a word that IMPERIUM, composed in 1947, does not also contain. Each day it is reconfirmed that Japan emerged from the Second World War victorious, as was noted in IMPERIUM. Russia's break with Jewry marks the beginning of the end of Bolshevism. It is called forth by the true, religious Russia, which abhors politics and technics, and which has been dominated by Petrinism and Moscovite Bolshevism alike. Of course, this break was only a beginning, but the final, inner collapse of Bolshevism is unavoidable. The possibility-indeed, I must say, the inevitability-of the destruction of Bolshevism by the true Russia is posited in IMPERIUM.

The Enemy of Europe is complete in itself, and its thesis in regard to the nature of America is true without qualification. Having lived for several decades in America, I have seen with my own eyes the distorted development of that country since the Revolution of 1933. For the most part, the resistance to the progressive distortion of America is merely passive-the resistance which any material whatever opposes to that which is acting upon it. Where the resistance is active-and the dimensions of such resistance are scanty-it finds little support, since idealism and heroism do not flourish in an atmosphere wherein economics is the ruling spirit.

Europe can attach no hopes to this resistance in America. For practical political purposes, the "White America" which still existed in its strength in the 1920's has today ceased to exist. Whether that submerged spirit will rise again in some remote future is unforeseeable. In any case, Europe cannot allow itself the luxury of dreaming that a revolution in America by the pro-European elements will lead to Europe's Liberation.

Europeans are familiar with America's propaganda for export, but less familiar with its internal propaganda. This propaganda utterly dwarfs, in its scale as well as its effect, anything Europeans can readily imagine. The Washington régime's leading internal thesis-which has not changed since 1933-is that Americans must be "tolerant" of the alien elements (which now number roughly 50% of the population), since, after all, these aliens are "brothers." "Brotherhood" is glorified on all public occasions, by all public officials, is taught in the schools and preached in the churches,

2

which have been coordinated into the master-plan of the Culturally-alien Washington régime. Newspapers, books, magazines, radio, television, films-all vomit forth the same "Brotherhood." The "Brotherhood" propaganda is a ghastly caricature of the Christian idea of the Fatherhood of God and the Brotherhood of Man, but there is no religious intent to the propaganda. Its sole purpose is to destroy whatever exclusiveness, national feelings, or racial instincts may still remain in the American population after twenty years of national leprosy. The result of the "tolerance" and "brotherhood" campaign is that the alien enjoys a superior position in America-he can *demand* to be "tolerated." The American can demand nothing. The tragic fact is that the attenuation of the national instincts has proceeded so far that one cannot envisage how a Nationalist Revolution would be even possible in America.

So long as America was dominated by men of stocks from Culture-European soil, America was a European colony, even though sometimes vocally rebellious. But the America that has been distorted by the Revolution of 1933 is lost to Europe. Let no European dream of help or cooperation from that quarter.

What has occurred in the world since the publication of IMPERIUM, how the inner development of Europe has progressed, makes it clearer than ever that the world-outlook and heroic ethic manifested here are the only thing that yet offers Europe a hope of fulfilling its mighty Destiny.

All wars are in some way related to politics, and the aim of Politics is to obtain power. If a state emerges from a war with less power at its disposal than it had at the beginning of the war, then it has lost the war. Whose troops return from the battlefield and whose troops lie dead on it does not matter: military victory may involve real, *political* victory, or it may not. Incidents outside the military arena can transform a mere military victory into an actual political defeat.

Thus it happened that the chief losers in the First World War were England and Germany. The chief victor was Japan; it won no military victory, of course, for the simple reason that it had not actively participated in the conflict. Russia, directly after its revolutionary transformation, found itself in a position that gave it an enormous increase of power, since Germany and the Austro-Hungarian Empire had been eliminated as European Great Powers. America was a political victor, but, lacking political experience and a leader-stratum, it was completely unable to consolidate its new power-position; hence it had to abandon most of its winnings.

Germany's losses are obvious: loss of twenty percent of its territory, complete loss of its foreign credits and its colonial empire, loss of the greater part of its rolling stock and its mineral wealth, loss of its prestige-it was robbed of everything under the Versailles dictate.

But England had to resign itself to even greater losses. To America it completely lost its influence in the Western Hemisphere and, just as completely, its former supremacy at sea; to Russia it had to surrender its position in Central Asia; to Japan and America its power-position in the Pacific; and to the coloured world-revolution its international prestige. The War undermined the British Empire, and more particularly, it thoroughly undermined the British Raj. Led by revolutionaries like Gandhi, the subject peoples of India began to take matters into their own hands. Soon the White rulers discovered that their voice had lost its authority. They saw themselves forced to negotiate at every moment with the active, awakened, native population, and, both personally and officially, they had to learn to behave with great circumspection. Similar things occurred among the

4

subjugated peoples of Europe's other colonial powers. Everywhere in the Coloured World the White European lost power and prestige. In this manner, not only did the two leading European states, England and Germany, lose the War, but so did the entire Western Culture, although that organism, *in toto*, had not participated militarily in it. Neutral Holland thus suffered a political defeat in the War, proving once again that political defeat does not depend on military defeat.

In the case of France, political and military *victory* coincided. Before the War, France was the weakest of the Great Powers; in the 1920's, it was the master of Europe. Indeed, it felt itself able once more to play the rôle of Napoleon, the opposition vis-à-vis England, and during the transitory political hegemony of France over continental Europe the diplomatic struggle between France and England was the most dynamic on earth.

The temporary supremacy of France during the Interbellum-Period shows the nature of power. *Ultimately, power depends upon inner qualities.* Mere possession of fleets, weapons, and masses of troops cannot provide a safeguard for power. Such things are only *appurtenances* of power, and possession of them is not its *source*. Within the political world, power is constantly in motion. There are strong but shallow currents of power which can temporarily work against the deeper, truer, farther-aiming power-currents. France was, in regard to its military, industrial and natural resources, to all appearances absolutely secure in Europe for the immediate future. In 1923, ignoring England's protests, it undertook a military invasion of Germany. At that time, two German thinkers were discussing the European situation. When the one expressed his opinion that within a decade Germany would again be the centre-of-gravity in European politics, the other, who was a "realist," rudely broke off the conversation. Hermann Keyserling was "realist" enough to recognise "reality"-any banker's apprentice can do that-, but Spengler was thinking of the *source* of power in Europe, of the Destiny of the Western Civilisation.

During the 1930's, French mastery over Europe dwindled away like a morning mist. There was no great crisis at that time, no epochal war. The very fact of the European Revolution of 1933 dissolved French hegemony

5

without a struggle, without a trace of hostilities. France's position was due solely to material factors, to simple control of the apparatus of power. The inner qualities of the régime that had this power at its disposal were not equal to asserting and preserving it. This régime was the bearer of no World-Hypothesis, no Idea, no Ethic. Its dynamism was a crude desire for mastery: it utterly lacked the feeling of a superpersonal Mission, lacked a world-outlook, a European Hypothesis. When it was confronted with the European Revolution of 1933, its power simply evaporated. Bayonets can give one neither a good conscience nor the Inner Imperative to rule. The vassals defected, and France suddenly found itself in the position of a vassal *vis-à-vis* England. The choice of its lord and master was the last formal act testifying to the political existence of France as a nation.

A nation is simply an Idea, not a mass of people, not even the form into which that mass has been shaped. This form is the expression of the Idea, and the Idea is primary. Before the Idea there is no nation; when the Idea has fulfilled itself, the nation has disappeared *for ever*. It matters not whether custom, form, nomenclature, diplomacy, and the material apparatus of power remain to convince yesterday-romantics that the nation survives. The Holy Roman Empire survived as a form until 1806, but as a political fact it had ceased to exist with the decay of the power of the Hohenstaufens after the battle at Legnano in 1176. However, in Politics, *facts*, not claims, not names, nor legalistic fictions are normative. In religious times, in an age of faith, men may again use in the realm of Politics words that have long ceased to describe facts. But in this Age of Absolute Politics, political fictions have lost their charm for stronger minds, no less than their effectiveness.

The death of a nation is a Ponderable, an event that must come to expression, and its *When* can be foreseen with sufficient accuracy to be made the basis of long-range policy. A nation shows that it is dying when it ceases to believe in its Mission and its superiority. It begins to hate everything new and everything that would drive it forward. It looks about, and seeks to make defensive preparations in every direction. No longer does it strive to enlarge, but is content merely to

6

maintain, its power-position. *To preserve power, however, one must continually increase it.* A nation need not die tumultuously in a great military defeat. As a rule, nations die quite peacefully, sinking deeper and deeper into sterile conservatism and shrinking back more and more from great decisions.

THE LIQUIDATION OF ENGLISH SOVEREIGNTY

English policy was senile already at the beginning of Joseph Chamberlain's career in government. Even his grand idea of English-German-American world-hegemony, though still a forceful, virile, aggressive policy, was basically *static*: behind it lay the age-old dream of bringing History finally to a close. After Chamberlain's time, English policy became completely toothless, and names like Grey, Lloyd-George, MacDonald, and Baldwin show the depths of the descent into national oblivion, when compared with names from more youthful days: Walpole, Pitt, Castlereagh, Canning, Gladstone. The great Empire Builders were eager for every large conquest; their dim successors indulged in lamentations over the *status quo*, expending their feeble energies on protecting it from young and virile "aggressors." These pallbearers of the Empire tried to build a wall against History by describing *Politics* in terms of *Law*: The *status quo* is "legal," every change therein, however, is "illegal." Political dynamism is "illegal:" Power-relationships must be continued as they were at the time of the Versailles dictate. After Versailles, England no longer had the national-political energy to increase its power; hence everybody was to be morally prohibited from doing so, and this moral coercion was codified in sacred "treaties," which were signed on the muzzles of cannon. To maintain England's political supremacy was "moral" and "legal"-respect for "international morality and the sanctity of treaties" it was called. "Observing international law," "orderly procedure in international relations," and similar political absurdities were promulgated. This was not the first time that one engaged in politics in order to put politics in legalistic wrappings. The politician who resorts to law and morality to disguise his power-position is suffering from a bad political conscience, and the politician or the state with a bad conscience is decadent. Ascendent politics is not afraid of being politics. Decadent politics passes itself off as religion, law, morality, science-in short, as anything other than Politics.

Of course, England's attempt to impose its form on the world by the simple trick of employing legalistic jargon was completely futile. Only the English population was deceived thereby, just as later with the propaganda about the invulnerability of Singapore. But on the power-currents of the world, which reflect the development of superpersonal organisms, the jargon had no effect whatsoever.

From the original standpoint of regarding the *status quo* as inviolable only insofar as the English power-position was concerned, one went on to that of regarding the *status quo* everywhere as sacrosanct. Thus English policy, in complete distortion of English interests, was made to support the Serbian, Roumanian, and Bohemian states against the power-currents that were destined to destroy those artificial political structures.

The cost of a distorted policy must be set high. The state with a distorted policy can gain no accretion of power; thus even its military and diplomatic victories are defeats. During the third decade of the 20th century, England gradually handed over its sovereignty to America in order to continue pursuing its distorted policy, a policy devoted to the world-wide preservation of the *status quo*. Naturally, such an unpleasant fact was not admitted by the representatives of a certain mentality, and-naturally again-those who bore the responsibility for the transfer of power shied away from defining the new relationship precisely; for had they done so, the whole policy would have been spoilt. Nevertheless, when Baldwin announced in 1936 that he would not deploy the English fleet without consulting America beforehand, he informed the entire political world in unmistakable terms that the end of English independence had come, that English sovereignty had passed over to America. Independence means being able to act alone. Sovereignty means being answerable to nobody except oneself. Neither Independence nor Sovereignty was characteristic of the English government that started the Second World War with its declaration of war on Germany in September, 1939.

When a nation loses its sovereignty, any foreign peoples and territories it controls pass, of organic necessity, into the sphere of influence of powers that are sovereign. Thus Denmark, for example, as a result of the Second World War, was absorbed into the American world-system. This occurred quite automatically; it was simply a process of the Organic law of the

Political Plenum,* which ordains that a power-vacuum in the political world is an impossibility.

A state is not to be regarded as a power unless it can make decisions alone. Units like Switzerland are artificial structures whose *raison d'être* is to serve as buffers for the adjacent powers, and thus owe their existence to the mutual jealousy of those powers. They are anomalies that can exist only so long as their territory has no particular strategic value for the surrounding Great Powers. During the 19th century, Switzerland was exactly the opposite of a power-vacuum. It was the point-of-convergence for the powers surrounding it and was likewise penetrated by the power-currents surrounding them. The statecraft of the Swiss "politician" consisted in abstaining from all politics and in dodging all decisions. As soon as Switzerland ceased, in 1945, to be the convergence-point for the bordering powers, that very moment it became an American vassalage, without hopes, wishes, fears, or even official recognition of its status. Throughout the 19th century, the Netherlands was only an English bridgehead on the continent, first against France (until about 1865), then against Prussia-Germany. The Netherlands had no sovereignty, and its military forces stood at England's disposal, very tactless though it would have been to speak about this in England or its protectorate.

The simple, terrifying truth is that, through the diplomacy of its leaders, beginning with Lloyd George, England lost its independence, parted with its established mode of political conduct, and passed into the same vassal-like relation *vis-à-vis* America into which, say, Holland or Norway had passed *vis-à-vis* England in the 19th century. It is utterly pointless to connect the national demise of England with the complete fecklessness of parliamentary government in the Age of Absolute Politics, to attempt to construct a causal relationship out of it. For nations have a certain time-span before them, and their political phase also has an organically predetermined rhythmic course. Material factors have nothing to do with the greater movements of the

*Cf. IMPERIUM, p. 190 ff.

power-currents within the political world. The merely ephemeral supremacy of France in the 1920's, based solely upon material factors, is the best example of this in recent times.

ORIGINS OF THE WAR

To understand the origins and the morphology of the Second World War, it is necessary to grasp the fact that England passed into the American sphere of influence not *after*, but *before*, the War. In 1942, a member of Parliament stated that it appeared to him as though England had the choice of becoming an eastern outpost of America or a Western outpost of Germany. His statement did not cover all the possibilities, and was imprecise, but it was at least based on the political fact that England's independence and sovereignty had ceased to exist.

English independence began to dwindle away from the moment in History when English policy sought to *preserve* rather than to *enlarge* the overseas Empire. Inwardly, this point was reached when England's Conservatism, which had formerly meant respect for the Past, shifted to hostility towards the Future. The establishment of American hegemony over the Island could be proved by citing documents, diplomatic agreements, overseas telephone conversations, and the like. But such things, indispensable as they are to the historian, the journalist, and the armchair politician, are all quite unimportant from a larger point of view. For the great, indisputable facts of politics themselves show sufficiently the underlying power-currents. *Neither power nor its movements can be concealed.* What are those facts?

The aim of Politics is to obtain power. As we have seen, an elderly organism aims expressly at maintaining the present circumference of its power, although the precondition for maintaining power is the acquisition of more power. From the actual nature of Politics (and accordingly one could also say, from the nature of superpersonal organisms and the human beings in their service), it is evident that a political unit must not recklessly enter upon a war that cannot increase its power. To the entire world it was obvious that England could not have increased its power through a war against Germany.

A war that a political unit is not capable of pushing through to victory on its own cannot increase the power of that unit. The term "political unit" is used here in the strict sense, of course, and means a unit that possesses true sovereignty and thus has the ability to decide on

12

its own initiative the War-Peace question; therefore this term cannot be applied to areas like Brazil and Canada. If allies are *indispensable*-not merely practicable and useful-for bringing the war to a victorious conclusion, then these allies will be the real power-beneficiaries of a successful war. The term "allies" describes only other, real political, units which can make the War-Peace decision on their own initiative; and here, too, areas like Colombia and South Africa are excluded. Obviously, not even with the remnants of its Empire and with its dependencies, France and Poland, could England have defeated Germany. It must be assumed that what was known to the entire world was also known to official circles in London. Nevertheless, in September, 1939, England began a war against Germany.

After the American declaration of war in December, 1941, it was officially admitted in England that the primary goal of pre-war English diplomacy had consisted in winning American military aid. What was not admitted, but was just as notoriously certain at the time, was that England's war-declaration had been made, first, with complete and unlimited confidence in America's assistance in every form; second, to carry out a policy that had been set in Washington and that in no way meant the continuance of English national policy.

It does not matter who begot the miscarriage called "collective security"-a mixture of legalism, naïveté, stupidity, envy, and senility. The fact is certain that only two powers in the world benefited from this policy: Russia and America. The government in London did not willingly favour Russia, but it worked, with full awareness of what it was doing, under pressure from the Washington régime, exactly according to its instructions.

The salient point here is that this fact, although satisfactorily proved by war memoirs, confessions, documents, and such, is manifest in the great decisions themselves. By way of example: If a power enters a war that it cannot win militarily, and that would not cause any power to accrue to it even if it did win a military victory, it requires no searching through history books to know that "power" is not acting in its own interests. In other words, *it is a protectorate.* From the standpoint of the Washington régime, the remnants of the English

State were useful as a means of entangling America in a war against Germany, according to the 1916 formula, and the English Island was valuable as an "unsinkable aircraft carrier" - in the words of the American General Staff- likewise as a conduit for men and matériel.

In these events, the relationship of England to America did not differ essentially from that of, say, Poland or Serbia. The Washington régime had England just as much at its disposal as it did Poland and Serbia. Only the strong power in a coalition can be said to *have* allies; the others merely *are* allies. In 1948, the post-War French government officially appealed to America as the "ally of France." This appeal requires no explanation. History consists of the ridiculous as well as the sublime.

A state that *needs* allies can never obtain them; it can become the ally of another, more powerful state, and fight for the increase of that power, but the state that needs to ally is the subordinate one. An alliance is never the sentimental grouping of a club, dripping with friendship, that the journalists are wont to make it out to be. On the contrary, every alliance has as its basis Protection and Obedience.* Taken strictly, Washington and Moscow had no alliance during the Second World War, since the relationship showed obedience, to be sure, on the part of the Washington régime without protection (which is a corollary of authority) on the part of Russia. In a Protection-Obedience relationship, the protectorate is within the sphere of influence of the Protector, and therefore *must* obey it. However, America's self-robbery on behalf of the Russian war-effort was thoroughly voluntary, even though it was in complete opposition to America's national interests.

Two degrees of political stupidity are to be found in diplomacy. The first is short-range: lack of political skill, inability to carry on any negotiations successfully and to recognise short-term advantages. The second is long-range: lack of political far-sightedness, ignorance of deeper power-currents and the Ponderables of the Becoming. These two kinds of political stupidity stand in the same relation to each other as the Military stands to the Political. The Military is the weapon and the servant
*Cf. IMPERIUM, p. 194, ff.

14

of the Political. Only disaster can come of military thought dominating political thought. "Win the War!" can never be an expression of *Politics*, for Politics is concerned with identifying the power-currents, choosing the Enemy, and weighing in relation to the national interest all happenings, inner and outer, according to how the war develops. To elevate the slogan "Win the War!" to the rank of policy, as America did during the Second World War, is the equivalent of saying that there is nothing political about the war. Military thought is simply not political thought. The permanent ambition of all military thought is to win a military victory; the corresponding ambition of all political thought is to win more power. That may or may not be implicit in a policy that seems to desire military victory at whatever cost, for one can probably adduce just as many historical examples of political and military victory occurring separately as of both coinciding neutrally. Likewise, if short-range political thinking constantly prevails over the long-range in the policy decisions of a state, the only possible result is that state's political extinction. No matter how skillfully executed its political manoeuvres, if a state has ignored the larger power-currents in puzzling out its policy, it will suffer a political defeat.

All these explanations and definitions apply only to real political units, for the microscopic destinies of such dwarfish "states" as San Marino, Monaco, and Belgium are completely determined by the Destinies of the true political units, the Great Powers, as the diplomatic concert of the 19th century liked to call them.

The Polish officials of 1939 were politically stupid in the first sense. Their country encircled by two Great Powers that had just concluded a non-aggression pact, they nonetheless chose to enter upon a war that would mean for it direct, permanent political extinction in the least desirable form: occupation and partition. Actually, it is pure charity to call the political dealings of those officials stupidity instead of treason, for shortly after the beginning of the War, they disappeared, going abroad to live on the capital they were able to amass owing to their policy. Treason and political stupidity are closely related to each other. In *The Proclamation of London* it is stated: "Treason is nothing but incapacity when it becomes resolute." As used here, the word "treason" refers to

15

treasonous conduct on the part of *individuals*. An individual may be able to better his personal-economic circumstances through an act of treason, but no group, no class, no organic stratum within a country is ever able to better the power-position of the country through a large-scale act of treason. In this sense, all treason is political stupidity.

The English officials of 1939 were politically stupid in the second sense in that they completely failed to identify the larger power-currents and likewise totally lacked statesmanlike feeling for the Definition of Enemy: *The Enemy is the state that one can defeat and thereby gain more power..* Thus military victory over an opponent whose defeat proves so costly that one must take in the bargain a greater loss of power elsewhere must be called political defeat.

These English officials approached diplomatic preparations for the Second World War according to the old tried and true methods. They attempted to isolate Germany, concluding wherever possible war-alliances with Germany's neighbours (the "Peace Front"). They counted on American aid, trusting in the Washington règime's assurances that it would be able to lead America to war-despite the geopolitical position of America, despite the unanimous opposition of the American people, despite the conflict between intervention and the national interests of America, and finally, despite the fundamental spiritual indifference of Americans towards even a victorious war against Europe.

The question they failed to ask was: *What is the final political aim?* Or in other words: How will England's power be increased through a victorious American war against Germany? Had they asked this question, it would have been obvious to them that, since England could not win this war alone, any extension of power derived from a defeat of Germany would be for the benefit of America, or some other power. The result of their failure to ask this question was England's total defeat.

The suicide-policy of the English régime in 1939- it was continued throughout the War -has various roots, and the ultimate explanation of it will
*Cf. IMPERIUM, p. 137 ff.
16

keep scholars and archivists busy. The essential facts are already well-known. First, political stupidity alone is not to blame: Some members of the government consciously and deliberately pursued a policy that was not pro-English, only anti-German. Second, some members of this régime were not officially part of the government, indeed, not even part of the English organism. Third, and most importantly, with Joseph Chamberlain the rich political tradition of England had been laid to rest. The succeeding statesmen were of lesser calibre; class-warriors, like Lloyd George and MacDonald; pure egotists, capable of representing any alien interest, like Churchill and Eden; even obsessed psychopaths, like Duff Cooper.

Thomas Hardy did well to introduce the Spirit of Irony into his Napoleonic drama, *The Dynasts*, in which the paradoxical and the ironic make up the favourite conversation of Clio. How ridiculous in retrospect now seem the efforts of those officials in London during the period from 1939 to 1941: They sought to drag America into the War! In reality, the War was from beginning to end a creation of the Washington régime. If it ended in victory, victory could mean only an increase in power for that régime, or some other political unit, but in no case for England. The English nation was impressed into the War as a vassal that had been made to believe it was acting independently, and it emerged from the War with every characteristic of a colony. Only the definitive, legalistic formulation was wanting. Those at the head of the London régime who were honest, if also stupid, schemed to use America for their purposes. And precisely because of their scheming, they were used to forward the ambitions of the Washington régime

STRONGER POWER-CURRENTS
IN THE AGE OF ABSOLUTE POLITICS

Before the First World War, the most comprehensive single power-current in the world was the movement of power out of Europe to the colonial areas-to America, to the Far East, to the Near East, to Africa. Power is spiritual in origin. That can mean only that Europe, seen from without, from Asia, Africa, and the Americas-was in spiritual decline. England was the nation that was then custodian of the Destiny of Europe. Other European powers had far-flung possessions and interests in the world, but none other than England could boast of a World Empire. To the outer world *England was the West*. However, the English national Idea had been completely fulfilled in the course of the 19th century; the English nation, as distinct from the English People, was too used up and too worn out to bear the burden of the Destiny of Europe. This fact could not be concealed, and so the scales of power between the West and the Outer Forces tipped over more in favour of the Outer Forces.

Thus it was England's political weakness that ignited the Asiatic masses' anti-European will-to-annihilation. In 1900, the English Empire, including the seas on which England was indisputably supreme, covered 17/20ths of the surface of the earth. To maintain this structure in that form the entire political strength of Europe would have been needed. Joseph Chamberlain's project of an Anglo-German partnership was based upon this insight. Other political minds that had the art of empathising correctly apprehended the power-current at the time, and the whole world was familiar with the expression Kaiser Wilhelm II coined for these stirrings: The Yellow Peril. The great fact of the "Yellow Peril" dominated the political world-picture before the First World War.

Within Europe, the great power-current went from England to Germany. The lesser powers France and Austria were both in the process of dissolution, and both passed into vassalage: Austria to Germany, France to England. But already England had entered the organically inevitable stage in which power moves according to the laws of centrifugal force. Power-currents moved from England to the strongest outlying powers, to Russia in Central Asia, to Japan in China and the Pacific, and to America in the Western Hemisphere. To Germany, Japan, and America, England gradually lost its position in world commerce, and on the seas it had to yield to the same three political units.

The metapolitical explanation for the intra-European power-current from England to Germany is simple. The decline and inevitable demise of the English Nation-Idea was part of the development of the Western Culture from the first phase of Civilisation, the Age of Economics, to the second phase, the Age of Absolute Politics. It was Destiny that England, the nation with the state-less articulation, to which the Ideas of predestination and laissez-faire had been given, to which they were *instinctive*, to which expansion meant a business-like plundering of the conquered territory with as little political disintegration in it as possible, was the guardian of the Western Civilisation during the 19th century. Likewise it was Destiny, and not chance, that the coming to an end of that age of liberalism, parliamentarism, economics, laissez-faire, and trade-imperialism also meant the coming to an end of England's power. The new age, the Age of Absolute Politics, in which Politics rules unconditionally over every aspect of life in the Western Civilisation, demands a different type of nation, a different Internationale,* a different Universal-Hypothesis to fulfil the Cultural Mission of the 20th century and the centuries to come. The Prussian-German nation is that one of the Western nations whose national Idea thoroughly corresponds to the Cultural Imperative in this Age of Absolute Politics. For the solution of its tasks this Age demands the old Roman virtues: a soldierly ethos and honour-feeling, political-organisatory talent, firmness, conscientiousness, devotion to duty, will-to-power instead of will-to-plunder. Since the Prussian Idea agrees with the Spirit of the Age, power flows organically, naturally, irresistibly to the focus of this Idea.

That a general war would break out, all statesmen and political thinkers were agreed; only its form was not foreseen, nor could it have been. The natural form corresponding to the power-problems posed by the power-currents-would have been England and Germany *versus* Russia and Japan. Since England and Germany belonged to the same Culture and had a

*Cf. IMPERIUM, p. 198 ff.

19

common Destiny, as they always shall, any war between these two states had to benefit powers outside Europe to so great an extent that neither one of them could have profited from it, and that quite independent of which won a military victory and which suffered a military defeat. Therefore, it was in the interest of each of the two, for its own well-being no less than that of the Western Culture, to undertake power-struggles only against extra-European forces.

After the War erupted into a false form, viz., into a form that in no way corresponded to the power-problems posed by the power-currents, the outward movement of power from Europe vastly accelerated.* The European Raj in India was undermined; Japan was freed from all fetters to Europe, and left with America as its sole power-rival. America became the ruling power at sea, despite the Five-Power-Naval Treaty of 1921, under which it scuttled 750,000 tons of new shipping. That folly hardly changed anything, simply because of America's increased ability to build ships, which may be ascribed to the War, and because of the powerful spiritual impetus of the War, because of America's awakening from its century of isolation, an isolation comparable to that of a silkworm in its cocoon. After the Bolshevist Revolution of 1917 and the consolidation of the Asiatic Moscow régime, Russia entered the political world as its most secure power. In Europe, France inherited the continental hegemony that England had striven to take from Germany.

Germany lost power, true; however England lost even more. It shared in a local, military victory as part of a world-coalition and paid for it with a general, political defeat. With results, England had applied the great fundamental of strategy precisely in reverse: it employed all its strength on inconsequential points while reserving as little of it as possible for the decisive point. Vis-à-vis the Coloured-Asiatic world, England was still the custodian of the Destiny of Europe, to be sure, now more enfeebled than ever, a pale shadow of the Imperialist England at the time of the Silver Jubilee of 1887. England no longer had the feeling of a Mission, no longer felt itself called upon to rule-one no longer spoke of an Empire, but of "Mandates"-, *it no longer believed in itself.* Even domestically England was in moral and material chaos. The War had resulted in the New Age, with its new values, and the discarding of much that was

*Cf. IMPERIUM, p.565 ff.

formerly significant, and the old Idea of parliamentarism and laissez-faire was ineffectual in this bewildering new state of affairs. A superpersonal Idea that has fulfilled itself can evolve no further. In a healthy, organic evolution, England would have adopted the new superpersonal Idea, the new Hypothesis, and been absorbed into the new Internationale, but the catastrophic form of the First World War prevented the normal evolution. The West was not represented before the world by a powerful, firm alliance of England and Germany, militarily and politically victorious over Russia and Japan, but by a superannuated English Capitalism.

Had the War assumed the organic form, an English-German coalition against the rising Asiatic menace, it would have ended in a European victory and brought the whole planet under the influence of Europe. But in the form events took, the West lost so much of the 17/20ths of the surface of the earth it had controlled that only about 4/20ths remained subject to it.

And so the two great power-currents continued unabated, the centrifugal current from Europe to the Outer Forces and the centripetal current from England to Germany.

Power in embryonic spiritual form streamed from England to Germany. All Europe looked increasingly to the Prussian Ethos for guidance. This idea gained irresistibly in moral force, strength of its Inner Imperative, and Cultural prestige. Within Europe, another, lesser power-current flowed, from France to Italy, this time actual political power. The source of this current was the Genius of a single man, Mussolini. He effected the transformation of Italy by infusing it with the Prussian-German Socialist Ethos. Since the petty-nationalism of the 19th century had not yet been overcome in Italy, as elsewhere, Mussolini was forced to associate his new State-building Ethos with the name of Imperial Rome. Italy and the entire Western Civilisation have no inward connexion with Imperial Rome, nor did it stand in any relation to them. Therefore, it may not be amiss if the true inspiration of his Genius is mentioned here. Mussolini himself designated Nietzsche and Sorel as the two teachers who had inspired him. Both were opponents of laissez-faire, both were anti-parliamentary, anti-liberal, anti-democratic; both had strong authoritarian leanings.

The centrifugal power-current from Europe outwards flowed more strongly to Japan, Russia, and America. Weak heads in England looked disconsolately to the American colony, symbolised in its spiritual endowments by its politically moronic leaders, like Wilson, Lansing, and Harding, and hoped for spiritual leadership and material support from it. That kept on even after Americans demonstrated loudly and clearly that they were quite indifferent to European politics, as their Congress showed when it refused to ratify the Treaty of Versailles and thereby rejected membership for America in the League of Nations. In consequence of the longing for American domination on the part of a certain group of Europeans-especially numerous and influential on the Island-, the totally altered American leadership that resulted from the American Revolution of 1933 found an open road to the financial-diplomatic conquest of France, England, and the Netherlands. Thenceforth America intervened in all intra-European affairs, always with the intention of promoting the same negative policy, meaning "collective security," which can be called both anti-German and pro-Bolshevist.

Here are outlined the epochal events of the Interbellum Period
1919-1939:

1919-Versailles dictate; French hegemony established in Europe. Spengler'swork *Preussentum and Sozialismus* appears.

1921-Mussolini emerges in History; the first open revolt in Europe of Socialism against Capitalism, of Authority against Money, of Faith against Criticism, of Discipline against Laissez-faire, of Duty-Consciousness against the ideology of "happiness," of Hierarchy against Equality, of the Will-to-Power against the Will-to-Plunder.

1923-France invades Germany; high point of France's power in its domination of continental Europe.

1931-Collapse of the international financial structure of Capitalism; economic catastrophe resulting therefrom; economic depression throughout the Western Civilisation.

Japan successfully raises its claim to power-monopoly in the Far East with its annexation of Manchuria.

1933-On 30th January: The **European Revolution**. Revolt of the Spirit of Authority against Money, of Socialism against Capitalism; over-throw of the 1918 pseudo-victory of Capitalism.

The **American Revolution of 1933**.* Assumption of power by the Jewish entity. Lasting transformation of American policy through abandonment of nationalistic isolationism and the introduction of an internationalist policy. Formation of the Jewish-American Symbiosis begins.

End of French hegemony over Europe.

1936-**Four-Power Pact**: England, France, Germany, and Italy forever renounce waging war among themselves; the first collective attempt to form an organically determined European Imperium.

August-September: America successfully intervenes to prevent the ratification of the Four-Power Pact, to abort the European Imperium and to make possible a second World War-this in order to destroy the power of Europe and to forestall the rise throughout the world of Authoritarian Socialism to the detriment of Finance Capitalism.

This is the year in which the English Prime Minister Baldwin made his statement about the dependence of England and France on America.

1938: Munich Agreement for the pacification of Europe. The Four Powers act together to end Czech domination over Germans, Slovaks, Hungarians, and Ruthenians. Last of the great European efforts to overcome petty-statism and to establish a provisional European Imperium without an intra-European war.

American meddling in England succeeds in annulling the mutual English-German renunciation of war and forces a reorientation of English policy towards setting up a warfront against Germany.

*Cf. IMPERIUM, p. 493 ff.

1939-Formation of the "peace front," a war-alliance of the Americanised England against Germany as diplomatic preparation for the Second World War.

September: Final success of the American policy. Outbreak of the English War against Socialism and the Reawakening of Authority.

1941-Attack on Russia by the provisional European Imperium. The War gains a second aspect.

November: The Washington régime presents its war-ultimatum to Japan as a means of provoking a Japanese attack that would facilitate the intervention of America in the European War against the wishes of the American populace.

December: Japan responds militarily to the ultimatum, whereby the Washington régime knows in advance the time and place of the attack. Complete destruction of the American fleet at Pearl Harbor by Japan-this because the Washington régime deliberately delays every defensive measure. America declares war on Europe; Europe becomes the chief enemy and is designated the main front The War expands into and shows itself from a third aspect.

THE THREE ASPECTS OF THE WAR

In this Age of Absolute Politics, *Culture* provides the motivation for Great Wars. From 1000 to 1500 A.D., the inner-Politics of Europe was determined by *fealty*. The motivation for the intra-European power-struggles during the centuries up to the Congress of Vienna was religious and dynastic; during the 19th century, it was nationalistic and economic. After 1900, the whole planet became increasingly active politically. The decline of England's power awakened in the Coloured World the illusion that the entire Western Culture found itself in a state of decreasing power. That was false indeed, but the outbreak of the First World War and the world-wide verdict against Western Power and Western prestige seemed to confirm this misconception, since the scale of political activity has become planetary, only two spiritual possibilities for a conflict remain: first, the Western Idea of world-rule (and for over two centuries, directly or indirectly, the West actually did rule the greater part of the world); and, second, the Outer Revolt, which is simply the negation of this Western Idea. Manifestations of the Western world-empire Idea were: the British Empire, and all other European overseas-empires; the Americans' conquest of their continent, American imperialism in the Pacific; Germany's enduring desire for expansion into the Slavic areas and its pushing back of the eastern frontier of the Western Culture during the millennium 1000-2000. Manifestations of the Outer Revolt were: the Chinese Opium War against England; the Indian Mutinies of 1857 and 1947; the Zulu Wars; the Mexican revolt against Maximilian, the Mexican revolution of 1910; the Chinese revolution of 1911; the Philippine insurrections against Spain and the latter Philippine uprisings against America, 1900-1946; the Bolshevist Revolution of 1917; the Japanese War Against the West, 1941-1945.

Thus the power-front is seen to be based on Culture as the dominant spiritual front in world politics, and all other politics, be it primitive, local, or personal, is overshadowed by this tremendous disjunction.* On the planet there is only one High Culture in the process of fulfilment, the Western Culture. Outside that Culture, there are only remnants of dead Cultures, whose peoples have once again become primitive, fellaheen, like the Chinese, Hindu, and Islamic; savages, like the African

*Cf. IMPERIUM, p. 234 ff.

25

and American aborigines; barbarians, like the Russians and certain tribes in Central Asia. All peoples living outside the West have perforce taken over many Western customs and characteristics, since the uniquely powerful imperialism of the West lays claim to the whole earth, and its performance has forced the people of the world to acknowledge the undeniable intellectual and material superiority of Europe. This does not mean, however, that "Westernisation" can ever be anything other than superficial. When the Western Culture says Yes to its Imperialistic urge, it naturally calls forth a reaction among those who do not belong to it. Their organic response is an equally passionate No. When they take up Western methods, it is only to use them against the West: If spears cannot defeat Whites, let us learn how to build factories and produce machines!

From a Cultural standpoint, the Second World War consisted of three organically separable wars. The first of these was an intra-Cultural war: England *versus* Germany. In the terminology of Ideas, it was a war of Capitalism *versus* Socialism. But as these two great outlooks have an organic relation to each other, it was actually a struggle between the Past and the Future, for Capitalism belongs to the Past, Authoritarian Ethical Socialism to the Future. Since the Past can never overcome the fact of the Future, except in semblance, this intra-Cultural war had only two possible results: Victory of the Idea of Ethical Socialism or Chaos within the entire Western organism.

The second of these wars began with the attack by the provisional European Imperium on Russia, the leader of the Outer Revolt against Western world-rule. The natural, organic form of this war would have been Europe with all its colonies-America, South Africa, Australia, Argentina, *et al.* -against Russia and the other Asiatic powers. Thus it would have ended in the political destruction of the Asiatic powers, including Russia, and in the establishment of Western world-rule in a stricter, more absolute form than the Western Empire, let us say, of 1900.

The third of these wars was related to the second: the American war against Japan, like the European war against Russia, was a war of the West against the Outer Revolt. In this war, America's rôle was that of a Western colony, and its victory over Japan was also a victory for Europe, just as a victory of Europe over Russia

26

would have been a victory also for America.

The first, the intra-European war, very quickly lost the character of such, since England's total war-effort was brought ever more under the direction of the Washington régime, and England, likewise its remaining overseas possessions, was occupied by American troops. Thereby the Washington régime wanted to ensure that England would not attempt to bail out of the War. With the American occupation of England and the remnants of its Empire, the intra-European war of England versus Germany ended. From then on, there were two organically dissociated wars: Europe *versus* the American-Russian coalition and Japan *versus* America. Wherever the English military forces fought on, it was only for the extension of Russian or American power, for now there was no longer an English political unit whose power could be extended by a victory.

Thus America became involved in all three organically dissociated wars. Its participation in the Second World War was a struggle for the victory of the West, in regard to Japan, and simultaneously for the defeat of the West, in regard to Russia. America fought for an Asiatic victory and against an Asiatic victory.

The outcome of the second organically dissociated war, that of the European Imperium *versus* Russia, was complicated by America's policy *vis-à-vis* Russia. At the beginning of the War, Russia was prepared to conclude peace with Europe, but the Washington régime, in accordance with its purely negative, anti-American policy of defeating Authoritarian Socialist Europe at any cost, even that of national suicide, promised to give economic support to Russia's entire war-effort, so long as it would stay in the War, promised to share with it in a Russian-American world-condominium in the post-War period. America's conduct *vis-à-vis* Russia has never had its like in world-history. During the War, America deprived its own armed forces of huge masses of war matériel, which it delivered to Russia without charge and without any terms of repayment. America supplied Russia with: 14,795 aircraft, 7,056 tanks, 51,503 jeeps, 35,170 motorcycles, 8,071 tractors, 375,883 lorries; other machinery valued at 1,078 million dollars; 107 million yards of cotton products and 62 million yards of woolen products. (This listing is incomplete and does not include ships, foodstuffs, railway matériel, etc.) At American orders huge quantities of armaments and other vital equipment were withdrawn from the English Army and delivered to Russia, including 5,031 tanks and 6,778 aircraft. Deliveries of raw materials reached the value of 39,000,000 pounds. The American viceroy in England, Churchill, confessed in his memoirs that one of his diplomatic problems lay in persuading the Russians to accept these gifts without suspicion and with good will. Throughout the War, the Communist underground movements the whole world over received from North America weapons, munitions, explosives, clothing, medicines, foodstuffs, and financial support-this in Europe, in Serbia, and in the Far East, especially Celebes, Sumatra, Indochina, and China.

It is clear-once again from the simple Organic Laws of Politics-that the Washington régime in no way pursued an *American* policy. A nationalist policy can never be negative. When a nation's policy becomes negative, something has prevailed over the national interest. All during the War, American propaganda was governed by a single great imperative: *Destroy Germany!* In the background was the weak echo: Destroy Japan! The propaganda left no doubt, however, about the relative importance of these two negatives.

Without America's intervention as the all-sacrificing lackey of Russia, the war of Europe *versus* Russia could have ended in two ways: political destruction of Russia by Europe, or negotiated peace. After the American war-entry, the second possibility was eliminated. In its main aspect, the Second World War was no longer a war of Europe against Russia, but *a fortiori* a war of America against Europe, and this war had only one possible outcome; political destruction of Europe. The innumerable Russian troops fought practically under the same command as the troops of America and its satellites. Faced with this coalition of powers, the European Imperium could only sue for peace. The American formula of "unconditional surrender" made that impossible, however.

The third of the organically dissociated wars, Japan *versus* America, had three possible results: political destruction of Japan, negotiated

28

peace, or expulsion of the American power from the Pacific. A political destruction of America was, and is, impossible, owing to America's geographic breadth and position. Only America's overseas-empire, in the Mediterranean, in Africa, in the Persian Gulf, in the Pacific, and in the Caribbean can be destroyed, not however the American political basis, autarkic and inaccessible as it is to large armies from another continent.

RESULTS OF THE WAR

After the American occupation of England, there was no longer a war between England and Germany, for the ability to wage war against an enemy of one's own choosing is the mark of a sovereign power, and England's sovereignty had ceased to exist.* But there was still a spiritual-ethical "war" between the English idea of Capitalism and the Prussian-German idea of Ethical Socialism. Since, in this Age of Absolute Politics, Politics takes unto itself every aspect of Life, this spiritual-ethical conflict had to be decided by the politico-military conflict. Thus the 19th century idea of Capitalism won a pseudo-victory over the 20th century Idea of Ethical Socialism, and that meant Chaos throughout the Western Civilisation. The Past cannot win an enduring victory over the Future. The later Stuarts and Bourbons learnt that, so did Metternich. It is an old lesson that must ever be learnt anew.

In its spiritual ethical aspect, the War, since it did not destroy Europe, came to its sole possible result: It weakened the Idea of Capitalism and, in the same tempo, strengthened the Idea of Socialism, by giving Socialism a victory at least in the field of Technics. After the War, the only possible way of governing and maintaining order in every Western country was through complete political regulation of economic life, in other words, through the application of Socialist *techniques*. Everywhere laissez-faire is dead, both nationally and internationally, except in the very highest economic sphere, that of bank and bourse. For the time being, that domain is spared state-intervention, simply because it is where the governments are chosen. Behind the parliamentary puppets stands the Master of Money.

The second war, that of the provisional European Imperium against Russia, yielded military and political victory to Russia. That politico-military victory, based on American aid, given with a largesse unique in world-history, made the Russian Empire into the world's foremost power, owing to its geopolitical position and to the poor quality of its only remaining opponent, notwithstanding that this opponent dominated

*Cf. IMPERIUM, p. 183 ff.

a greater part of the planet than it did. England's pseudo-victory was owing solely to the Washington regime's policy of sacrificing Americanand European interests to Russian interests. It is a fact of great importance that the Washington régime quite consciously and deliberately created the present Russian Empire as an instrument of its absolute anti-German, anti-European policy.

The third war, that of America *versus* Japan, was, from a Cultural standpoint, a war of Western Civilisation against the Outer Revolt. To superficial observers, its outcome seemed to be political annihilation of Japan. Yet *this* war ended in a negotiated peace. The most important fact about Japanese history, society, and politics is that Japan contains a nationbearing stratum, a level of the population that feels itself charged with an organic Mission. America did nothing to weaken this stratum's feeling of a Mission. Through peace negotiations, the Japanese nation, state, aristocracy, and other institutions were preserved; the Japanese Army was disbanded honourably, and the Emperor, the Japanese national Idea, suffered no Oriental loss-of-face. An American army occupied the Island, and even the commander of that army spoke openly on behalf of an early termination of the occupation. This war resulted in a military and psychological victory for America, and at least for the moment, the West reasserted itself in a part of the world where it had been in retreat for 75 years. At the time, however, in IMPERIUM, I called Japan a political victor of the Second World War because its outer Mission, the expulsion of the West from Asia, had been accomplished, and its inner independence, though temporarily suspended, had not been really abolished.* The Washington régime, which had but little interest in the matter of Japan, permitted its occupation forces considerable autonomy. The leaders of those forces had no idea at all of the types of power and of the overcurrents of power in the world. Their notion of exploiting the victory was on a journalistic plane. They regarded the main effort of the occupation not as political but as moral. In all seriousness, this leadership wanted to "educate" the Japanese nation, as though it were a child, and teach it "democracy."

*Cf. IMPERIUM, p. 587 ff.

The extent to which the military victory of America over Japan was also a political victory over Japan for the entire Western Civilisation is thus very slight indeed. The Washigton règime's policy of reconstructing Japan undermined the greatest part of the victory. Its surrender of China and Manchuria to Russia, the leader of the Outer Revolt against Western Civilisation, undermined it even further. The last remaining step, the restoration of Japanese sovereignty, is only a matter of time, for here the initiative lies with Japan. So long as the Japanese monarchy and the Japanese nation-bearing stratum, with its feeling of a Mission, survive unimpaired, a revival of Japanese sovereignty, Japanese militarism, and the Japanese Empire against America is certain.

The Outer Revolt against the West was only locally contained by America's military victory over Japan. In other parts of the Far East, the revolts were successful. The Chinese, Malays, Indonesians, and the primitive denizens of the Philippines expelled their Western masters.

In the metapolitical sense, the Western Civilisation lost the War against Japan, despite the local, purely military victory of the Americans.

THE POWER PROBLEMS OF THE WAR

The two great power-currents in the world before the Second World War were the centrifugal flow of power from the Western organism to the Outer Forces (especially away from the Continental European nations, since the obsolescence of the English national Idea led to the power-current England-America), and, then, the centripetal flow of the attributes that alone make power vital and lasting, from England to Prussia-Germany.

To set forth these two power-currents as *power problems* - from the European standpoint -, the first problem was: How is European world-hegemony to be restored? And the second was: How is Europe to be imbued with Ethical Socialism, the only viable world-outlook and nation-building force in this Age of Absolute Politics?

These two problems were the actual issues of the Second World War. Men and governments cannot *create* power-problems; rather, these arise when superpersonal organisms collide with existing power-currents. Both lie far beyond any human control. In navigating the seas, one can sail with the currents, or try to sail against them, but one cannot produce new currents. Thus it is with the Organic: The possibilities are *given*, and are not subject to alteration or dispute. One can either accept an organic possibility, or abandon oneself to disappointment, disease, and chaos. If a possibility is frustrated long enough, it will one day no longer be there to accept, for the Organic always has a duration of existence.

The more important of the two power-problems in determining the form of the War was the first: The European Imperium voluntarily decided to give the problem of Europe's world-position precedence over that of Europe's internal constitution. It was hoped that solution of the latter problem could be postponed until a time when it could be resolved more easily and without endangering the European world-position. This decision not to occupy the English Island was the personal decision of the Hero who was custodian of the Destiny of Europe during the Second World War. From the time of that decision on, from June, 1941, the European Imperium's invasion of Asiatic Russia was the real war. Europe expended its energy mainly on winning that war, wherein a victory would have secured the Destiny of the European Culture for the coming century.

Now the War could not take its natural course, that corresponding to the organic power-problems, viz., England and Germany *versus* Russia and Japan, with America and the other colonies either neutral or allied to Europe. Instead, it was forced by the Washington régime into a distorted form: England and the European colonies attacked Europe from behind while it was struggling for its Cultural-political-economic-social-military-technical survival.

Since the form of the War was unnatural, having stood in no relation to the organic power-problem posed by the powercurrents, its results were unnatural, too. As the Organic Laws of Politics show, such a distortion as the Second World War can result only from the intrusion of a Culturally-alien group into the political affairs of the host-organism. *The Second World War was the most monstrous manifestation of Culture-distortion in the history of High Culture.**

The Culturally-alien group that conjured up the War could symbolize its triumph over the West through the infamous "tribunal" at Nuremberg, a year after the War, but its victory was as unnatural as the War itself. Nor can a Culturally-alien group occupy any kind of lasting political position within the host-organism. It summons forth its own opposition, Cultural antibodies, through which its power will eventually be dissolved. Power, to be perfect, must be openly exercised; however, a Culturally-alien group can hold power only so long as it works through others, through individuals, organisations, classes, governments, and groups of every sort that it manipulates to direct their forces temporarily into its own channels.

Likewise, Russia's ascendancy as a result of the War is unnatural. It does not bring organic actualities to expression, but contradicts them. Europe possesses the true sources of power, which are spiritual-ethical; the Russian Empire is only a formless grouping of barbaric tribes with a purely negative mission. In this, its Imperial Age, Europe is simply not ripe for a long domination by barbarians.

*Cf. IMPERIUM, p. 535 ff.

34

Thus it was a war of spent energies and lost power, of territory lost and cities destroyed, a waste of life, wealth, effort - a waste everywhere but in the realm of Heroism and the Spirit. In the spiritual domain, the great process of forming the Imperium continued unrelentingly, and one saw the curious spectacle of the Washington regime's puppets, the Churchill's, taking up the aim of the Hero they had helped Washington and Moscow to destroy. They began to talk about the "unification of Europe." A few months before they hated the Europe that had been united - indissolubly united through blood spilt on the tundras and steppes, in the forests of Russia, and to destroy it they were prepared to betray their European Fatherlands and their own souls. After the War, the hottest-headed of the puppets shrieked in horror, in the style of his war-incitements, that Asia now stood at the Elbe. When the frontier was at the Volga and in the Caucasus, he did everything in his power, little as that was, to bring this frontier into the middle of Europe.

The Heroic world stands infinitely above the economic-technical disjunction *utile-inutile*. Nor is the military test of "victory" valid in the realm of Heroism. It was Cromwell who inspired generations of leaders long after his death and subsequent disgrace, not the later Stuarts who had caused his body to be dismembered by wild horses. It was Napoleon who inspired a whole century of leaders after him, not Louis XVIII, nor Metternich, nor Talleyrand. About 1840, Napoleon triumphed, he whose name one could praise in Europe twenty years before only at one's peril. Napoleon's Idea conquered the spiritual-political realm, his personality the Heroic realm. Who would *reproach* him now with the fact of the lost battles of Leipzig and Waterloo?

So it shall be with the Hero of the Second World War. He represented a new ethical type that will inspire and inwardly form all coming leaders of significance of the West. The bewailing of his "mistakes" after the Second World War was simply contemptible. Every journalist and every braggart knows better than the great man - they would not have made this mistake or that. Indeed, they would never have been in the place to do anything at all!

Heroism is and can never be wasted. So long as men survive a Hero, they will be influenced by him and his legend. He lives on in spirit, and continues to act upon the world of facts and deeds.

THE AMERICAN OCCUPATION OF EUROPE

After the Second World War, the opponents of the Hero of that War were still dominated by his compelling personality. Either they took up his ideas and declared them their own, or they continued to fight against him. Of a new Idea, independent of that Hero, there was not a trace. This can be explained by the issues in world politics being yet the same as those of the Second World War, for the War solved no power-problems, having neither followed nor changed an organic power-current.

During the War, some Europeans entertained the comfortable illusion that the Washington régime was hostile only to certain states in Europe, certain Culture-peoples in Europe, certain ideas in Europe. Nevertheless, the Washington régime's real enemy was *Europe*, which means, above all, the Culture-bearing stratum of Europe, that invisible stratum of the population that by virtue of its sensitivity to Cultural Imperatives is the custodian of the Destiny of the Western Civilisation, and will remain so, too, until the end of Western history. This stratum of approximately 250,000 souls is distributed throughout Europe, but, naturally, it is concentrated primarily in Germany, which can be attributed to the organic fact that the Prussian-German nation is destined to actualise the European Imperium. Since this stratum is invisible - who could have looked at Rembrandt, Goethe, Napoleon, Bismarck in the cradle, and seen what they were to become? - the Washington régime began its post-War task of liquidating this stratum by attempting to kill all of those who had already proved themselves an elite.

Herod sought to kill the Christ Child by slaughtering all male infants in Bethlehem of two years and under. To the invaders it did not seem feasible to take over this technique in its entirety. Yet they believed that if they extinguished the elite of the past they would *ipso facto* prevent the formation of a new élite, that of the Future. Hence they proceeded with a monstrous Black Mass of scaffold-trials, unique in History, that were intended to kill off everybody whose war-service in a particular field had been of outstanding merit. These Black Masses, variously called "Entnazifizierung," "épuration," and the like, in various countries, were performed in all parts of Europe at behest of the Washington régime. Even in such countries as Sweden and Switzerland, which had not participated in the War, the Washington régime had certain people hunted down, "tried," and killed. By these methods, thousands of the best minds were liquidated. But that was still not enough. Huge masses of human beings had to be butchered. In a certain way, at least, Herod's method had to be applied.

Accordingly, "laws" were devised for *ex post facto* application: Everyone who *in the past* believed in the establishment of a European Imperium, and worked for it, was a "criminal." The "penalty" for this "crime" of obeying the Historical Imperative of our Age could not be simple imprisonment for a definite term; that would be impossible. Murder millions by steel and by cord? No, millions of individuals had to be ruined for the rest of their lives.

Hundreds of thousands of French, Walloon, Flemish, Dutch, Danish, and Norwegian soldiers returned home after years of battle against Asiatic Russia and found themselves accused of "treason" and condemned to death or sentenced to years of imprisonment in concentration camps. (In Belgium alone, the Americans incarcerated 400,000 from a population of 8 million.) For under the *Neuordnung* of the Washington régime, the struggle of Europeans for the survival and power of Europe was designated "treason." Thus an American colonel, acting as a "judge" in a "war-crimes trial," told a European soldier who had carried out the orders of his superior officers: "You could have deserted! "

After being released from the overflowing concentration camps, the "criminals" were robbed of every possession, sentenced to heavy fines, deprived of all civil rights, which made it nearly impossible for them to earn their livelihood, and forbidden to perform any but the meanest sorts of labour.

The American High Command fiercely pursued a policy that brought about a uniform impoverishment of the Europeans to whom it contemptuously referred as "the indigenous population." Years after the War, the High Command deliberately blew up European factories, or dismantled and shipped them to Asiatic Russia; chopped down giant forests in Germany that had provided timber years before Columbus discovered

38

America; confiscated large sections of European cities and forbade Europeans to enter them; drove from their homes, cruelly and unexpectedly, hundreds of thousands of European families so as to make room for those of the occupation soldiers of America and her satellite-regimes; set a daily ration of 1,000 calories for adults, which corresponds to only one third of the amount needed to sustain human life; forbade its occupation soldiers to give or sell Europeans food and clothing, even to speak to them. And, finally, it proclaimed to Europe that the Americans had come as a *Herrenvolk*, possessed of great understanding for political realities and morality, to liberate "Europeans" and "educate" them up to True Democracy.

Although the American occupation used the slogan "democracy," it did not make even a pretence of introducing 19th century democratic forms. The press, political parties, every kind of gathering, every move - everything required a "Licence." This was the substitution of a negative, mechanical *Führerprinzip* for the natural, organic Authoritarian State founded upon the inwardly imperative principles of Ethical Socialism, which is the destined state-form of Europe in this Age of Absolute Politics. This was the tyranny of capitalist liberalism, using the mere methods of the European state-form without understanding their spiritual content. The "freedom of speech" America brought to Europe by conquest is best shown through the example of Bevin, the English Foreign Secretary. In 1948, he spoke publicly of "financial servitude to Wall Street," and within one day, was forced to beg its pardon in public.

The American occupation brought into the open a whole stratum of the European population that had hitherto never been recognised as a unit. In Germany the expression *"der Deutsche Michel"* has long been current. It pertains to the type with anti-national instincts, an enthusiast for talk instead of action, likewise for anti-social individualism, laissez-faire, and parliamentarism, a person who cringes to aliens, a natural, instinctive, organic, *traitor*. This stratum of the German population worked systematically but quite instinctively, in two World Wars, for a victory of the enemy. Like the Culturebearing stratum, the Michel-type is distributed Europe-wide. In every European country, America has an inner-America, the Michel-stratum, as an advertisement for its political success, and pseudo-Europeans it uses to implement its policies locally. Such Europeans are called "churchills," after the best known member of their species.

Finally, the American occupation of Europe demonstrated irrefutably that England's policy of "isolation" from the rest of Europe, from the European family of nations to which it belongs, was a grotesque anachronism in the 20th century, the Age of Absolute Politics, of the struggle for control of the planet, wherein only Great Powers with a large geographic basis can take part, not tiny islands situated close to the Continent. In the Age of Economics and Nationalism, the policy of Isolation, likewise the "Balance of Power" idea, was justified. Much that was right, correct, natural, and justified in the 19th century is in the 20th century merely past history. In that century, it was possible for England alone to conquer and hold in check India. In this century, that no longer lies within the realm of possibility. In that century, sea-power could be employed *decisively*. In this century, sea-power is no longer decisive, since the entire hinterland is politically active.

It was tragic that England held so long to the isolation-doctrine, for that made possible Washington's policy of a second fratricidal war. The isolation-idea thus contributed its part to the loss of Europe's world-hegemony. However, this idea survives today only in the sclerotic brains of Culturally-backward old men. What is decisive is the fact of England's passing, together with all other European countries and peoples, into the common status of subjection to America, not the feigning of unimpaired English sovereignty by a certain stratum left over from the past. England's community of Destiny with the rest of Europe is now patent to everybody in the world, is everywhere binding, and can be denied neither in the individual nor for one moment.

In one of its results, the Second World War showed the entire world that the Age of Nationalism is forever past. Precisely those nations whose enmities had reached such fantastic proportions in that Age ceased to exist as political units. There is no relation of cause and effect here, for the Nation-Ideas have a certain life-span, just as every aspect of a Culture's existence, and every Western nation died when it was organically its turn. The last phase of a Nation-Idea is its political one.*

The oldest of the Western nations, the first to have attained the political phase of its development, was Spain. Its great period began with the unification of Aragon and Castile and reached its summit with the world-ascendancy of Charles V. The last act of Spanish history was the revolt against Napoleon, and even then the resistance was more primitive and racial than national. After that period, Spain no longer played an independent rôle in Western history, though, of course, it retained a common Destiny with the Western Culture, and was conscious of it. France entered its political phase in the time of Richelieu and appeared in Western history as a spiritually independent people until the turn of the century. The last affirmative act of this nation manifested itself in 1914 at the Marne. Austria was a Great Power from the time of Charles V until 1900, although in the course of the 19th century it became less and less sure of itself. The linguistic form of the Nation-Idea in the Western Culture, which dominated that century, weakened the Austrian Idea to the point where Austria's last independent political act - the ultimatum to Serbia in June, 1914 - was dictated more by pride than politics.

England's political history as a nation extends from Cromwell to Joseph Chamberlain. Before Cromwell, there was no WorldIdea in England, and after Chamberlain, an Idea no longer existed, could no longer exist, for national extinction, like every other organic phenomenon, is irreversible. Between 1600 and 1900, England's power increased to the extent that in 1900 it controlled by its fleets and armies 17/20ths of the surface of the earth. Spiritually, the entire Western Civilisation - particularly from 1750 onwards - was Anglicised.

*Cf. IMPERIUM, pp. 328-353.

The thought- and action-systems of 19th century were English: Marxism arose on the basis of English capitalist economics; Darwinism reflects the English individualistic-competitive world-outlook; Materialism, Legalism, Capitalism, Social-Ethics - all are of English provenance, and they were the foundations of the 19th century.

The Boer War occurred at the turning-point. At that time, wrote the Englishman Christopher Sykes, England suddenly became the most hated country in Europe. All at once, the spiritual centre-of-gravity shifted: Darwinism succumbed to the Mutation Theory of de Vries, the class-warfare of Marx to the organic State-Socialism of Bismarck, social-ethics to Political Ethics, Sensualist philosophy to the idealist, laissez-faire to state-intervention in the economy, Liberalism to the precursors of the Reawakening of Authority, pacifism to the reassertion of martial virtues, and daydreams of an eternal peace were shattered in the global arena of the Age of Absolute Politics.

This was the end of the intellectual-spiritual Anglicisation of Europe - but not of America, for colonies have their own organic rhythm, as the History of High Culture shows, and all colonies are perforce Culturally-retarded. And it was the beginning of the new Nation-Idea of the West: the entire Culture itself constituted as a Nation, i.e., as an Imperium.

As nations, Germany and Italy were destined by the advent of the new Age, namely that of Absolute Politics, to be stifled before they had yet lived through the mature political phase of their existence. Unlike France, Spain, Austria, and England, however, these two nations are inwardly alive, i.e., their Nation-Idea, their National Mission, is not fulfilled.

Spain fulfilled itself *before* the Age of Nationalism, France and Austria *during* that Age, England and the Age of Nationalism unfolded concurrently, and Germany and Italy must fulfil themselves *after* the Age of Nationalism. Thus these two nations will not fulfil themselves in a nationalistic form in the old sense of the word. They will fulfil themselves as the custodians of the Destiny of all Europe, and the new Nation-Idea of Culture-as-Nation will be the instrument of their fulfillment

As political units, of course, Germany and Italy are dead. It lies beyond all possibility that one or the other could ever regain its sovereignty except as part of a sovereign Europe. Both stand in the shadow of America and Russia, which falls over all Europe. However, the German and Italian peoples possess the instincts that alone guarantee a rôle in History. The three great instincts upon which all power is based are: the absolute will to self-preservation, to procreation, and to increasing power. The first and last instincts directly describe superpersonal organisms, the second only indirectly through the human beings that compose the body of the higher organism. A nation that welcomes foreign troops is no longer fit to live - such a thing is rendered impossible by the absolute instinct for self-preservation, which excludes submission to any other organism, whether "friend" or "foe." A nation in numerical decline is moribund: the size of the population is the result of the National Mission. A nation that no longer strives for power and possessions is dying, and the actual renunciation of power - even by traitorous churchills - means the nation is dead, for a living nation simply does not surrender its power.

The great nation-forming Ethic in this stage of European history is the Prussian-German Idea of Ethical Socialism. Only this living, wordless Idea can banish the overshadowing extra-European powers, form the European Imperium, and lead the West to the fulfillment of its World-Mission. Imbued with the new Ethic and free of petty-statist 19th century nationalism, the European nations will climb out of the abyss as a unity, or they will never climb out at all.

Germany is the only surviving nation of Europe that contains formative possibilities, and so it has become identical with the West. Since the Destiny of Europe is at once that of the Imperium, which can take only an Authoritarian Socialist form, Prussia-Germany is the custodian of the Destiny of all Europe. This is an organic *fact*, and it is wholly independent of human logic or wishes. Destiny is at work in what exists, not what disgruntled old men wish existed.

This relationship of Germany to Europe was confirmed by the Second World War. While the War continued, there was power based in Europe. The very moment the European phase of the War ceased, there was no longer any power in Europe, all power-decisions being made in Washington and Moscow or with their permission. The German resistance to the American Russian invasion was no 19th century nationalism, since the whole Culture-bearing stratum in Europe took part in this struggle and troops for the battles came not only from German-speaking territories, but voluntarily from every other part of Europe as well.

Words that in the 19th century described Nation-Ideas, describe in the 20th century only geographic areas. Today the words German, Spanish, English, Italian, French describe only languages and territories, but no longer peoples, nations, political units or superpersonal Ideas. Since a mysterious force inheres in the words when they are used polemically, a policy for European Liberation that would attain success will not use the geographic and linguistic words, England, France, Italy, Spain, Germany in a political sense, but will use the word Europe alone.

The advance of History has destroyed the old significance of these words, and a dynamic policy needs its own terminology. Today 19th century nationalists are the instruments of the occupying forces, which follow the old maxim: *Divide et impera*. What *European* would dare speak openly in favour of the American occupation of Europe? What *European* would declare himself against Europe's organic Unification, against its resurrection as a sovereign unit of Culture-State-Nation-People-Race?

Using the old appellations of nationality, one can say without paradoxical intent that in the 20th century an Englishman, an Italian, a Spaniard *is* a German. In this century, it is of scant importance what language a European speaks and in what geographic area he was brought up. Of importance only is the spirituality that permeates his inner life. Europe's churchills and toynbees prove that it is possible for Americans to be born and raised in Europe. The example of Mussolini shows that an ethical Prussian can be born and raised in the Romagna, and the examples of Ezra Pound, William Joyce, Robert Best, Douglas Chandler, and others show that Europeans can be born or raised in America.

44

In this century the idea of vertical race is dead. We can now view race only in horizontal terms-the race one feels in oneself is everything, the anatomic-geographic group to which one belongs means nothing.* In this stage of our Cultural development, the principle of individuality reasserts itself, as it asserted itself in the earliest days of the Gothic. During the dark age of Materialism, it was believed that heredity and environment were everything; with the decline of Materialism the human Soul regains its former dignity. Everyone must now openly admit that the engrafting of the outworn nonsense of the vertical race notion onto the glorious European Resurgence of Authority brought about by the European Revolution of 1933 was an enormous tragedy - all the more so since the coupling of these two ideas was in no way necessary or even logical.

In the Classical Culture, any man who was *ethically* equal to the Inner Imperative of Roman spirituality could rightly say: "*Civis Romanus sum.* " In this, our Western Culture is somewhat akin to the Classical. Our touchstone of comradeship and belonging is spiritual-ethical, not the old one of birth-place, cephalic-index, eye-colour. In the 20th century, the century of elective affinities, materialistic tests are pure stupidity.

One last word on the relation of Germany to Europe. The adoption of the German formative-ethic of Authoritarian Socialism by all Europe means, of course, the automatic disappearance of Germany as a petty-state. The Anglicising of Europe in the 19th century did not mean the Europeanising of England, for the 19th century was the age of petty-nationalism. However, with the coming to an end of that age, the ethical Germanisation of Europe is simultaneously the Europeanisation of Germany. In Germany, as elsewhere, petty-statism is dead. Europe will have a Prussian-ethical Future, or none at all. Either Authoritarian Socialism will win its victory and liberate Europe from its enemies, or else Europe will be reduced permanently to Chinese conditions. Either Europe will unite in this Ethical Idea, or it will ever remain a collection of provinces over which the Outer Forces will wage their wars of plunder.

* Cf. IMPERIUM, pp. 273-316.

The test of *rationality* is completely invalid in History; the test in that field is *organic possibility*. As to Politics, Europe has but one organic possibility, the Imperium, and but one Ethic, Authoritarian Socialism. The nations are dead, for Europe is born.*

What names this mighty Imperium will bear in History, what language its people will speak, where its capital will be - these are secondary questions for us in the middle of the 20th century, and no one alive today will decide them. All that matters now is that unless Europe forms itself into an indivisible national-political entity by dint of its nation-building Ethic of Authoritarian Socialism, the Europe of 2050 will be essentially the same as that of 1950, viz., a museum to be looted by barbarians; a historical curiosity for sight-seers from the colonies; an odd assortment of operetta-states; a reservoir of human material standing at the disposal of Washington and Moscow; a loan-market for New York financiers; a great beggars' colony, bowing and scraping before the American tourists.

In the face of Europe's terrifying position between the Second and Third World Wars, the old differences between the remnants of the old Nation-Ideas collapse into nothing. Every man of significance in our times is History-oriented, for one cannot profoundly understand our times, their Inner Imperative and Mission, unless one ponders deeply the meaning of Leibnitz' aphorism: *Le présent est chargé du passé et gros de l'avenir*. In his inner life, Western man now cannot take sides in the bygone struggles between Wallenstein and Gustavus Adolphus, Olivares and the Cortes, Richelieu and the Fronde, Stuarts and Parliament, Bourbons and Habsburgs, Church and State, England and Spain, Italy and Austria. Today the loftier European identifies himself with *both* sides in these titanic struggles, with the totality of our precious Western History, for that History is his *own* spiritual biography written before him in large letters. He, too, had his Gothic, Reformation, Enlightenment, and rationalist-revolutionary phase - his youthful religiosity and crusades, his Democratic-Liberal-Communist phase; and now, in his fullest maturity, he has entered, spiritually and

* Cf. IMPERIUM, p. 58 ff., 110 ff., 613 ff.

materially, the Age of Absolute Politics, in which the struggle is planetary and its motive Cultural. That means not 19th century petty-states and nations, but that only the Culture-State-Nation -Imperium can take part in it.

With its successes and failures, its "flaws" and brilliancy, its advances and retreats, Western History describes *ourselves*. Even with the first World War, we are still able to experience inwardly what both sides felt. But with the Second World War, the higher type of European experiences only one side, for that War was in its main aspect a war of the West against Asia, and all men of the West who, knowing that, sided against the European Imperium were traitors to the West, inner enemies of their own Culture. In 1914, it was England *versus* Germany, but in 1939 this was no longer the case. By 1939, the England of Walpole and North, Canning and Gladstone, Kitchener and Joseph Chamberlain was dead and buried. Replacing it was the "England" of Eden and Churchill, Cooper and Belisha - not even a recognisable caricature of the youthful England of the Independents. These were no far-sighted Empire Builders with unerring power-calculations, but only liquidators of the Empire, American agents, greeters of the "valiant Red Army." As their enemy they named the European Culture, the organism of which England is a vital part and with which it will always share a common Destiny. Every English statesman of the old tradition would have recognised the growth of events during the third decade of the 20th century from a European to a global scale. But these wretched epigoni with their boundless jealousy and muddled instincts closed their eyes to it and sold the English Island to the Washington régime for a little pseudo-power and the fleeting glory of a suicidal "victory."

In this historical orientation, the Westerner of the higher type, who alone has Cultural value and significance, regards events in which the West was pitted against the Outer Forces with a completely subjective eye. Thus he sees in the Crusades, for example, only one side of the question - I am speaking here not of any ethical, religious, moral, aesthetic, or other such questions, of course, but solely of the organic question of *identity*. He is for Charles XII against the Russians, for England against the Indian Mutiny, against the Zulus, and against China in the Opium War; for the Teutonic Knights against the Slav at Tannenberg; for Maximilian against

Juarez; for the American Colonists in the Alamo against Santa Ana; for Napoleon against Russia; for Mussolini against the negroes of Abyssinia; for the Hero and his Army against Russia in 1941-1945. In these events, it was left only to chance which of the Western nationalities fought the Barbarian. The victory of any Western nation over an outer military force, whether Chinese, Hindu, Zulu, Islamic, was a victory for all Europe and Barbarian. The victory of any Western nation over an outer military force, whether Chinese, Hindu, Zulu, Islamic, was a victory for all Europe and its colonies. Any European who gloats over the defeat of a Western nation brands himself politically and Culturally feeble-minded. For what distinction does the Barbarian make between the Western nations? During the Second World War, the Japanese called the Germans "friendly enemies" and the English "hostile enemies." To Jewry all men of the West are "goyim;" to Islam they are "giaours" and "Franks," and in Persia during the First World War Waßmus had the greatest difficulty in making clear to the tribal chieftains why the two "Frankish" powers were fighting each other. For a European to emphasise any trifling differences between the Western nations today is stupidity, if not treason.

Yet Anglophobia, the mode of yesterday, is back in style again; Germanophobia has been transformed by the Outer Forces of Washington and Moscow into a veritable hate-religion for the masses. In this direction lies the Sinoisation of Europe.

Treasonous propaganda in Europe between the Second and Third World Wars has its origin with the Outer Enemies of Europe. Spreading it is taken care of by the Inner Enemy of Europe.

An inner enemy is more dangerous than an outer one, because while he seems to belong, he is actually a kind of alien.

The Inner Enemy of Europe is at once a stratum of the population, a world-outlook, and a Culture-illness. The Michel-stratum is Europe's Inner Enemy, the stratum that commits treason organically and instinctively. Its world-outlook is that of the past Age of Nationalism, Economics, Democracy, Capitalism. Because it looks backward and resists the Imperative of the Future with pathological intensity, this stratum is the embodiment of the Culture-disease called Culture-retardation.*

An inner enemy is dangerous in two respects: first, because of his own activity, and, second, because of his usefulness to the outer enemy. During the Second World War, the European Michel consciously worked for the defeat of Europe and the victory of the American-Russian coalition. Examples of this conduct were Churchill and Attlee in England, Badoglio and Mauggeri in Italy, Halder, Hassel, and Goerdeler in Germany, the Communists in France, the Netherlands, Spain, and Scandinavia. Without this organic, professional treason on the part of the European Michel, the Outer Forces could never have defeated Europe. After the War, the American occupation of Europe and the despoliation of Europe were made possible only by the Michel-stratum, which hired itself out to the enemy to establish vassal-governments, churchill-régimes, in every province of Europe. During this period between the Second and Third World Wars, the Michel as an American agent is more dangerous than he would otherwise be in himself. The reason for this is the advance of History since the 19th century has rendered his world-outlook completely useless to him, even for purposes of sabotage, while to the Americans it is still useful as a means of control over Europe. Thus the Culture-disease of Culture-retardation remains in the body of Europe only because of the American occupation.

If "capitalism" is understood not simply as an economic technique, but, above all, as a spiritual-ethical principle, we may designate the world-

* Cf. IMPERIUM, p. 410 ff.

outlook of the Michel as Capitalism. In the 20th century, *Capitalism* is inwardly dead, both in the broader sense of a Cultural-ethical world-outlook and as an economic technique. The fact that it is dead is shown every time its representatives approach some new problem in the world of facts. Their solutions are uniformly *rigid* and in every case misfire, even when the problem is purely economic. After the Second World War, the English government that called itself "socialist" decided to "nationalise" the railways. The sole possible *raison d'être* for nationalisation of the railways lay in reducing costs for the ultimate consumer, thus granting a sort of general rebate. But there resulted a doubling of all fares and a continuation of the separate identity of the lines, even to the point of competitive advertising. The programme remained in existence only for the sake of the principle of nationalisation. All other "nationalisation" schemes that originated with this capitalistic, class-war inciting Marxist régime ended similarly.

The singularly unhappy career of the capitalist system was continued throughout Europe after the Second World War, to be sure, because of intervention coming from the Culture-periphery. Unhesitatingly, the Washington régime employed the resources of the North American continent to shore up the tottering system. Thus it is only the extra-European power of the Washington régime that subjects Europe to the negative world-outlook and outworn economic system of capitalism. A European revolt against capitalism is *ipso facto* a revolt against America. A Socialist Europe, founded on the principle of the sovereign, organically articulated State, would be an independent Europe and master of its own economy. This economy would not be established for reasons of class-war, nor for the purpose of realising any rigid, abstract ideas. On the contrary, it would be an economy that overcomes the economic problems of Europe in the spirit of the 20th century, and, indeed, in their sole possible way of solution: the State as organism and its economy as part of an organic *totality* to which all private and class interests are subordinate.

Before the First World War, the European power-monopoly, the monopoly of trade and technics, secured all requisite markets for the products of Europe, and with these products Europe paid for the raw and other materials it ordered from abroad. The First World War undermined this system in that, for its duration, it deprived the overseas consumers of European merchandise, and thus gave them the stimulus to construct factories of their own. After the War, the capitalist international economy was never again able to solve its problems, not even through extensive state-intervention in the form of protective tariffs, and the like. This development was concluded by the Second World War. The old system passed away.

The only solution for the economic problems of Europe consists in the most intensive possible rationalisation of all existing possessions and in the acquisition of new resources for the European economy. Naturally, America insists that Europe keep the capitalist system. A Socialist Europe does not need America, whereas a capitalist Europe is a beggars' colony of America.

In the basic world-outlook of both the American population and the ruling economic caste the world is still *the object of plunder*. America is not interested in forming and organising the world, but in creating the widest possible opportunities for financial-economic penetration of other countries. It is driven even to military conquest to attain this goal securely. Again, this is 19th century motivation, and its corrosive, pathological revival in our Age is a symptom of Culture-retardation.*

To the finance-capitalist politico-military thought is merely a tool, albeit that it may seem to predominate at times. It is a dangerous weapon. The possibility is ever present that a political general might like to rule the roost. The political general is the nightmare of the finance-capitalist, and therein lies the explanation for the inferior businessman-type and feebleminded liberals that make up the American generalcy. All officers of strong will and superior intellect are weeded out before they attain to the rank of general; and in 1941 the Army regulations were so revised that automatic promotion to general - which had been the rule in the American Army since its beginnings in the 18th century - was eliminated, and promotion to that rank made dependent on "service," i.e., subservience to the Washington régime, or in other words, on the lack of any earnest will and strong instincts.

* Cf. IMPERIUM, p. 517 ff.

To recapitulate everything: the Inner Enemy of Europe may be described in three ways:

1. With regard to his Culture-biological value.
2. With regard to which stratum embodies him.
3. With regard to his conception of the world.

1. The Inner Enemy is the bearer of Culture-retardation.
2. The Inner Enemy is the Michel-stratum; his leaders are the churchills.
3. The Inner Enemy is Capitalism, whereby the word is used in its total meaning of a Cultural-spiritual-ethical-economic principle.

In contrast to the foregoing, the true European spirit may be likewise sketched:
1. It is Culture-health, i.e., the actualisation of the Inner Imperative, accepting the challenge of the Future.
2. It is in the charge of the Culture-bearing stratum, the highest élite of the population, which stratum comprises no more than *circa* 250,000 souls.
3. It is the grand Idea of Imperialism, the world-outlook that is suited to the coming European Imperium of Culture-State-Nation-People-Race-Society.

For the purpose of demonstrating with the utmost clarity the elements of the two world-outlooks in this period of Western History between the Second and Third World Wars, a paradigm is appended:

Imperialism	**Capitalism**
Faith	Rationalism
Primacy of the Spirit	Materialism
Idealism	Sensualism
Will-to-Power	Will-to-Riches
World as object of organisation	World as object of plunder
Rank as social distinction	Wealth as social distinction
Society as organism	Society as a collection of individuals
Fulfilment of Duty	"Pursuit of happiness"

Ascendant instincts:	**Decadent instincts:**
1. Absolute Western self-preservation	1. Acquiescence to the Outer Revolt
2. Absolute will to biological fertility	2. Race-suicide, birth control, Puritanism, Bohemianism
3. Absolute will to increase power	3. Surrender of the World hegemony of the West
Hierarchy	Equality
Discipline	Freedom, ethical laissez-faire
Authority	Parliamentarianism
The superpersonal organism as *State*	The superpersonal organism *as society*
Aristocracy	Plutocracy
Society as an organic unity	Class-war
Sexual polarity	Feminism
Europe as Imperium	Petty-statism
Europe as Nation	Chauvinism
Europe as Fatherland	Petty-nationalism
Order	Freedom
Stability	Constant motion, business-cycles

Responsibility, all public power exercised and administered openly	Irresponsibility, anonymity, public power in the hands of private persons, finance capitalists, labour-dictators
Resurgence of Authority	Communism, Democracy Liberalism
Ideal of Chivalry, faith in oneself	Separation of Word and Deed, systematic hypocrisy
Respect for the political enemy	Replacement of respect by hatred, "war-crimes trials," ideals as a substitute for Honour on the battlefield
Cultivation of soldierly virtues	Cult of bourgeois virtues, the derision of soldierly virtues
Eroticism as legitimate source of joy and fertility	Eroticism as vice, the cult of immorality, general spread of clandestine and illegal prostitution, an Erotic without consequences
Affirmation of War and Conquest	Pacifism, preparation of the coloured populations for "self-government," the "right of self-determination"
Separate status of Culture-alien	Equality with the Culture alien, the "melting pot"
Western Man as an individual human being, completely different from primitive non-Western humans, Western Man in the service of a great Mission: the fulfilment of the European Culture	Rousseau: Man as Savage Darwin: Man as Animal Marx: Man as economic creature Freud: Man as sexual creature Science-as-Religion: Man as Machine, capable of limit-

	less existence, "Victory over disease," etc.
Art practiced in conformity with the Cultural task	"L'art pour l'art"
Politico-military expansion	Financial-military-economic expansion

From a cursory glance at the list of examples it is obvious that the reigning forces of Culture-retardation make use of the ideas and instincts of Imperialism whenever and wherever they find it necessary and possible. For instance, they subordinate Art to Politics. They have set up a new, inverted hierarchy in which the American and the Michel are the patricians and the true European is the plebeian. They preach "democracy" while ruthlessly imposing their will on the masses and pressuring them in so-called elections; they deny the rightness of the Idea of Conquest while occupying Europe with their troops and forcing its people to take on heavy political, military, and economic burdens in the interest of the extra-European powers, and so on.

This is the Age of Absolute Politics, and everyone who acts in this Age, acts in its spirit, whether he knows it or not, whether he wishes it or not. If he reflects, makes use of, values that run counter to his stated political beliefs and aims, then he is either hopelessly stupid or is pursuing some other goal than the fulfilment of the Destiny of Europe - the formation of the Western Imperium in the spirit of Ethical Socialism.

There are two designs here: the first is the design of the European Michel, who seeks only his own advantage (the churchills) or that of his class (the finance-capitalist class; the proletarian usufructuaries of the looting of the body of Europe). The second design is that of the Cultural-outsider, the total alien, who in his boundless rancour directs a political will-to-annihilation against the West, who negates its Inner Imperative, who would strangle its Destiny and divert it from the Future. Geographically, he may act from outside the Western Culture, or inside, in the form of Culture-distortion. In each case, it is his spirituality that clinches the matter, and the Culture-distorter is one of the Outer Enemies of Europe.

When used in Politics, the word *enemy* has a meaning completely different from what it has when used in regard to Culture or private life. In private life, we call him our enemy who bears us ill will. Applied to world politics, this definition is meaningless, for no state bears ill will in any private sense. That is true even in those cases in which a political unit is animated by a purely negative will, and would express it politically. For the form-world of Politics itself conditions all political activity and transforms its whole content into power activity. However, Politics seldom does supply its own motivation - that is to be sought in another realm.

The motivation of the global power-struggle in our Age of Absolute Politics lies in *Culture*. On the planet there is only one High Culture in the process of fulfilment, the Western Culture, and as a *spiritual* front it naturally assumes the following form: the West against the Outer Revolt. The spiritual motivation of the politics of all outer forces whatever is the will-to-annihilate the Western Culture. In a power-struggle between Europe and any outer force, each contestant will, however, strive for power, that means *control over the other.* The motivation of the contestants will become apparent only *after* a power-decision in the struggle. Thus it is obvious that the West does not have the desire to destroy the peoples, territories, resources, and low cultures of the outer forces, whereas these outer forces most emphatically wish to destroy the peoples, landscape, resources, and the High Culture of Europe, as the Russian-American occupation of Europe after the Second World War demonstrated.

In the purely spiritual sense, then, Europe has but one "enemy," the Outer Revolt against the World Hegemony of the West. From this great, fundamental fact we know that the Outer Revolt will provide Europe with political enemies so long as the Age of Absolute Politics lasts. A European victory in the struggle for the planet will not extinguish the Outer Revolt as a spiritual front; it will simply prevent it from again rising to the level of political intensity. At present, this spiritual front is divided into two political units: Russia and America-Jewry. Culturally, it is anomalous that America and one of the outer enemies of Europe are interdependent, for America belongs by its origin and fate to the Western Culture. All the same, it must now be counted among the enemies of Europe, since ethically and politically it is dominated by the Culture-alien Jewish entity of ChurchState-Nation-Society-Race. Just how this domination came about is of less concern to Europe than the fact of it. The objective events of world-history since 1933 show that in not one instance has America pursued an American nationalist policy, but exclusively a policy in the interests of the Jewish entity.

In order to bring the metapolitical realities of this period between the Second and Third World Wars into clearer focus, each of the Outer Enemies of Europe must be examined separately.

America is, and shall always be, a colony of the Western Culture. A colonial spirituality determines the fate of colonies. So it has been with every previous Culture. When on the Home-soil the parent-Culture becomes extinct, everywhere the colonies perish. Population-streams may continue in primitive form; landscapes, of course, remain, but they are desolate and tyrannise the human beings that just yesterday dominated them; edifices may yet stand, but their symbolism is no longer understood. A colony is linked by a mystical bond, as though by a spiritual umbilical cord, to the parent organism, a bond just as inexplicable and just as real as the one that binds the Culture to the soil on which it was born. A colony thus shares a common history with the parent-organism, and its life reflects - with a natural and organic retardation - the development of the Culture. In the case of America, this retardation generally corresponds to the life-duration of one generation. This lagging behind is not the same thing as Culture-retardation, for it is natural and unavoidable. Still, that tardiness is serviceable to the Culturally-parasitic group which is now contriving to prevent the American colony from reflecting the development of its parent-organism. This pathological design is unattainable, of course, but any such deviation from Culture-health must have enormous effects on the host before the parasite is expelled.

The Jewish entity is a Cultural form-world of its own stamp, and can therefore *never* be assimilated by the Western Culture.* Since

* Cf. IMPERIUM, p. 376 ff.

58

this entity finds itself inside the West - geographically speaking - and since it must seek its political actualisation, it necessarily influences Western politics in the direction of *its own interests*. Though it be of alien origin, it must not appear alien; its politics must be regarded as though it were legitimate politics, and not the alien politics it is. The Western ideology of the 18th and 19th centuries was admirably suited to the political needs of the Jewish entity, but with the passing away of that ideology and the birth of the Age of Absolute Politics, the preconditions for the successful political activity of the Jewish entity on European soil completely vanished. The fictive constructs of *"Liberté, Egalité, Fraternité"* have entirely died out in Europe; hence the political history of the Jews, as quasi-members of the Western nations, has also ended. Even so, the colonial tardiness in Cultural development and the disease of Culture-retardation make it possible for Jewry to retain its uncontested domination over the American people.

In this period of history, America and Jewry form a Symbiosis. The head of the organism is the Jewish entity, the body is America.

The problem of the existence-duration of this Symbiosis is of only secondary importance to Europe. No one predicted the French Revolution in regard to its time or its form. No one predicted the Russian Revolution of 1917, or the European Revolution of 1933, or the American Revolutions of 1775 and 1933. No one can in any way presage the time or the form of a Third Revolution in America which will take the power away from the Jewish entity and place it in the hands of a new American ruling-stratum.* That Revolution is an organic possibility - indeed, even more: it is an organic *Unavoidable*. But since the time of its outbreak is still an Imponderable, the possibility of such a Revolution can play no rôle in the formation of Europe's policy, for a policy cannot be based upon Imponderables, though it must be flexible enough to adapt itself when they emerge from the realm of the Unforeseen. When the Revolution starts, it will bring in America a re-awareness of European politics and a re-

* Cf. IMPERIUM, p. 549 ff.

evaluation of Europe's meaning.

The Symbiosis of America and Jewry in this moment of history between the Second and Third World Wars is decisive not only for America, but also for Jewry. During the centuries of its "dispersion," the Jewish entity never attained to the position of absolute sovereign over the fate of a Western host-people. But now it has come to that, and Jewry has identified itself for political purposes with America before all the world. In that Jewry became the overlord of America, it lost the most important of its other possessions and bases. Before the Jewish hegemony over America, the height of Jewish power was in Bolshevist Russia. In 1945, the superficial observer might have gained the impression that the total political power of the planet was being gradually collected into *one* political unit. That was in fact the aim of the Jewish leadership, and the means of creating the "world government" was to be the resurrected "League of Nations."

As has already been shown in IMPERIUM,* a world-state is an organic impossibility, and likewise a logical one. *State* is a political term, and political power results from polarity. A state is thus a unit of opposition. Although in theory a world-state would not have an opposition, if one were founded, it would at that very instant split into two or more political units. These would develop along regional, cultural, class, or economic lines - even along the lines dictated by a dominant political figure. Ignoring the concrete example of failure afforded by the "League of Nations" after the First World War, the Jewish-American Symbiosis attempted through its "United Nations" to create a power-monopoly for itself.

One great obstacle was present: *Russia*. It had been hoped, even taken for granted, that Russia would remain sufficiently under the control of the Jewish entity to collaborate in the scheme and, together with America, formally surrender its legal sovereignty to the "United Nations." But the rise of the American-Jewish Symbiosis undermined the position of the fragment of the Jewish "diaspora" in Russia. So long as Jewry acted alone, it was politically effective in Russia. The worldwide identification of Jewry with America aroused Russian nationalism, with
* Cf. IMPERIUM, p. 166 f; 170 f.

the result that the Culture-alien Jewish entity of Church-State-Nation-Society-Race lost its status as a member, so to speak, of the Russian national structure and was re-classified as a foreign element, thus losing completely its political effectiveness inside Russia.

As we have seen, the sole great spiritual-Cultural "enemy" Europe has is the Outer Revolt, against the West, the great No to the Western World-Mission, and this spiritual-Cultural front is divided into two political units, of which Russia is the second. Between the First and the Second World Wars, Russia was generally acknowledged to be the leader of the Outer Revolt, but in the Russo-Japanese War, 1904-1906, it was *vice versa*. At that time, Russia figured as a Western power against the Outer Revolt, which was led by Japan as the only sovereign power outside the Western Culture. In between lies the Bolshevist Revolution of 1917.

The Bolshevist Revolution was more than political; it was Cultural. Power was tranferred from the Westernised elements in the church, state, army, aristocracy, and intelligentsia to a group basing itself upon the instinctively nihilistic stratum of the Russian peasant masses. The primitive Russian Soul, unsure of itself, had been forced by the Romanovs and the powerful inroads of German culture in Russia to submit to Westernisation. Consequently, there arose in Russia a dreadful tension of polarity between the two Souls, the Western and the proto-Russian. Dostoievsky's *The Possessed* depicts how it fermented nihilistically beneath the surface. It was this underground Russia that, led by the Jewish entity, broke away in 1917 from the West. By 1923, the civil wars had ended, and Western culture was for the time banished from Russia. A community of destiny with Asia and its revolt against the West, rather than with a Europe whose form-world it had just expelled from Russian soil, more nearly answered the expectations of the new Russia.

The Russian Soul is too virile ever to be strangled by something alien. Hence the Jewish entity, despite the dominant position to which it had attained with the Revolution of 1917, was incapable of maintaining its unconditional rule. The expulsion of Trotsky in 1928 marks the downward turning point for Jewry in Russia.

And yet the Bolshevist Revolution did not eliminate the polar tension within the Russian Soul. So long as the Russian Soul, chaotic and full of longing, animated by a strong will yet of weak resolve, exists within the sphere of influence of a Western organism that is conscious of its World-Mission, there will remain in Russia a powerful urge towards reunion with the West. The European Revolution of 1933 found an echo in Russia, and when the European armies entered Bolshevist territory in 1941, they were hailed everyplace there as "liberators." Marshal Vlasov could have raised armies of millions and affiliated them with the European military forces, but, unfortunately, the European Command did not make use of such aid until it was too late. The possibility indeed exists that a second monstrous upheavel - with a pro-Western Cultural aim - will overthrow the Bolshevist régime. This possibility might be realised either through a renewed Western invasion or through the appearance of a new Peter the Great. It is a further Imponderable. Today Europe must reckon with Russia as part of the Outer Revolt against its World-Mission.

Since there are only two political powers in the world, the world situation can assume only the form of preparation for war between them: America-Jewry *versus* Russia.

If Bolshevism is understood as the urge to destroy the Western Culture, then these two extra-European powers form an anti-Cultural Interregnum in Western History, the Concert of Bolshevism. Both powers are formless and personal; neither is the expression of a superpersonal Soul, a higher Destiny, an organically necessary Imperative to a World-Mission. The Outer Forces, whatever the extent to which they have Western technics at their disposal, whatever Western customs they practise, whatever superficial display of literary connexions with the West they make, are, in fact, to be classed in the same category with the formless powers of Tamerlane and Genghis Khan, Sun Yat-sen and Kemal Atatürk, Lobengula and the Mahdi. Europe is still the bearer of a World-Idea, a great World-Hypothesis; it still has an inward necessity to view the world in a particular fashion, an Ethic whereby it conducts itself towards it in a particular fashion and reconstructs it in a particular fashion. For the single, all-encompassing reason of this *total* difference between Europe, on the one hand, and the formless extra-European powers on the other, Europe can have at bottom no interest in the projected Third World War within the Concert of Bolshevism *per se*. Nor would it make any difference in this if the War broke out in 1960 or 1975.

Nevertheless, Europe is linked *politically* to the projected Third World War, and it must exploit every possibility in the diplomatic preparations for that war to push through its Liberation. Europe must recall its Destiny and its WorldMission. It must assess the differences between the two powers in the Concert of Bolshevism, and adapt itself so that it will profit from their changing fortunes in the events to come. Europe must form its policy.

THE DEFINITION OF ENEMY

As we have seen, the word "enemy" has a different meaning when applied to Culture, private life, Politics. In the Cultural sense, Europe has only one "enemy," and that is the Outer Revolt against the World-Mission of the West. It embraces all primitive populations, even in those cases in which they live geographically within the Western Culture, as in North and South America, and includes all fellah-populations now inhabiting areas where High Cultures once fulfilled themselves, for example, the Islamic, Hindu, and Chinese populations. Likewise it embraces populations in whose areas a High Culture has never existed, for example, the barbaric Russians and Mongols, the savages of Africa, South East Asia, and the Pacific islands. The Jewish entity comes from the Magian Culture and will always belong to it spiritually, that Magian Culture which during its life-span gave rise to the Arabian, Persian, Nestorian, and Parsic peoples, among others. While some of these entities may have lost *individuals* to the West, alien units cannot be assimilated by the West in their entirety. Superpersonal realities on both sides forbid it. It is an organic impossibility. The world-wide Cultural front against the West is divided into two political units, Russia and America-Jewry, and the word enemy is used quite differently in Politics.

Politics means so living life that its possibilities are exhausted. In the course of events, Politics divides its world into political *friends* and political *enemies*. Before Politics undertakes this division, all outer units are potential enemies, and it is the task of Politics to select one or more units as enemies, then, if possible, to win the other units as friends.

The choice of enemy is the most important decision in the entire realm of activity called Politics. The mighty English Empire, which dominated the world for more than a century, foundered on its simple but profound mistake of choosing the wrong enemy in two World Wars. The whole adroit ancillary diplomacy, the total war-effort, and the military victory itself did not succeed in preventing the disappearance of the greatest Empire in history and the destruction of England's own sovereignty. The English homeland was not even spared the ultimate humiliation of occupation by foreign troops, and, what is more, these troops came from its erstwhile

64

colony. The formulation of policy is *esoteric*, and this is proved by the selfsame example: Notwithstanding the collapse and disappearance of the English Empire, notwithstanding the reduction of England itself to the status of an "unsinkable aircraft carrier" for foreign air-forces, the Culture-retarding stratum and the broad masses were successfully persuaded by foreign propaganda that a great "victory" had somehow been won for England.

Political blunders can be made at two levels: at the highest level, where the enemy is determined and friends can be obtained, or at the lowest, where the policy based thereupon is carried out. The word *error*, in the strict sense, can be used in Politics only with regard to the future. Thus one must reproach England for choosing Germany as its enemy in the Second World War when it was obvious that its choice was an error. The great von Moltke defined strategy as "the art of making one less error than your adversary." This definition can be likewise applied to Politics. Considered in retrospect, Life is a fabric of errors. No one can foresee the Future.

Politics is concrete; it is the art of the possible, not of the desirable, not of the moral, not of what is worthy of aspiration. Politics is an *art*, and it is the grandest of all arts, since its material is human life and its completed work the blossoming of a superpersonal Destiny. When a work of art is executed by an inferior, an imitator, an academic, the result is a piece of bungling. The indispensable gift of the politician is the gift of *vision*; after it comes finesse in political activity. Without prior vision, the whole fateful proceeding comes to naught.

A statesman comes nearest to the gift of vision when he is aware of his own strength of will and that of his people and perceives the power-currents of the political world. A steady adherence to both of these fundamentals will preserve him from the far-reaching error of choosing the wrong enemy. It is tantamount to waging war against oneself. In the Second World War, England sacrificed both the remnants of its Empire and its own independence for the benefit of America and Russia. There are still people who would deny this fact, but only facts are positive, not the sclerotic opinions of half-blind dotards.

The Political Genius is a superlative artist, and thus free of all negativity in his creations. To his task he brings no hatred, no malice, no envy, nor any will-to-destruction that does not serve his will-to-power and will-to-creation. He is incapable of pursuing a policy that is basically "anti"-oriented, for example, a policy that has the slogan "Win the War!" as its "war-aim." Such slogans may have certain propaganda value for the policy of a political Genius, but only the shamelessly hate-filled reactionary of the Churchill sort makes a policy of his hatred and asserts that "victory" at the cost of self-destruction is something worth seeking. Naturally, the political Genius removes from his path all forces opposing him, so far as he can; but this "anti"-tactic he employs for the sake of increasing his power, not from jealousy, prejudice, hatred, or mere dislike.

The problem of choosing an enemy is the same for Europe today, i.e., for the Culture-bearing stratum, as it would be for us if Europe were constituted as an actual political unit. Today Europe is an area and a People. If it pursues the right policy. tomorrow it will be a power - by virtue of its Inner Imperative alone, which proceeds from the unfulfilled Destiny of the Western Civilisation. The fact that Europe has a World-Mission guaranteees that it will play a rôle in the centuries to come. Whether this rôle will be an active one, or merely passive, will become evident in our decades, and will be determined by the policy of the European Culture-bearing stratum.

The choice of an enemy is not arbitrary: We can designate a political unit as enemy only if, first, we can overcome that unit, and, second, by overcoming it gain power. Clearly, in this second Interbellum-Period Europe cannot overcome any power militarily because there does not and cannot exist a European military force as long as Europe is not constituted as a sovereign state. Any military force directly or indirectly under the command of the Washington régime cannot be called a "European military force." The nationality of an army is that of its political leadership, not of its common soldiers or its officer-corps. In these circumstances, Europe is compelled to win power by spiritual-intellectual means. It must extract power from one or both of the Outer Forces, Russia and America-Jewry. That one of these two units from which Europe can draw true political power, viz., unlimited control over its own land and people, is the political enemy. It cannot be emphasised enough that the enemy-definition does not entail, from the European standpoint, any judgement of especially bad ethical, moral, aesthetic, or cultural qualities on the part of the enemy. Culturally, aesthetically, morally, ethically, there is no choosing between Russia and America-Jewry. Yet, *politically*, Europe is compelled to distinguish between them, by its organic necessity to translate its Inner Imperative into action. It would be impossible for Europe to play a passive rôle in History, even if it wished, or it were wiser to do so. While   Life advances, there is no standing still.

The Definition of Enemy is a problem that must be solved in the total historical frame-of-reference of our Epoch. Thereby the power-currents of the century, the power-problems resulting therefrom, and the relative danger for Europe must be considered.

THE POWER-PROBLEMS OF
HE SECOND INTERBELLUM PERIOD

Owing to the false form of the first two World Wars and to the presence of a Culture-disease in the Western Civilisation, the power-problems in this period between the Second and the Third World Wars are the same ones that have confronted Europe for half a century, but now intensified to the highest possible degree.

In the year 1914, the power-problems were the following: how to preserve Europe's world-hegemony and how to make possible the conversion of Europe from an accumulation of petty-states with the hand-me-down world-outlook of a nationalist-capitalistic parliamentarism to the determined shape of Europe for the 20th century, viz., an Authoritarian Socialist structure of Culture-Nation-People-Race, the Imperium of the West. The form of the First World War, shaped by Culture-retarders like Grey, prevented a natural, organic solution of this power problem.

Between the First and Second World Wars, important steps were taken within Europe for the organic solution of the second problem, the transition of the 20th century phase of the European organism into the world of reality. Hardly anything was done for the solution of the first problem, owing to the precarious world situation at that time, although the ItalianAbyssinian War did bring a general increase in power for Europe.

But this organic move forward was halted by the meddling of America-Jewry in intra-European affairs, and, as we have seen, this meddling brought about, in the same sterile form as the First World War, the tragedy of the Second World War. About 1939, the power-problems consisted in the re-establishment of the world-hegemony that had been almost entirely destroyed by the First World War, and in the completion of the halfactualised Imperium of Europe. The Second World War, occasioned by the extra-European, non-Western force of America-Jewry and by the churchills of France and England, once again thwarted the organic solution of these two problems.

As a result of the Second World War, it can be seen that the power-problems are essentially the same two. Only their order of precedence has changed, so that now the problems are, first, the Liberation of Europe from extra-European rule, for the entirety of Europe is ruled from alien capitals; and, second, the fulfilment of Europe's World-Mission, i.e., the reconquest of its world-hegemony and the establishment of its World Empire.

Every power-problem contains a disjunction between the distribution of spiritual power-sources, on the one hand, and the distribution of acknowledged power and its attributes on the other. The spiritual power-source - the possession of a World-Mission, a calling, a mighty, positive Inner Imperative, and a nation-forming ethic - are found concentrated almost entirely in Europe. The spiritual resources that exist outside Europe, in Russia, America-Jewry, and Japan, are merely a reflex of the European - a European Will that is inspired there by Europe. In actuality, the Outer Forces are seeking to realise the World-Mission of Europe, even though they lack the Inner Imperative to it. Their motivation is completely negative. Thereby is explained the circumstance that the immense concentration of power in the Washington and Moscow regimes has brought no Order to the world, that both regimes perpetuate the Chaos left over in the 20th century from the 19th century. Only Europe can give back to this chaotic world the Principle of Order.

THE AMERICAN POWER-ACCUMULATION

The American power-accumulation can be called an "empire" only in a loose, transferred sense. Within the Symbiosis America-Jewry, neither the Jewish entity nor the subordinate American element thinks in terms of American Imperialism. Thus the American head-of-state specifically declared to the populace that no people on earth was *in any sense* subject to America, that America's "defense" of other peoples did not entitle it to demand reciprocity from them, and, moreover, that under no circumstances would America "dominate" another people. What is of particular significance in this is the anti-imperialist ideology, not the fact that all these principles are completely disregarded in the political conduct of America-Jewry. The intention here is to prevent the rise of *American Imperialist* thinking, for that would run counter to the anti-nationalist policy of the dominant part of the Symbiosis. But if the Imperialist urge within the American people were of deep, imperative force, and pregnant with the Future, it could not be suppressed, and the power-accumulation that the Washington régime at present administers would be organised into an American Empire.

However, a true American Empire that is hierarchically organised and politically administered will never be, since it is not among the formative possibilities of the American character. Now, a *nation* cannot arise by happenstance - a people, yes - but a nation is the outflowing of a High Culture.* Though America can never belong to any other Culture than the Western, in American life Western culture is only a veneer. Its inward influence on the American population was too slight, for example, to have prevented the invasion of Culturally-alien units. There is no American Idea, no American nation, no American ruling-stratum - three ways of expressing the same thing. To be sure, there is an American *People*, whose members are in fact characterised by an *individual imperialism*, which is instinctive, racial, economic. But this individual imperialism can never lift itself to political heights. The true American People is a unit based upon matriarchy. By its own choice, it leads a cocoon-like life within a closed system. The soul of this

*Cf. IMPERIUM,p. 328 ff., p. 334 ff., p. 398 ff.

People is too oriented to the feminine pole of existence, and it therefore cherishes peace, comfort, security, in short, the values of *individual* life. War, conquest, adventure, the creation of form and order in the world - these do not interest the American People. Empire-building demands sacrifices; yet, for sacrifices to be made, and not just *sacrificial victims* slaughtered, there must be an Idea.

The American power-accumulation arose without sacrifices through America's chance intervention at two decisive moments in world affairs. In the First World War, America's sole war-aim - according to the public and private utterances of all leading Americans who were in favour of intervention in that War - was to defeat "German tyranny." As was shown in the analysis of Politics in IMPERIUM, to have the defeat of an arbitrarily chosen enemy as a "war-aim" is to have no war-aim at all. Thus America had no *political* aim in that War. The rôle England played in America's entry into the War is not important here. Important only is the stock of ideas that were played out to set the American People in motion. In the Second World War, America's internal propaganda was exclusively non-political. Again, the chief "war-aim" was to "defeat Germany," and the one attempt to display a positive "war-aim" was a series of negative proposals - all of them reflecting the feminine values of a matriarchy - to free the world of hunger, fear, etc. The psychological orientation of the American People prevents American governments in peacetime from clearly expressing a demand for war. In wartime, it is obligatory to speak only of "peace." "Victory" is supposed to bring only "peace," and not an extension of power. Above all, the purpose of victory is not an American Empire. After the extinction of the Federalist Party in 1828, no political grouping in America publicly advocated the creation of an American Empire. The average type of party-politician ensures, however, that every public man would advocate political imperialism were the idea popular.

The American power-accumulation in this epoch between the Second and Third World Wars has arisen without sacrifice. Had sacrifice been necessary for it, then it would not have arisen.*

* Cf. IMPERIUM, p. 472 ff., p. 482 ff.

Before 1914, America controlled only a small section of the world-surface: the North American Continent, Central America below Mexico, small areas of northern South America. Not even the Caribbean Sea could be called American, since European bases were numerous there and the American fleet was inferior in number to more than one European fleet. In the First World War, 10,000,000 men lost their lives on the battlefield. Of this total sum America's tribute amounted to 120,000; for this slight toll in blood, America acquired sufficient new territories and bases, obtained enough power for itself at sea, to have 1 /5th of the earth's surface under its control: North America, the whole of Central America, including Mexico, the entire Caribbean, much of South America, and half the Pacific. After the War, in accordance with the feminine-matriarchal orientation of the American People, the greater part of these power-acquisitions was abandoned - this occurred through the Washington Naval Treaty of 1921, under which America obligated itself to sink half its fleet without demanding the equivalent from England or Japan. Yet the fact remains: America acquired a power-area that was four times larger than its original with the vanishingly small blood-toll of 120,000.

By 1939, America had gained control, *pari passu* with the steady decline of England's power, of 1/5 of the earth-surface. At the end of the Second World War, America controlled 18/20ths of it. That is the largest power-accumulation ever to come about in the entire history of High-Cultures. The total number of dead of all belligerent states amounted to approximately 15 million. America's portion of this loss was 250,000. In the Second World War, then, America acquired control of more than half the world without its having to make a blood sacrifice worth mentioning in connexion with such an operation.

Not even such unparalleled political successes fill the soul of the American People with satisfaction. America, as a People, is organic, and will forever remain isolationist. Isolationism is the only American characteristic that can be called "nationalism." The American soul does not delight at all in this world power. It finds in it no

* Cf. IMPERIUM, p. 472 ff., p. 482 ff.

72

reason for pride. When in 1947 the Washington régime calmly handed over China to Russia, that is, the focus of America's quarter of the world's power, Americans took no notice. The diplomatic intermediary in the transfer was publicly honoured and draped with medals. Only a few years after the War, ships were taken from the American fleet and delivered to Japan *en masse* to Serve as the basis of a new Japanese navy. No American nationalist protested, for in America there are no nationalists, only victimised isolationists.

It is a strange phenomenon, and History will deal with it as with so many other transient paradoxes, that between the Second and Third World Wars American troops were stationed all along the perimeter of the political world, viz., the northeast quadrant of the planet, and this wide dispersion of American armed forces did not involve any kind of national exultation for Americans. The reason for that is Americans are primarily economics-oriented. The Masculine Principle is to realise higher ideas through art, warfare, Politics. Nothing could be further from the American ideal than that. The Feminine Principle is to nourish and preserve life - that is the American ideal. Americans therefore do not delight in an "empire" that continually lays claim to their wealth and constantly demands a reduction in their standard-of-living. In its traditional isolation, America needed no armies, garrisons, subventions to foreign countries, and Great Wars. The superficial politisation of America has brought the American People economic injuries, and thus confirmed it in its isolation.

The American casualty lists in the first two World Wars, slight as they were numerically, hit the American People in a sensitive spot. No mother rejoices in the death of her children, and matriarchy informs the American soul. Americans do not love their victories, whereas the deaths they count bitterly. Long before American intervention in each of the two World Wars, there was already a *de facto* state-of-war between America and European or Asiatic belligerents. In each case, the possession of numerous "allies" provided Americans with a certain solace. In the Second World War, long lists of American allies were published, and considered effective propaganda even though few of the "allies" were still power-factors or even existed. Indeed, with the alternative: war *now* with allies, or war later, *standing alone*, America can be forced into a war. The old European proverb: *Viel' Feind, viel' Ehr* finds no resonance in matriarchal America.

This American character-trait is a Ponderable of which Europe must take account in shaping its policy. In the American mind (and likewise in the policy-decisions of the Culturally-alien Washington régime), Europe is the basis of every war-plan against Russia. This Ponderable might be used by Europe in either one or the other of two ways, as will be shown later. Moreover, Europe's Culture-bearing stratum must keep in mind that it does not matter at this time whether America, as a People, can regain its independence and sovereignty or whether it will remain simply the instrumental part of the Symbiosis America-Jewry. For political purposes, America and Jewry have become a unit; what name this unit receives is not important.

It remains for us to compare and evaluate from a political standpoint the psychology of the two extra-European powers, America-Jewry and Russia.

Neither Russia nor America-Jewry belongs to the Western Civilisation, though America, considered abstractly in and of itself, as it was before the Revolution of 1933, is still a European colonial-people.

Hence there is no Cultural *casus belli* in the coming Third World War between these two powers. They both belong to the Outer Revolt against the world-supremacy of the West, and the collective term for this revolt, which turns, destroying and negating, against the creative affirmation of the Western Destiny, is *Bolshevism*. Within the Concert of Bolshevism there are, of course, differences as well as similarities. Both must be evaluated.

With both world-powers, the reigning ideology comes from a bygone Western world-outlook. The American ideology of "freedom," "equality," and legalism stems from 18th century Europe, as does its underlying philosophy of materialism. The Russian ideology of Marxism comes from 19th century English Capitalism, of which Marxism is a supplement. In Russia, Marxism is treated as a *religion*, for the prime characteristic of the Russian soul is its religiosity. Whatever this soul takes seriously, be it even the absurd end-product of Western materialism - Pavlovian reflexology, scientific psychology -, it deals with in a religious way, that is, in a way transcending action. Nowhere in Russian life is there anything that in any way corresponds to the Marxist schema. The Russian soul is not yet politically mature, and Russia continues to use Marxism as a political export article, even though a market for it no longer exists, since the First World War buried the form-world of the 19th century for ever. America-Jewry, which is similarly maladapted to the New Age, exports to Europe the shop-worn ideology of Montesquieu, Constant, Mill, Bentham, and hopes that on this basis it can turn the Destiny of Europe back two centuries.

In America, on the other hand, Marxism is not a theory but a fact. In the realm of facts, Marxism means class-war. America is the classic land of finance-capitalism and trade unions, the two organised groups that systematically plunder the national economy.

Not only Marx, but all 19th century theorisers were obsessed with economic doctrines - Malthus, Darwin, Mill, Spencer, Shaw. American life is *essentially* oriented to economics, and every aspect of Life is simply referred for its justification thereto.

Feminine-matriarchal life is routine; hence American life is routine and technicised. Books instruct the population "How To Win Friends," how social life, family life, sexual life are to be conducted. Yet this uniformisation of life is not perceived as burdensome or ignominious-the American population is entirely passive and feels quite at home in this atmosphere of a nursery. The social instincts predominate over the individual instincts, and every American child is taught from his earliest days that the essence of leading a successful life consists in "getting along with people." There is no other way to realise this ideal than to renounce one's individuality. That is the explanation for the difficulty of kindling any kind of political opposition in America. As soon as a policy secures a foothold and becomes popular, it is right and respectable. Radical or persistent criticism is impossible in America; the term "individualist" is nearly an insult. The extirpation of strong individuality precludes the rise of a true elite, an aristocracy, a ruling-stratum, for these are always based upon strong individuality and the feeling of uniqueness. All feelings of superiority, of higher self-esteem, of uniqueness are educated out of the American while he is still in kindergarten. It is impressed on him that his existence, his problems are exactly like those of everybody else.*

An elementary demand of Life, however, is that every group possess a stratified social articulation. America's "élite" for economic, technical, industrial, social purposes is the businessclass, those thirty-thousand technical-managerial brains that permit American life to function. For *political* purposes, the "elite" is the Jewish entity, which enjoys a monopoly of power in all matters but is especially conspicious in the direction of foreign affairs. The technical-managerial caste has no sense of carrying out a mission; it does not regard itself as superior
* Cf. IMPERIUM, p. 502 ff., p. 524 ff.

in nature, but only as more proficient in intellectual-technical matters. This type of social-technical differentiation resembles that which exists among the social insects, for example, the bees and ants.

Russian life is fundamentally barbarian. The barbarian is to be distinguished not only from Culture-men, but from savages, primitives, fellaheen, and decadents as well. Barbarian is a word full of promise, for the barbarian is inwardly in motion. The Germanic tribes that occupied Imperial Rome were barbarians, and from this Germanic stock came, many centuries later, men who wrought the Western Culture. The barbarian is the pre-Cultural form of humanity, just as different from the fellah, the end-product of a Culture, as from the savage, the proto-human type that stands in no relation whatever to a High Culture. The barbarian is strong-willed yet irresolute. He can be readily converted to new doctrines - witness the Russian "conversion" to Marxism -, but the conversion must be superficial, for mere verbiage cannot abolish the difference between Culture-man and barbarian. The barbarian is rough and tough, not keen-witted, full of artifice, and certainly not legalistic and intellectualised. He is the opposite of decadent. He is ruthless and does not shrink back from destroying what others may prize highly.

America's ideology - 18th century materialistic egalitarianism and 19th century capitalism - and Russia's ideology - 19th century proletarian capitalism - are both permeated with the spirit of their respective populations, the American ideology with that of the amalgam of negro-Jewish-Asiatic-Indian-European elements, as modified by the peculiarities of the landscape, the Russian ideology with that of the nomadic tribes of Asia, which are imbued with the enormous impersonality of the Asiatic steppes.

The Culture-man outside the Culture-sphere stands in danger of losing his Cultural-orientation - what the British civil administration in India used to call "going negative." During the expansion of the American population over the vast plains, the American colonial lost well-nigh every contact with Western tradition and Western happenings, and his Western culture was diluted. Only in one part of

Chinese or Hindu, he would have retained his Cultural-orientation in fullest measure, for conflict with the Alien strengthens the Proper. But he fought merely savages and, more often, the landscape itself, the hardships of Nature. In the inward contest between Culture and Landscape, Landscape was largely the victor. Because comfort is one of the main ideals of the American, his vital impetus finds expression primarily in the domain of technics. Unrestrained by tradition, by political or social considerations, he fell head over heels into *absolute technical development*, and - in technics - he made his the foremost among the Western Colonies. Thus, as a result of his century of stateless expansion, the American succumbed, on the one hand, to the primitivity of his vast and empty continent, while, as a result of the concentration made possible for him by the absence of power-struggles, on the other, he made himself in some respects superior to Europeans. This had as its consequence yet another peculiarity.

The simultaneous presence of primitivity and over-civilisation in the American shaped his relationship to Europe into an unhealthy one. With his strong technical aptitude, he came to regard Europe as *inferior*; with his primitivity, he failed to comprehend Europe's Cultural Imperative in the 20th century. Hence he offered no resistance when the Culture-distorting régime foisted on America the idea that it had to *educate* Europe.

This idea could be all the more inculcated since America is by nature feminine-matriarchal and attributes great value to formal education. In America the autodidact will find neither political, academic, professional, nor social recognition. This peculiarity of the American character has been aggravated by the Culturedistorting element, and American schools and universities have been made into scholastic factories that produce uniform biological units. They have eradicated human individuality, so far as that can be attained at all in the human species. All values imparted through this "education," such as comfort, security, and social uniformity, may be found on the purely animal level in man. None appeal to the specifically human level, which is embodied at highest potential by the unique and individualised human being, with his loftier values.

While the American is a Culture-man, *reprimitivised* on the one side of his being, *over-civilised* on the other, since he is completely and entirely animated by the ideals of peace, comfort, and security, the Russian is a barbarian, and still wholly primitive. Centuries of Petrinism never touched the underground Russia. No matter that it figured as such for centuries, Russia never became a nation of the West. America is a genuine Western colony, though, to be sure, it must now be counted part of the Outer Revolt.

The orientation towards technics is common to both: America is technical by instinct; Russia has become so under compulsion from its leaders, who have only politico-military reasons for embracing technics. In the field of philosophy, America's sole contribution to the Western intellectual heritage was Pragmatism - the doctrine that Truth is "what works." In other words, Truth is not a function of the Soul, but of Nature. Pragmatism is at once a primitive and over-civilised philosophy, primitive, because its position *vis-à-vis* Truth is devoid of higher culture; over-civilised, because it makes all Truth merely an attribute of *Technics*. Expressed in terms of the American psychology: "True is what procures me more security, more comfort." In America, obsession with technics is the expression and content of life of the population. It is *instinctive*, and America naturally seeks to export it to whatever countries its armies and bomber-squadrons have conquered. In Russia, on the other hand, the technics-obsession merely serves political and military ends, and is imposed on the Russian population only through the apparatus of a political dictatorship. The Russian experiences things primarily in a religious way; hence the incredible spectacle of his worshipping *a machine.*

Russia exhibits the same education-obsession as America: In the words of Lunacharsky: "Education, distributed according to Marxist principles, can make even the most mediocre Oriental intelligent." Once again, a common denominator with America. There, too, "intelligence" is regarded as something that can be acquired, and, moreover, as the only distinction between human beings. Both Russia and America hold that the External forms and conditions the mind. Both emphasise totally environment and experience, negate dogmatically Spirit and Soul. For both the collective man is the ideal and the prevalent type. In both there naturally exists the most extreme intolerance towards anything other than the mass-ideal.

In Russia, the craze for uniformity, including the educationmania, is likewise imposed from above to carry out a political programme. The emphasis on the power of environment, the adoration of reflexology, the idolisation of machines, of statistics and percentages, and of economic theories generally - all this is in Russia simply *technique*, and it is all essentially *negative*: the Russian peasant-barbarian soul is a religious ferment, and, as such, abhors economic theories, machines, science, and nationalism. The programme of Moscow-Bolshevism represents a means of quashing the hyper-individuality of a people of Pugachevs, Aksakovs, Kropotkins, Nechayevs, Dosto-ievskys, Rasputins, and Shoptsy. *Primarily, Moscow-Bolshevism is a method for politicising the religious-barbarian Russia.* That the Moscow régime uses Marxism as an export-article is simply political idiocy, and the possibility constantly exists that it will one day discard it because of its ineffectiveness.

For Europe the following distinction is important: American-Jew-ish Bolshevism is the instinctive destruction of the West through primitive, anti-Cultural ideas - peace, comfort, security, abolition of individuality -, through over-technicisation, through the imposition of Culture-distortion and Culture-retardation. Russian Bolshevism seeks to attain the destruction of the West in the spirit of pan-Slavic religios-ity, i.e., the Russification of all humanity.

Thus American-Jewish Bolshevism poses a real spiritual threat to Europe. In its every aspect, American-Jewish Bolshevism strikes a weak spot in the European organism. Even in Europe there exists a stratum, the Michel-stratum, the inner-America, which is animated by the purely animal American ideal of peace, comfort, security, abolition of individuality. Even in Europe there is an element that would like to replace culture with machinery. Even on Europe Culture-retarding regimes can be imposed, if necessary with American bayonets. Even in Europe Culture-distortion is present: the dictature over Europe

80

of the American-Jewish Symbiosis itself. And even in Europe, in the midst of the Age of Absolute Politics, the Cato-type exists: You can watch him babbling, misty-eyed, about democratic ideals while the Barbarian and the Distorter occupy the sacred soil of the West. The 20th century European Cato would rather see the West destroyed than have finally to toss the rubbish of democratic ideals on the scrap heap of history, where the corpse of Democracy lies stinking and putrescent after a half century of decay.

Russian Bolshevism is simply barbarism, and therefore finds no resonance anywhere in Europe. Even Europe's lowest spiritual stratum, the inner traitor, the Michel-stratum, has nothing whatever in common with the pan-Slavism of barbaric population-streams. Russian religiosity has been temporarily and, from a Cultural standpoint, falsely raised to political intensity as a reflex of the great Western spiritual development, the Resurgence of Authority, the genesis of the Imperium-Idea. Without the Western Culture, there would be no such structure as Russia, only marauding tribes of barbaric horsemen like the Cossacks in *Taras Bulba*.

Russian Bolshevism is therefore less dangerous to Europe than American-Jewish Bolshevism, for no aspect of its menace corresponds to a weakness in Europe's spiritual armour. Europe actually has an inner America, the Michel-stratum; however, Europe has no inner Russia. Obviously, the so-called Communist Parties are not at all the reliable tools wherewith a Russian occupation of Europe could be built. In fact, the work of these Communist Parties is already done. They were useful instruments of early Bolshevism's foreign policy, especially in the period 1933-1939. During the Second World War, they helped save Russia's existence as a political unit; after the War, they helped create the Russian power-accumulation, extending from Hanover to Hong-Kong, the largest contiguous poweraccumulation in the history of the world. Yet, today, between the Second and Third World Wars, all Communist Parties, including the American, are politically insignificant.

The Communist Parties of the West are simply class-war units, not bearers of barbarism and Russian pan-Slav nationalism. In the 20th century, all are forced to think in terms of facts and not merely words, so far as Politics is concerned, and Russia's connexion with Western class-war rests simply on words. Russia claims to be the bearer of class-war in the West. Nevertheless, during the Second World War the Moscow régime forbade the American Communist Party to engage in class-warfare. Actually, the entire policy of using Marxism as a political export-article is now political stupidity, for Marxism has lost its former rabble-rousing value in the West. The highpoint of class-war in the West has passed.

In particular, it was the re-orientation of Russian world-policy after the Second World War, the turning against the Jewish entity of Church-State-Nation-People-Race, that sealed the doom of every Communist Party in the West, the one in America included.

The blow that the American-Jewish Symbiosis has dealt the European organism is well-known. The values of this Symbiosis are purely animal, anti-Spiritual, anti-Aristocratic, anti-Cultural, anti-Heroic, anti-Imperialist, and therefore appeal to the worst element in the European population and to the worst in every individual European. In each point of its attack, America-Jewry opposes the values of Capitalism to those of Imperialism, the heroic world-outlook of the Age of Absolute Politics. With the spiritual-ethical values of Capitalism, America-Jewry is planning to kill the Western organism. But since the Past can never destroy the Future, only attempt to thwart it, that means American bayonets imposing the anti-Cultural Interregnum on Europe, and therein lies the possibility that for Europe will follow many decades of degradation, chaos, darkness, stultification, misery, and wasting away.

The effect that a Russian occupation of Europe would have on the Western Culture is not yet equally well-known, and can be determined only by uncovering its organic basis.

The Russian is a barbarian; the European is a Culture-man in his late-Civilisation phase. Before this moment in History, barbarians have violently invaded Culture-areas. In the 16th century B.C., Northern barbarians invaded the Egyptian Culture-petrifact, to enact the chapter of history that is called the "Hyksos"-era. About 1700 B.C., the Kassites conquered and occupied the Babylonian Culture-area, and, around the same time, the Aryans in a barbaric wave from the North flooded into and conquered the Culture of the Indus. Chinese history in its first stirrings is the epic of a barbarian invasion by the Chou. Imperial Rome - even Republican Rome - was invaded more than once by the barbarian Germans and Gauls. In none of these historical instances did the invasion of the barbarians destroy the body of the Culture; in each case the result was finally the absorption of the barbarian elements into the Culture-body or their expulsion. The barbarian comes to destroy and stays to learn. Spiritually, the barbarian is a tabula rasa. Labile and childlike, he is eager to apply the new doctrines, new life-forms, to which he has been converted. Hence the Romanov Petersburg of the 18th and 19th centuries displayed a higher degree of Western Politesse and social-form than any European capital before it.

The belief that a Russian-barbarian occupation of the whole of Europe would be similar to the Russian occupation of half of Germany after the Second World War is a completely false estimate of the possibilities. A Russian occupation of all Europe would involve an entirely different distribution of forces and a completely different psychological situation. In the first place, the Russian occupation after the Second World War originated as a gift from America. Cynically, Europe's border against Asia, which had been pushed back gradually over a millennium, was restored to its place of 900 years ago. Thus the history, honour, and traditions of thirty generations of Europeans were outraged. The atrocities committed during the first years of the Russian occupation were permitted, encouraged, and even imitated by America. Without American encouragement, Russia would not have been in the position to commit its atrocities. In the second place, Europe was not politically able to intervene to protect 30,000,000 Europeans, for every European country was governed by the churchill-régimes the Americans had appointed, and these puppet-governments greeted barbarian Russia as their "valiant ally" while their members exchanged decorations with those of the Moscow régime.

Russia's occupation of a small part of Europe and its domination over one tenth of the European population after the Second World War were made possible only by the Washington régime, which, in 1945, wanted Europe so divided that the Red Flag would wave over Berlin and Vienna. If the Washington régime, instead of giving Russia simply a small part of Europe, had abandoned to it all of Europe - and that is a possibility contained in the events to come -, the division of forces would be completely different. Instead of AmericaJewry, the whole of Russia, Eastern Europe, and most of Western Europe - under churchill-régimes - ranged against part of Germany, then against 200,000,000 Russians, would be arrayed the total body of the West, 250,000,000 men who are superior to them in intelligence, technical skill, organisational talent, and will-to-power. If this happens, America will be expelled from Earope, once and for all. Europe will have but a single enemy. That would be a unifying factor such as did not exist from the First Crusade until Lepanto.

A Russian occupation would develop along one or the other of two lines. The first possibility is an endless series of European uprisings against Russia that could result only in the expulsion of the demoralised barbarians. The second possibility would result from Russia's introducing a clever régime and according Europe extensive autonomy and magnanimous treatment. Within a few decades, this Europe would naturally aim at infiltrating horizontally the whole Russian seat of origin, its technical, economic, social, and, finally, military and political life. Instead of the Russification of Europe, as Dostoievsky and Aksakov dreamt of it, would result the Europeanisation of Russia once again, and this time in far stronger degree. This would occur from pure historical *necessity*, since this is the Age of Absolute Politics and Europe is politically shrewd whereas barbarian Russia is formless and politically inept, fluctuating between senseless vehemence and inner doubt. Not even the most brilliant statesmen in Russia could use this barbarian material to subjugate Europe in this Imperialist stage of its Destiny. An attempt by Russia to integrate Europe into its power-accumulation peacefully would eventually result in the rise of a new Symbiosis: Europe-Russia. Its final form would be that of a European Imperium. An attempt by Russia to chastise and terrorise Europe without the help of America would result in Russia's expulsion from Europe for good, by a Europe whose own dormant barbarian instincts had been thus reawakened.

If Russia should occupy Europe and attempt to imitate the American policy of encouraging petty-statism, to divide and conquer, it would fail utterly. America has been successful in that policy only because of its access to the European Michel-stratum with its lickspittle churchills. The Michel yearns for American capitalism and liberalism, but trembles with abysmal cowardice before Russian barbarism. The Communist Parties would be of slight use to Russia in any attempt to set up puppet-governments on the model of America's churchillregimes. The leadership and membership of these Communist Parties is composed of inferior European types, not of pan-Slavs or religious Russian nationalists. The barbarian, immature and unversed in the subtleties of the art of Politics, trusts only those who are of his own religion, and the true religion of the Russian is not Marxism, but *Russia*. The first victims of a Russian occupation of Europe would be the European Communists, who would be liquidated at the slightest suspicion of disloyalty. Their "Communism" stems from books, their pro-Russian sentiments from hatred and envy of their European surroundings, their utopian orthodoxy about Russia comes from a lack of realism and an exaggerated intellectualism. The Russian knout and the Russian revolver would soon teach them what they have not learnt from their books, would shatter their utopian ideals and give their hatred a new focus.

Russia's effect on petty-statism and petty-nationalism would in no way resemble America's successful perpetuation of these Culture-pathological phenomena. To carry out its policy in Europe, America *needs* petty-statism. Not only does it work in the spirit of the principle, *divide et impera*, it also cannot think outside the narrow framework of it. After the Second World War, the Washington régime, which held absolute power to force its will on enfeebled Europe, announced its policy of a "united Europe." It then proceeded to Balkanise Europe politically and atomise it socially in unparalleled fashion. Numerous congresses of toothless and infantile old men from the 19th century passed even more numerous resolutions, but the result was continued disunity and chaos. The childish dotards had received permission from Washington to jabber about the "unification" of Europe as much as they liked, but they were not allowed to say a word about the Liberation of Europe. That is why all these congresses led to nothing. For the Unification of Europe and the Liberation of Europe are one and the same process: seen from within, it is Unification; from without, liberation.

The fact that Russia used the fiction of "independent" states in its post-War occupation of Eastern Europe offers no criterion for its policy in the event it should occupy Western Europe, the Europe that is synonymous with the Western Culture. In any case, simply the presence of the barbarian, let alone his policy, would dissolve the Inner Enemy of Europe, the Michel-stratum, and thus liberate all creative forces within Europe from the tyranny of the Past.

Without the Michel, without his leaders, namely the churchills, without American bayonets, the distribution of forces would be as follows: the European will-to-power and the European Destiny against the sheer military might of a barbarian horde. The dissolution of the Michel-stratum would automatically destroy petty-statism, for petty-statist ideals and theories are preserved only in Culture-retarding brains. The barbarian, whether he wished it or not, would complete the spiritual unification of Europe by removing the only innerEuropean obstacle to that unity. From the Spiritual to the Political is but one step.

The following would be the results of the two possible kinds of Russian policy, the far-sighted policy of striving to integrate Europe into an enormous Russian Empire, embracing the whole world, and the policy of attempting to rule Europe by terror and violence.

Should Russia aim at a lasting incorporation of Europe into its Empire, it could succeed only if it granted Europe significant concessions. The first of these would have to be administrative autonomy for Europe as a unit, for that is the desire of all Europeans - the Michel-stratum and its leaders, the senile churchills, of course, excepted.

Should Russia attempt to terrorise Europe, it would summon forth in the European People the will to counter-terror. Faced with the barbarian, all Europeans, even the simplest minded liberals, would learn the necessity of inner firmness, of a stern will, the virtues of Command and Obedience, for these alone could force the barbarian to accept demands, or else retreat to his tundras and steppes. All Europeans would realise that not parliamentary babble, class-war, capitalism, and elections, but only Authority, the Will-to-Power, and finally, the military spirit could ever drive out the barbarian. The expulsion of England's army of 40,000 men by a few hundred Irish guerrilla-fighters in the years 1916-1923 would be repeated on a larger scale. In a great, unrelenting War of Liberation, Europe would unite itself, and cast the barbarian back to the distant plains of Asia.

To conclude: Between the two powers in the Concert of Bolshevism that dominates this Second Interbellum-Period, there are numerous similarities, some profound, others superficial. Neither of the two is an organism with a positive Mission; neither of the two exhibits the inner qualities that alone can found and preserve a world-system; neither of them has or can have an aristocracy; in short, neither of them is the seat of a High Culture. In both the element of Landscape predominates over the cultural component in every stratum of the human material; both make use of an antiquated Western ideology that is completely ineffectual in the world-situation of the Age of Absolute Politics; both have not the faintest inkling of the Imperium-Idea, the necessary fulfilment whereof is the total historical meaning of this Age; both believe it possible to attain a static world-order in which History would have ceased to exist, and this belief makes both dangerously relentless; both believe Europe can be destroyed as a politico-Cultural unit, and degraded to the level of China.

Thus, from the European standpoint, there is in a *Cultural* sense no choice between these two powers, for both represent fundamental opposites to European Cultural imperatives. In their political relation to Europe, however, the two extra-European powers widely and fundamentally differ. Owing to the presence of a European inner America, the Washington régime is able to establish or maintain in every European country: Culture-distortion, petty-statism, finance-capitalism, democracy, economic distress, and chaos. Regardless of its intentions, Russia produces a spiritual aversion throughout Europe. If America, deliberately or otherwise, relinquished to Russia the whole of Europe, Russia's occupation would have to be based either on terror or large-scale concessions to procure collaboration. Both occupation policies would end in the domination of Russia by Europe, either through a peaceful inner conquest or a series of Liberation Wars that Europe would wage as a unit against Russia. Barbarian Russia can only awaken Europe's sterner instincts. The American-Jewish Symbiosis, composed of fellah-Jews and American colonials who are at once primitive and over-civilised, appeals to the lowest stratum of Europe and to the lowest stratum in every European, the stratum of animal instincts, laziness, cowardice, avarice, dishonour, and ethical individualism. America can only divide Europe-no matter what its policy. Russia can only unite Europe-no matter what its policy.

From their comparative relationships to Europe, it follows quite clearly that a Russian-barbarian domination of all Europe, if such a thing were brought about by American policy-and that is the only way such an event could occur-would be less injurious to the Destiny of Europe than a continuation of the American-Jewish domination, for the barbarian, by his very presence, would dissolve the Inner Enemy of Europe, the Michel-stratum, and unite Europe spiritually.

This brings us to the concrete question of political decisions for Europe. The political question would be: How is power to be enlarged? But since Europe has no power, the question is: How is power to be obtained? There are only two political units in the world; hence the question is simply: From which political unit can Europe wrest away power? Or in other words: *Who is the Enemy?*

The armistice that concluded the Second World War left Europe divided between Russia and America-Jewry. Russia received ten per cent of Europe's population, America-Jewry was allotted ninety per cent. By Europe is meant here, of course, the Cultural Europe, viz., Germany, France, England, Italy, Spain, together with tiny provinces like Switzerland, and not the geographic "Europe" that is an historically worthless concept.

The Washington régime naturally seeks to convince its European subjects to identify the interests of America-Jewry with their own and therefore prepare Europe for war against Russia in alliance with it. The propaganda that aims at enlisting Europe's participation in this war has three main points: first, Russia is not a "democracy"; second, it "enslaves" other peoples; third, a Russian occupation of Europe would result in the slaughter of the whole European population or a considerable part thereof.

The first point is politically meaningless, nor is the second point worth taking seriously. To enslave two hundred and fifty million people who are spiritually, ethically, scientifically, technically, militarily, and politically the most highly developed in the world is impossible. So far as Europeans can be enslaved at all, they are already enslaved by America-Jewry. Today the people of Europe work with every possible exertion for the enrichment and aggrandisement of the financiers, industrialbarons, politicians, and generals of North America. Slavery no longer means the rattling of chains, rather shortages of currency and materials, rationing, unemployment, occupation soldiers and their families, puppet-governments, re-armament and military programmes on a gigantic scale.

The third point seeks to *frighten* Europeans into a war to destroy America-Jewry's sole dynamic opponent, thus placing the masters of New York and Washington in control of the entire world. But again, to kill a considerable part of the European population through short-term violent measures would be impossible. The well-planned and systematically executed starvation of Germany by the American-Jewish occupation during the period 1945-1948 killed approximately 3,000,000 people. That is probably the largest number of people that could have been killed by such methods. Overheated brains that could be persuaded that Europe "killed 6,000,000 Jews" can readily imagine the course a Russian massacre of hundreds of millions of human beings would take. People who believe in such nightmares lack a sense for exaggeration, and their psychology is entirely wanting. No great number of men can be trained to kill, directly and systematically, as a daily performance, from morning till evening, over an extended period, unarmed men, women, and children. Certainly, the mere sporadic killing of the kind involved in every military invasion could never reduce the population of Europe to any great extent.

If a selective killing should be the method in an attempt to behead the European organism, then Russia would be likewise incapable of that. This was the method of the American-Jewish "war-crimes" programme, the most extensive terror in the history of the world. America-Jewry attempted to isolate the elite and string up its members one by one; but there, too, it missed the mark. Russia did not practise any systematic "war-crimes" terror, in spite of encouragement on the part of America-Jewry, since it was more interested in individuals as material for the Future than in settling past accounts according to Mosaic Law. Furthermore, the American Colonials and their exotic leaders understand much better than the barbarian how to go about isolating and exterminating superior individuals, for the inner structure and cohesion of the Western Culture are much less familiar to him and much less understood by him. A profound ignorance of the outside world goes hand in hand with Russian xenophobia.

America-Jewry insists that Russia could overwhelm Europequite mechanically and automatically-were not American colonial troops here. Yet the *fact* remains that only America's intervention in the Second World War prevented Europe from destroying Russia as a political unit. The present Russian power-accumulation was thus created by America-Jewry. Never in the five centuries of Russian history has Russia been able to make way into Europe unless supported by one or more European states. Against Frederick the

Great Russia received aid from France, Austria, and Sweden; against Napoleon Russia received aid from England, Austria, Prussia, Sweden, and Spain. In 1945, Russia penetrated into Germany only with America's assistance. Before American intervention, Europe had hurled the barbarian back across the Volga. Russia is a threat only to a divided Europe; a united Europe could destroy the power of Bolshevist Russia at the moment of its choosing. That Europe has need of America-Jewry to defend itself against Russia is a crass lie.

Only America can grant Russia entry into Europe; this was true in 1945, and will be just as true in 1967 or 1975. There are two ways in which America-Jewry could deliver Europe to a Russian-Bolshevist occupation: by voluntarily making Russia a gift of it, as it did with China in 1947, or by losing a war against Russia from European bases.

In any case, Europe-that means here above all the Culturebearing stratum-will choose its own enemy because the 250,000 men who are mystically charged with fulfilling the Destiny of Europe are by nature inwardly free of Culturally-alien influences. Enemy propaganda, however great its extent may be, cannot frustrate the Destiny of a High Culture, for that Destiny is above mechanism and technics, and propaganda is simply a technique. An enemy occupying Europe can probably round up herds of civilians by means of its puppet-governments and call the result an army, but beyond that it cannot go. An army means, first, morale; second, an officer-corps; third, a high command; and, fourth, the human material of the troops. A herd of civilians conscripted under foreign coercion would possess no morale and have no European officer-corps and European high command. Without these, they would be only an armed mob, and, as such, not a formidable match for the barbarians.

We have seen that it is a deep spiritual need of the matriarchal American People to have many and strong allies in a war; and of the ruling-stratum in America it must be remarked that the rider is always limited to the abilities of his mount. We have also seen that Europe is the basis for America's every war-plan against Russia. Europe may be able to exploit these facts.

91

To secure the collaboration of Europe in the war it is planning against Russia, America would grant Europe huge concessions--in inner autonomy, in commerce, in military affairs, and even in administrative unification. But since America has the Michel-stratum at its disposal, and this stratum holds office everywhere in Europe, no demands are put to it. Thus the Washington régime can treat Europeans as something less than peons-peons at least receive *a wage*. The churchills of every country make no demands lest they disquiet the American bayonets upon which their tenure of office depends. To expect pride and independence from the stratum of professional traitors is simply unrealistic.

The second way in which the American People's spiritual need to have allies might be exploitet would be through an unswerving, voluntary, neutralisation of Europe vis-à-vis the projected war against Russia. Once the Washington régime was forced to accept European neutrality as a fact, it would have to abandon its plans for a European theatre-of-war and evacuate Europe.

Either of these possibilities, if realised, could bring about the Liberation of Europe before the Third World War. The first possibility could be realised only if the Michel-stratum were removed from public life, for the churchills would scarcely place Europe's interests above their class and personal interests, which are protected only by the foreign occupation.

To act creatively in Politics, one must begin with the right choice of enemy. If one selects an enemy from whom one can win no power, the end-result is suicide, as we saw with the self-destruction of the English Empire in the Second World War. Were Europe actually to fight for an enemy, that would be proof that Europe had in fact died, but the continuing mystical relation between the European Culture-bearing stratum and the European population would prevent Europe from doing so. Should the Third World War occur, Europe will participate in it only on its own terms. That is an absolute mystical certainty. Perhaps a herd of hapless conscripts without morale, without European officers and a European high command, can be thrown on the battlefield to fight for an enemy, but that would hardly be European participation worthy of the name.

All this has long since answered the question: *Who is the Enemy?* The enemy must be a political unit at whose expense we can gain power. America-Jewry has the power in Europe, and if Europe would win back its sovereignty, it can do so only at the expense of America-Jewry. Politics is concrete, and thus the argument that Russia wishes to conquer Europe has but little force. Perhaps India would like to do that as well, but Europe must reckon on facts and not on threats. America has the power in Europe, and, therefore, America is the Enemy.

Two facts dominate the politics of Europe in this historical period: Europe will never fight for its Enemy; Europe will survive the Third World War and its aftermath, regardless of the new weaponry.

These are *metaphysical* facts; they possess Destiny value and cannot be removed by human action. They correspond to all life-furthering, life-affirming, power-increasing instincts of the European People, to the superpersonal Destiny of the Western Culture. In view of these facts, the enemy propaganda of the Russian bogey can be called simply idiotic. America-Jewry is the bearer of the Russian menace, today, as in the Second World War. If it brings about a Russian occupation of all Europe, then all Europe will persevere and overcome that happening. Should America be expelled from Europe before the Third World War, the form of the war would be completely different. Instead of America-Jewry *versus* Russia, it would then be the European Imperium *versus* Russia, and in that form the war would end in the destruction of Russia as a political unit. For the European Imperium, the result would be external security for the coming centuries. Should America attempt to intervene, as before, this time its efforts would be of no avail, for the European Imperium will naturally include England and Ireland. It was only America's fortuitous possession of those bases that enabled it to stab Europe in the back during the Second World War. From North America or Africa, AmericaJewry could do little or nothing to help Russia.

The Age is mighty and its tasks enormous, but if we hold fast to our honour and pride, harken to our own instincts and the Inner Imperative, we will win the upper hand in every instance. Although the opponents are gigantic, they are formless; behind their patchwork power-accumulations is a spiritual void which, like a vacuum, will draw back their dispersed forces. Neither America-Jewry nor Russia is a structure inwardly adapted to the Age of Absolute Politics. The American People is matriarchal, isolationist, and interested only in economic matters. When the power-adventures at the antipodes run into too much money or demand real blood-sacrifice, the Washington régime will no longer be able to force it to tread the false path of senseless World Wars. In the World War, Germany lost 739 Generals, whereas America had the death of a single General to mourn. This fact just symbolises the truth that America has enjoyed success without having to pay the price of it. The moment the adventures become too costly, the Washington régime will have to retreat, for even its "victories" mean nothing to the American People. An apolitical people cannot win an enduring political victory; it does not need it, or want it, or even know how it would use the power proceeding from it.

The Russian barbarian does not understand power; he has no knowledge of the meaning of this Age. Neither the halfWesternised Bolshevists nor the pure-Asiatic masses possess the qualities needed to build an empire. The spiritually unadulterated Russian, whose limitations are binding for the Moscow régime, is *religious*, hence *inward*; he is rural and land-hungry, but there is no nobility and no religion in Russia that attend to his material and spiritual cares. Marxism is a collection of dead and sterile phrases, and can no more strongly inspire the Russian than it can the European. Pan-Slav religiosity does not seek an empire; with it an empire cannot be built.

This is the Age of Absolute Politics, and its meaning is the fulfillment of the Destiny of the Western Civilisation: the formation of the European Imperium and the actualisation of its World-Mission. In this Age, a power that would impose its will on the world must be endowed with the inner qualities that alone can establish and maintain a world-system, the qualities of the Spanish Europe in the 16th century, the English Europe in the 18th and 19th centuries, the Prussian Ethical Socialist Europe in the 20th century, which will survive the 21st century. The one, great, all-embracing quality that is absolutely necessary for such a task is *the consciousness of a Mission*. That cannot come from human resolves; it can come only as the emanation of a superpersonal soul, the organ of a higher Destiny, a Divinity. The American-Jewish and Russian ideas of negative world-conquest are but vague caricatures of the true, Western European Idea of *Imperium Mundi*, a travesty of History on the world-stage.

Europe recognises its Cultural enemies and its sole political enemy. Thus it sees the only path it can follow. The basis of Europe's politics is *faith* in but under no circumstances fear of the Future. If we follow now the path that our instincts, our intelligence, and our Inner Imperative have prescribed, whatever befalls us shall be *good*. For us there is but one crime, one misdemeanour, and one mistake: that is to be untrue to ourselves and follow alien leaders and hold alien ideals.

Europe also recognises its Inner Enemy: Whosoever pursues another policy than that of a sovereign Europe, whether this be the policy of America-Jewry or Russia, is the Inner Enemy. Petty-statists and petty-nationalists sink to the level of spies and foreign agents. Loyalty to Europe excludes every other political loyalty. No European owes the petty-state of his birth any allegiance whatever, for all these tiny erstwhile-states are now simply anti-European tools in the hands of our Enemy, the Washington régime.

Europe is equal to its historic task. Against the anti-spiritual, anti-heroic "ideals" of America-Jewry, Europe pits its metaphysical ideas, its faith in its Destiny, its ethical principles, its heroism. Fearlessly, Europe falls in for battle, knowing it is armed with the mightiest weapon ever forged by History: the superpersonal Destiny of the European organism. Our European Mission is to create the Culture-State-Nation-Imperium of the West, and thereby we shall perform such deeds, accomplish such works, and so transform our world that our distant posterity, when they behold the remains of our buildings and ramparts, will tell their grandchildren that on the soil of Europe once dwelt a tribe of gods.

THE ENEMY OF OUR ENEMIES

A CRITIQUE
OF FRANCIS PARKER YOCKEY'S
THE ENEMY OF EUROPE

Revilo P. Oliver

LIBERTY BELL PUBLICATIONS
PO Box 890
York, SC 29745

Printed in the United States of America

CONTENTS

THE ENEMY
OF OUR ENEMIES

WHEN Francis Parker Yockey completed and published *Imperium* in 1948, he wrote a comparatively short sequel or pendant to his major work. This sequel, which he later entitled *The Enemy of Europe*, is now lost, but he had his manuscript with him when he was in Germany in 1953, and, after revising two passages to take account of events since 1948, he had it translated into German and printed at Frankfurt-am-Main in an edition of two hundred copies. Yockey's work displeased the Jews, who accordingly ordered their henchmen to raid the printing plant, punish the printer, smash the types, and destroy all copies of the book. Yockey escaped and fortunately had already sent several copies abroad, and it is from a photocopy of one of these that Mr. Francis has tried to restore Yockey's English text, so far as possible.

The Enemy of Europe is a work of great philosophical, historical, and political significance because

(1) In it Yockey applies to the contemporary situation of the world the philosophy of history that he elaborated in *Imperium*, much as Spengler in *Die Jahre der Entscheidung* applied to the world of 1933 the philosophical theory he had expounded in his *Untergang des Abendlandes.*

(2) It is the earliest coherent expression of a political attitude in Europe which first became manifest to Americans in the late 1950s and which at the present time largely determines the conduct of the various European nations in their relations with the United States and the Soviet Union. This attitude, which is generally misunderstood because, for the most part, Europeans cautiously use in public only equivocal or vague terms to intimate or disguise what Yockey said explicitly and without diplomatic subterfuge, was quickly imitated in other parts of the world and is commonly designated by such terms as 'neutralism,' 'uncommitted nations,' and 'The Third World.'

(3) Yockey's analysis of the situation when he wrote poses today the most urgent question before intelligent Americans

1

and, indeed, all other members of our race — a question of political fact that each of us must solve, at least provisionally, before he can estimate the chances that our species will survive on this globe.

It will be proper, therefore, to examine, as summarily as possible, each of these three aspects of *The Enemy of Europe.* Before we do so, however, it behooves us to say something about the only text in which Yockey's work is now available.

THE RETROVERSION

Yockey's manuscript, as I have said, has disappeared and must be presumed lost.[1] We may conjecture that it was in Frankfurt when the subjugated Germans' Thought Police[2] burned, as they thought, all copies of the German edition, and that they found and burned it at the same time. So far as I know, the identity of the translator, who did the work for a

---

1. Yockey seems not to have made a carbon copy, an unfortunate omission. The distinguished foreign correspondent of the *Chicago Tribune,* Donald Day, wrote a veracious account of events in northern Europe, especially the Baltic countries, during the period in which preparations were being made for Roosevelt's War. His book, *Onward, Christian Soldiers,* was published by a well-established firm in New York, but all copies were destroyed on the orders of the diseased degenerate whom the Jews had put into the White House as their front man. Day, however, had kept a carbon copy of his manuscript and, despite vicious persecution by the alien government in Washington, which prevented him from returning to the United States, that copy was brought to this country and a mimeographed transcription of his suppressed book is now available from Jane's Book Service, P.O. Box 2805, Reno, Nevada 89505.

2. The raid was officially carried out by an agency of the nominally German government that was set up in the western part of the conquered territory and given "virtual sovereignty" in 1952, the Bundesnachrichten-dienst Abteilung K-16, a counterpart (or subsidiary) of "our" C.I.A. Its official functions are to control the Communists, work in which it has been notoriously unsuccessful, to terrorize Germans who seem not to have learned that they must venerate the Jews, and to help God's People hunt down Germans who were loyal to their country before it was destroyed in 1945 and have failed subsequently to cringe before the Master Race to which Yahweh, by a famous Covenant *(B'rith),* deeded ownership of the entire world and all the lower animals in it, including, of course, the fatuous Aryans.

small fee,[3] is now unknown, possibly even to the Jews, who, despite the efficiency of their espionage service, which is by far the finest and most formidable in the entire world, seem not to have known that a few copies of *Der Feind Europas* escaped the destruction they had ordered.

The Jews are almost invariably accurate in statements of verifiable fact that they include in the data compiled for the use of the cowboys who ride herd on their Aryan cattle. I note that in one such compilation, dated May 1969, they boast that Yockey's "pamphlet for distribution in the United States" was evidently printed but "confiscated by the Federal authorities," and that the manuscript of his unfinished book, *The American Destiny*, was seized when he was arrested by their Federal Agents.[4] Then follows, in the list of the writings of the hated

---

3. It is reported that a man, unnamed but identified as a German, was arrested in Frankfurt and punished as the translator of forbidden thought. Since, as I shall mention shortly, it is scarcely credible that the translator was a native German, we may conjecture that the man, who was perhaps caught with Yockey's manuscript in his possession, accepted the blame to shield the real translator (perhaps a woman), perhaps thereby facilitating Yockey's escape from Frankfurt. A memorandum in Yockey's handwriting indicates that when the book went to press, he still owed the translator $45.00; from this it may be inferred that the total fee was not large, perhaps twice that amount. A man whose knowledge of Yockey's career far exceeds my own believes that the memorandum was disingenuous and that Yockey himself produced the German version, and supports his opinion by a stylistic analysis that does show that, in all probability, the translation was made by an American. Since he admits that the only evidence is "indirect and circumstantial," I elect to accept Yockey's memorandum at its face value here and leave the decision to Yockey's future biographer. The details of an author's life may be interesting in themselves, but are seldom relevant to the worth of a literary or philosophical work. As Flaubert said, "L'homme, c'est rien; l'oeuvre, c'est tout."

4. Yockey, whose passport had been confiscated by the State Department to prevent him from returning to the United States, entered the country on a forged passport in San Francisco, where he was the guest of a Jew in whom he had, for some reason, placed confidence. He was arrested, thrown into prison, held under a vindictively exorbitant bail, and found dead in his cell, reportedly a suicide. The Jew in whose home he had stayed disappeared until after Yockey was dead, and was found to have sneaked into the United States under an assumed name with a fraudulent passport, but no one, surely, would be so "anti-Semitic" as to suppose that God's Own People are amenable to laws that are enforced against the lower races. You may be quite certain, of course, that the manuscript of

3

goy, this odd entry:

Enemy of Europe (completed book but never published as manuscript was to be translated into German).

It would appear, therefore, that they were satisfied that all vestiges of the printed edition had been successfully effaced.

I remark in passing that American "Liberals" are wont to yap about "book burning," but that is merely characteristic hypocrisy. Everyone knows that well-conditioned "intellectuals," their little minds sodden with the degrading superstitions that are injected into white children in the public boob-hatcheries, like well-trained dogs, never bark when their masters have enjoined silence. It is hard to believe, however, that the "intellectuals," unlike the dogs, never perceive the inconsistency of their conduct — not even when they refrain from complaining about the total destruction of books that are disapproved by Jews.

From a photocopy of one surviving copy of the German book an attempt to restore Yockey's English text has been made by Mr. Francis whom I know only through some correspondence and conversations over the telephone. No one will expect the retroversion to be precisely what Yockey wrote, but we must specifically note that Mr. Francis has acquitted himself of a very difficult task.

All that remains of Yockey's original are five paragraphs that do not appear in the German translation. It seems that when he sent his book to press, he extracted those paragraphs from his own "Introductory Note" and planned to have them printed as a preface signed by a friend who was going to contribute half of the cost of printing.[5] The friend evidently declined the honor:

The American Destiny will never be found, whether it was burned or is now in the files of the Federal Bureau of Intimidation. A short essay entitled "The Destiny of America," which may be an extract from the unfinished book, was mimeographed and distributed privately in 1955; by an audacious but not unprecedented plagiarism, a would-be "leader" of the American "right-wing" then published it, with additions, under his own name. The theme of Yockey's book may be deduced from an essay, "The World in Flames," that was published as a booklet by his friends in 1961, shortly after his death. Both essays are reproduced in the booklet, *Four Essays*, now available from Liberty Bell Publications.

5. Yockey added, for the proposed preface, an introductory sentence,

he may have been unwilling to expose himself to punishment by the Jews or he may have decided not to remit the $210.00 that Yockey believed he had promised.[6] Mr. Francis has restored these paragraphs to their logical place in Yockey's introduction. For all the rest of the book, he had to work from the German translation.

I cannot believe that German was the translator's native language. His occasional errors in syntax are not what one would expect of a young person whose education had been interrupted by the European catastrophe, and while some of the awkwardness of his version suggests the sloppiness of the worst German journalism, they correspond much more closely to the paraphrases and circumlocutions in which we indulge when we are speaking a foreign language in which we have not learned to

---

which he squeezed in at the top of the typewritten page. The clause in the first paragraph, "Having lived for several decades in America," was originally intended to refer to himself, being strictly true (he was born in Chicago, 18 September 1917) but designed to conceal the nationality of the author of *Imperium* and *Der Feind Europas,* which were published under the pseudonym Ulick Varange. In his introduction to the American edition of *Imperium,* Willis A. Carto explains the pseudonym thus: "Ulick is an Irish given name...and means 'reward of the mind.' Varange, of course, refers to the Varangians, that far-roving band of Norse heroes led by Rurick who...came to civilize Russia in the 9th Century....The name, therefore, drawn as it is from the Eastern and Western antipodes of Europe, signifies a Europe united 'from the rockey promontories of Galway to the Urals.' " Perhaps, but the Varangians are best known as the Norse mercenaries who formed the élite corps of Byzantine armies, and *Ulick* is the early Erse adaptation, from the Latin *Ulixes,* of the name of the great Aryan hero, celebrated for his courage and practical wisdom, who, at the very beginning of the epic, is described as having wandered for many years after the fall of the sacred city of Ilium, which his fellow Greeks destroyed, and having seen many foreign cities and observed the character of many tribes of men. Both names, therefore, connote a stranger in a strange land. Yockey felt himself a stranger in an America that had lost its early Western culture and become a colony ruled by its Jewish masters (see Part Two below). It would be otiose to speculate whether Yockey remembered the etymology of *Odysseus* in the epic (XIX.407 sqq.) or had in mind the fact that the Byzantine Empire was inhabited by diverse and mostly mongrelized peoples and infested by Jews.

6. The facts could doubtless be ascertained, but they are irrelevant to the philosophical and political significance of Yockey's book, and I leave the task of ascertaining them to a future biographer.

think, cannot call to mind a precise equivalent of an English expression, and try to make our meaning clear as best we may. And we may be certain that Yockey's command of German was not adequate to enable him to revise and polish a translation that is always pedestrian and sometimes worse. He could doubtless speak German sufficiently for ordinary conversation and to write short letters, but it is significant that he read and quoted Spengler in the English translation by Charles Francis Atkinson. It is true that Atkinson was a great translator whose versions from Spengler and Friedell accurately represent the German in English so impeccable, fluidly idiomatic, and, on occasion, eloquent that they set a standard that few translators from one language to another can hope to approach; but nevertheless, it is hard to believe that Yockey would not at least have read the original texts, had he felt at home in literary and philosophical German. That he did not do so may reasonably be inferred from the fact that, as Mr. Francis discovered, in the manuscript that Yockey gave to the German translator, he quoted Spengler in Atkinson's translation, and the translator, instead of supplying the corresponding text from Spengler's German, simply retranslated Atkinson's English into German, somewhat distorting the meaning in a way that gives us no high estimate of his competence in either language.[7]

Mr. Francis's retroversion is the accomplishment of an arduous task. He had to decide where the German translator was content to approximate the meaning of the English before him rather than render it precisely or even altered a logical sequence of ideas to shirk the labor of transferring the argument from one language into another in which the normal order of words and clauses is quite different. A comparison of some passages of the retroversion with the corresponding German satisfies me that Mr. Francis has approximated Yockey's original as closely as is possible in the present circumstances. In what follows here, my reference will be to pages of his work.

---

7. A good and probative example is the epigraph prefixed to Chapter I, §4 (p. 29 of the German edition), which is a rather loose translation of Atkinson's *The Hour of Decision*, p. 205, which is an accurate translation from Spengler's *Die Jahre der Entscheidung*, p. 148 in the first edition (1933). Even though Yockey's German translator was poorly paid, he can scarcely be forgiven such negligence, unless he had to work in great haste or under very adverse conditions.

I need not remark that the formulation, or the criticism, of a philosophy of history is a task suited only to the comparatively rare minds, probably found only in our race, who can attain a perfectly dispassionate and relentlessly objective attitude of intellectual detachment from their personal wishes, sympathies, and even instinctive loyalties, at least during their consideration of the problems involved. Persons who have psychic fixations on gods or other praeternatural powers in whose existence they find it comforting to believe, or who feel an uncontrollable impulse to eulogize the "greatest nation on earth" or some ideological savior, or whose vanity must be salved by faith in the immortal excellence of their race, caste, or clique, should be advised not to disturb their glands with reading that cannot fail to affect adversely their equanimity and their blood pressure.

It is less obvious, perhaps, that every man who tries to elicit natural laws from the records of human history will *inevitably* make errors in matters of detail that need not impugn the validity of his general theory. A synoeretical view of human history or of the history of our race must be based in large part on secondary sources, since no man can learn all of the relevant languages or find time, in the short span of human life, to read and ponder all of the practically innumerable archaeological and philological reports and studies that may (or may not) in some way alter our understanding of the past. To demand of a vast theoretical and philosophical construction absolute accuracy in all details, as the little men who have long been barking at Spengler's heels would have us do, is as absurd as to demand that every square centimeter of St. Peter's in Rome or Westminster Abbey be finished with the accuracy of a well-cut diamond. Even if a man is not betrayed, *humanitus*, by the lability of his own memory when it is charged with almost infinite details, he must, for a large part of his survey, depend on scholars who are reputed to be experts in the history of some particular region or culture and whose summaries and interpretations of data may not be endorsed by contemporaries of equal reputation in the same field, so that, as often as not, a man must acquire a very considerable knowledge of each subject before he can decide whose authority is to be trusted, even provisionally. Furthermore, in many areas of history and pre-history our knowledge is so fragmentary that the conclusions generally accepted today may become obsolete tomorrow as the result of some new discovery (as, for example, the discovery that solar radiation has fluctuated even so recently as during the past ten thousand years, which made it necessary to calibrate chronological determinations made from the radioactive isotope of carbon) or even detection of the spuriousness of evidence previously accepted (as in the example from *The Enemy of Europe* that I shall mention below).[8]

When I reviewed the American edition of *Imperium* in 1963, I called attention to a startling slip of memory. Yockey says (p. 288):

> When Charles of Anjou beheaded Conradin, the last Hohenstaufen Emperor, in 1267 *[October 1268]*, Germany disappeared from Western history, as a unit of political significance, for 500 years .... During these centuries, the high history of Europe was made by other powers mostly with their own blood. This meant that — in comparison with the vast expenditure of blood over the generations of the others — Germany was *spared.*

Yockey, writing from memory (hence the trivial error in the date) and perceiving the significance of the eclipse of the Holy Roman Empire as a European power, made a sweeping generalization, forgetting at the moment the Thirty Years' War (1618-1648), in which, according to the best estimates of cautious historians, *two-thirds* of the population of Germany perished and much of the country was made a waste land over which Protestants and Catholics fought, each to exterminate the other for the glory of God and the profit of the Jews.

The Enemy of Europe contains (p. 80) a compound error that is both obvious and an excellent illustration of what I have said above.

---

8. Although it is not strictly relevant to a judgment of his work, we may, as a matter of human interest, remember that Yockey was an astonishingly young man, only thirty years old, when he settled down in Ireland to write *Imperium,* and only twenty-four when his studies were interrupted and he was hauled into the Army for service in Roosevelt's War. When we consider the brilliance Yockey exhibited in his youth, we can only wonder what his incisive and versatile mind would have accomplished, had he lived in a happier age and been able to complete the long study and meditation requisite for the great intellectual task before him. We need not add that when he wrote in a hamlet on the lonely coast of the Irish Sea south of Dublin and Wicklow, he probably did not have at his disposal even the basic reference works that every serious writer keeps on his desk.

8

In the 16th century B.C., Northern *[nordische]* barbarians invaded the Egyptian culture-petrifact, to enact the chapter of history that is called the "Hyksos" era.

Aside from the superficial reference to Egyptian culture as petrified, which could be defended only with reference to a much later period in Egypt's history, there are two errors. The first of these is clearly a slip of Yockey's memory: he has confused the successive invasions of Egypt in the thirteenth century B.C. by the "Peoples of the Sea," who were predominantly Nordic (and who were defeated and expelled, finally by Ramses III in the following century), with the earlier take-over of Egypt in the seventeenth century[9] by the "Hyksos," who were predominantly Semitic — a confusion facilitated by the speculations of some historians who tried to reconcile conflicting evidence by postulating that the "Hyksos" were the Hittites, who were classified as Aryan[10] because they were ruled by an

---

9. Yockey's reference to the sixteenth century B.C. is to the recovery of Egyptian independence. The rule of the "Hyksos" lasted for a little more than a century. The dates here are fairly secure, although chronological precision in Egyptian history can be attained with certainty only with the Eighteenth Dynasty.

10. The word 'Aryan' is commonly avoided these days by writers who fear that the Jews will punish them for using it, but we do need a specific designation for our race and one that will permit us to restrict 'Indo-European' to use as a linguistic term, since, as everyone knows, race and language are quite different things, and language is not an indication of race or even nationality. (Jews are not Germans because many of them speak Yiddish, which is basically a corruption of a low dialect of German, and the Congoids residing in the United States are not Anglo-Saxon because their only language is a debased English.) The great pioneer in social anthropology, Vacher de Lapouge, would have us restrict the term 'Aryan' historically to the division of our race that conquered India and Persia and sooner or later destroyed itself by miscegenation with the aborigines they had subdued. (One has only to think of the mongrel population of modern Iran, of which the name, derived from *ārya* through the Zend *Airyana,* means 'land of the Aryans'!) He would have us use the Linnaean biological classifications, *Homo Europaeus* and *Homo Alpinus,* which correspond to 'Nordic' and 'Alpine' in the more common terminology; but the awkwardness of those terms is obvious. The Sanskrit *ārya* is not only the designation by which conquerors of India and Persia identified themselves, but also a word meaning 'noble,' which designates the qualities of heroism, chivalry, and magnanimity for which our race has always had a characteristic and distinctive admiration, and is therefore better than any neologism we might devise. So long as we intend to

aristocracy (which evidently came from the east to invade and conquer the country) and their official language was based on Indo-European.

The second error in that statement was not an error in 1948 in the sense that Yockey's assumption that the "Hyksos" conquered Egypt could have been supported by references to the works of some of the most distinguished Egyptologists of the time, although grave misgivings about the supposed conquest had been accumulating since 1892 (and perhaps earlier), as the discrepancies between the one long-known account (the late Egyptian historian, Manetho, as quoted and interpreted by Josephus) on the one hand and the Egyptian inscriptions and the archaeological evidence on the other became ever more glaring. It is now established that there was no conquest by force of arms — no sudden invasion by barbarians of any race.[11] What happened was that Asiatics,[12] most or all of whom bore Semitic names and came from the region in Asia Minor that is now called Palestine, by gradual immigration across the Sinai peninsula infiltrated Egypt and used, consciously or instinctively, the techniques of subversion, inciting or exacerbating class-warfare, regional differences, and the greed or ambition of discontented Egyptians until the nation was

consider objectively the phenomena of the real world, we should not be deterred by the threats of our biological enemies nor yet by the yapping of trained witlings of our own race.

11. The facts, so far as they have now been ascertained, are well presented by Professor John Van Seters' *The Hyksos,* Yale University Press, 1966. Although the crucial data come from an Egyptian stele found in 1954 and a papyrus that was first published in the following year, the evidence from archaeological and epigraphical sources had been accumulating for the better part of a century, but a clear understanding of what is known as the Second Intermediate Period in Egyptian history was impossible so long as historians felt obliged to try to reconcile the evidence with the statements of Josephus, a Jew who wrote in the first century of our era and claimed he was quoting Manetho, a very late Egyptian priest, who wrote in Greek in the third century B.C. Josephus, who naturally wails about what his race now calls "anti-Semitism" (i.e., resistance to its covert dominion), says what he thinks will impose on the *goyim* and is, naturally, a forger and a liar. His statements about a military conquest of Egypt by valiant Jews must be disregarded.

12. The proletarian revolution is described in the *Admonitions of Ipuwer,* one of the best-known works of Egyptian literature, now dated to the period of social upheaval that preceded the open dominion of the

reduced to a revolutionary chaos, fragmented under numerous local rulers, many of whom were native Egyptian puppets, and then again consolidated under Semitic overlords to whom the various provinces paid tribute. The Asiatics ruled Egypt for more than a century until a native tributary dared to revolt, and the Egyptians called their Semitic masters, whom many Egyptians served willingly and for profit, their 'alien rulers' — in the modern transliteration of hieroglyphics, which ignores unwritten vowels, the *ḥḳ3 ḫ3swt,* whence the long-misunderstood term 'Hyksos.' So much is now certain, although many details remain obscure, and we note the irony that Yockey, by a few years, missed an historical determination that would have been of the utmost value in the formulation of his own theory — the first clear example of conquest by immigration and subversion.[13]

"Hyksos." We do not know how numerous those Asiatics were, nor to what extent their subversion of Egypt was carried out by a conscious and concerted plan, as distinct from instinctive parasitism. It may be significant that some of them disguised themselves under Egyptian names, much as Jews now frequently masquerade under Anglo-Saxon names (e.g. Ashley Montagu!), and that the "Hyksos," although fanatical devotees of an Asiatic god of their own, often feigned "conversion" to the native Egyptian cults. It is thus often difficult to tell whether some of the rulers subordinate to the Asiatic overlord were Asiatics masquerading under Egyptian names or Egyptian collaborators who profited from the exploitation of their own people. The Asiatics obviously promoted a "multi-racial" society as a means of destruction and perhaps even a kind of "anti-colonialism," since the Blacks of the Egyptian colony in Nubia became "independent," and, indeed, the Egyptian revolt against Asiatic domination succeeded only because the "liberated" Nubians failed to follow instructions from the "Hyksos" to attack the insurgent Egyptians in the rear. The policy of mongrelization was so successful that we even hear of one of the Asiatics' puppets, supposedly the legitimate heir of an Egyptian king, who was known as The Black *(nḫsy).* The genetic ruin of Egypt was thus begun, although Egypt, after the expulsion of the "Hyksos" rulers (though many of the race doubtless remained in Egypt) knew a period of imperial greatness under the Eighteenth Dynasty until the accession in 1379 B.C. of a crazed religious fanatic, Akhenaten, who, although at least two of his grandparents were blond Aryans, was, as is obvious from his portraits, some kind of mongrel.

13. The Egyptians did not distinguish clearly between the various breeds of Asiatics, and therefore the available evidence does not authorize an inference that they were Jews or directed by Jews, tempting as that inference is. There is no historical identification of Jews at so early a date. Josephus tried to connect the "Hyksos" with the story of Joseph in the *Old Testament (Gen.* 39-50), which is, of course, just a folk-tale dated by allusions to a much later time. It is not impossible, however, that some

A philosophy of history is not invalidated by such oversights, any more than Copernican astronomy was invalidated by its author's inadequate and largely erroneous knowledge of planetary orbits.

The analogy incidentally reminds us that the English word most commonly applied to efforts to formulate laws of history, historionomy, is misleading, since it suggests a possibility of determinations and predictions as precise and certain as in astronomy. That is manifestly absurd, and the French term, *métahistoire*, with its implied analogy to the notoriously speculative and vaporous doctrines of metaphysics, is preferable, although it may conversely exaggerate the degree of uncertainty and insubstantiality. Whatever the name given to this comparatively new domain of inquiry,[14] it must be regarded as a philosophy, not as a science in the strict sense of that word. There is therefore a great difference between philosophical theory and practical perception of contemporary realities, although the two are combined in the work of every writer on the subject. The theory is neither strengthened nor impaired by the accompanying view of contemporary events.

The still great prestige of Spengler today does not depend on the morphology of history that he elaborated in *The Decline of the West*, for while it would be premature to make a final

---

actual events may have suggested the exemplary fiction about a Jew who got into Egypt, wormed his way to the top by adroit trickery (supposedly with the help of his tribal god), preyed on the good nature of an unnamed Egyptian king to import a swarm of his brethren, exploited the stupid king's superstitions with oneiromancy, got control of the whole nation, and, acting in the name of his royal dupe, cornered all the food and all the money in Egypt (see especially 47.14-21), and then starved the stupid *goyim* until they had to barter their cattle and their land for food and finally sell themselves into slavery, after which the wily Jew herded his biped cattle from their homes to other parts of the country to destroy what sense of community his slaves might have with their former neighbors.

14. For all practical purposes, it may be said to begin with Théodore Funck-Brentano's *La civilisation et ses lois*, published in 1876. The study, begun after the defeat of France in 1870 and the horrors of the Commune is now obsolete but should not be forgotten. Its author saw clearly the absurdity of many contemporary fictions, such as the notion that there are "human rights" (which is still used to make bird-brains cackle), and understood that nations inevitably rot when they fall under the dominance of peace-lubbers; and he even foresaw the extension of Russian power over the more civilized nations of Europe.

judgement before 2000 or even 2100, it is apparent that the course of our own civilization has drastically departed from what his theory predicted. [14a] Indeed, unless there is a total and epochal reversal of present tendencies in the next two decades, it will be possible to reconcile the facts to his theory only by claiming that the Faustian civilization was, like the Incan culture of Peru, cut off and destroyed before it reached maturity — a claim excluded by Spengler's own analysis of historical forces. For the time being, at least, the Spenglerian theory seems to have been fallacious and to be memorable only as a vast intellectual construction, comparable to Kant's philosophy, respectable as a monument of intellectual power, though mistaken in its conclusions, and as prime datum concerning the historical period in which it was constructed. But even if we flatly reject Spengler's historionomy, we must nevertheless acknowledge and admire the sagacity of a mind that perceived contemporary realities much more clearly than did the reputedly wisest of his contemporaries, as is evidenced by numerous observations made *ob iter* in his major work [15]

14a. Spengler's historionomy, as expounded in his major works and, indeed, everything that he published before his death in 1936, predicted that, as an *ineluctable* historical necessity, the coming war would be fought for hegemony of the West, and the many highly intelligent men who were convinced by his analysis confidently expected that that war would decide which nation of our civilization would become the analogue of Rome in the Classical world. When the war occurred, however, it was fought for the Suicide of the West as a necessary preliminary to realization of the Jews' millennial dream of subjugating the entire world. In no published work did Spengler show the slightest awareness of the terrible power of the international race or anticipate the now unconcealed Jewish domination under which the West is being driven to the precipice over which nations and races disappear from history. Some of his admirers today point out that he did not overlook the power of the great predators of international finance, some of whom are Aryans who have assimilated Jewish attitudes toward their own race, but in 1921 he assured his contemporaries that they were living at "the moment when money is celebrating its last victories, and the Caesarism that is to succeed approaches with quiet, firm step" (Vol. II, p. 507). Today, more than half a century later, is there any indication that "Caesar's legions are returning to consciousness"? The present is obviously the result of forces that Spengler ignored, and whatever our problematic future may hold, events have shown that his "morphology of history" was, at least, radically defective. (Cf. pp. 23 ff. below.)

15. E.g., his perception in 1921 (Vol. II, p. 457, n.2) that the Weimar Constitution would almost automatically lead to unlimited majority rule such as the Hitlerian régime after its consolidation in 1934-35.

and, above all, by *The Hour of Decision*, in which he, in 1932, saw, with a clarity and accuracy that is now indubitable, the grim realities of the world at that time and the imminent dangers to our civilization of which virtually no one was then aware. The essential accuracy of his prevision is made obvious by the disasters that have fallen so terribly upon us.

The theory of history that Yockey elaborated in *Imperium*, which is essentially a revision of Spengler in the light of subsequent events and his own reading and observations, is separable from his estimate of the world situation, and it is not impossible that his reputation in our problematical future will depend more on *The Enemy of Europe* than on his major work.

---

16. *The Hour of Decision* is incomplete, and Spengler's understanding may have been even more comprehensive than we now know. An unpleasant aspect of the Hitlerian régime was an atmosphere, perhaps inevitable in all mass movements, that prevented Spengler from publishing, and perhaps from writing, the projected second volume. There was no *official* hostility toward him, and his books remained in print constantly until the Jewish conquest in 1945, but an English reader can sufficiently perceive the essentials of the situation from the translation of *Spengler Letters, 1913-1936*, selected and drastically edited by Arthur Helps (London, 1966), to pages of which my parenthetical numbers will refer. Although sales of the first volume delighted his publisher (291) and certain bookstores filled their windows with his works (285), and although he had an evidently amicable interview with Hitler (290), his book was, as he said, "misunderstood by a section of the ruling party in Germany, and consequently attacked" (196), and, according to one of his friends, both the new book and the *Untergang* were attacked in an "unfounded, personally malicious, and rancorous way" by writers who were like vultures (300f.). Spengler officially protested to Dr. Goebbels the publication in one of the Party's organs, the *Kreuzzeitung*, of two articles "in which I was described, among other things, as a traitor to my country. It is impossible," he added, "to appear in public on behalf of Germany when at the same time articles of this kind appear. Personally they are a matter of indifference to me. For the last fifteen years I have endured so much abuse that I am sufficiently brazen-faced. But in regard to my efforts to work for Germany, they are a hindrance which must be got rid of" (290). Dr. Goebbels was apparently unable to suppress the attacks, which continued. There were rumors that he was an opponent of the régime (304) and unverifiable reports that the régime was opposed to him (297, 308), and although the second volume was "anxiously awaited" (301, 308), it never appeared, and Spengler devoted his remaining years to studies in ancient history. That he wrote no more of the *Hour of Decision* than the published volume seems unlikely, but we cannot go beyond the affirmation of his niece and literary executrix, Dr. Hildegarde Kornhardt, that no part of a second volume was found among the *Nachlaß* after his death.

14

Although *The Enemy of Europe* is formally presented as a pendant to *Imperium*, we must be certain that Yockey's perception of the present was not deduced from historical theory. He was a man of acute and discerning mind, as he proved in an article published in 1939, when he was twenty-one. [17] At that early age he saw much that was hidden from virtually all of his contemporaries, however experienced or learned they were. He perceived that the so-called "Economic Depression," which so effectively scared the Americans and made them docile, had been contrived by our enemies by use of the Federal Reserve System, which had been foisted on this nation in a campaign engineered by a Warburg, imported from Germany in 1902, while his kin remained at home to ensure the defeat of that nation in the European war that began, no doubt on schedule, in 1914. He foresaw — and this, mind you, before hostilities began in Europe in 1939 — that the "Depression," which was being cunningly prolonged to subjugate the American people, "break their spirits," and "make the greatest possible number dependent on the Government," would culminate in a planned war in which "American youth by the millions will be conscripted into armies to be sent to Asia and Europe to fight the battle of world Communism." (That, remember, was two and one-third years before our great War Criminal was able to stampede American cattle into the war that he and his masters had instigated in Europe.) Yockey understood — as many individuals do not, even today — that the gradual imposition of Communist slavery on the Americans began when Warburg, Baruch, and other Jewish herdsmen cozened the boobs into thrusting their necks into the yoke of the White Slave Act, officially called the Sixteenth Amendment, which imposed the admittedly Marxist device of an income tax. He perceived, as did few men of supposed financial acumen, that the bonds issued by the alien government in Washington

---

17. "The Tragedy of Youth" appeared, under the date of 21 August 1939, in *Social Justice*, a weekly periodical that was published by a Catholic ecclesiastic, Father Charles Coughlin, until the Jews bribed or frightened his venal superiors in the Church to suppress a publication that was making some of the serfs discontented. In the article, Yockey uses such terms as "a conservative, Christian view of life," perhaps as a courtesy to the editor. The term 'Christian' at that time and for decades thereafter was a convenient designation for the established traditions of our civilization as distinct from Jewish influences, which the word was thought to exclude, and it carried no necessary implication of religious beliefs.

were fraudulent and would never be redeemed for their face value in real money, although their owners might be given some counterfeit currency printed by the Treasury in Washington and progressively depreciated. And he also perceived that virtually the whole of the educational system had come under the control of typical American "educators" and "intellectuals," who will say anything for a fast buck, while the press, including both most of the newspapers and the popular periodicals, was even more directly controlled and often owned by the aliens, who were using it to defile and pervert the minds of the young and prepare them for use as expendable animals abroad or as obedient zombies at home.

All that is obvious now — except to the verbosely "intellectual" parrots who learn from the *New York Times* and its subsidiaries what line of chatter will keep them fashionable and hopeful aspirants to *bakhshish* from their masters — but if we can recapture in our minds the climate of opinion when he wrote, we cannot but be mightily impressed by the perspicacity of an adolescent of twenty-one. I will frankly admit that in the summer of 1939, although I was older than Yockey and had carried my studies into many areas of human history that he never had the leisure to investigate, and although I had no illusions about the fetid mass of traitors, enemy aliens, and looters in Washington, I grossly overestimated the intelligence of both the British (who held the pivotal position in Europe) and the Americans, and as grossly underestimated the power and even the racial solidarity of the Jews. And I knew of no one who estimated our plight more accurately. Had I read Yockey's article when it was published, I should have dismissed it as an alarmed apprehension of unlikely future contingencies rather than a description of what had already happened.

For the acuity of perception that he then evinced, Yockey had no need of an historical theory. But since *The Enemy of Europe* is written in terms of history, it will be necessary briefly to examine that philosophical structure.

CYCLICAL HISTORY

Imperium, as I have said, is based on *The Decline of the West*. In large part, its premises are Spengler's conclusions. A critique of the philosophy of history that the two works have in

16

common would require a large tome; it will suffice here to indicate some considerations that are crucial to an estimate of it.

That history is cyclical in the sense that nations and empires rise and fall by some strange fatality in constant succession, has been a commonplace since the first rational study of human societies and was specifically stated by Herodotus. The opinion that the fatality is quasi-biological — that civilized societies are themselves organisms that necessarily pass through the life-cycle of all living things, being born, growing to maturity, and ineluctably progressing to senility and death — is doubtless much older than the elder Seneca, to whom we owe the first clear statement of it. [18]

That the several human species have produced more than one civilization is indubitable. There have been numerous organized and powerful societies (e.g., the Huns) that we may classify as barbarous rather than civilized, but, no matter how strict our standards, we must at least recognize the cultures of Sumeria-Babylonia, Egypt, China, and India as civilizations in the full sense of that word, and also as civilizations separated from our own by an impassable abyss: we can observe their deeds, so far as the facts can be ascertained from written records or by archaeological research, and we can read what is preserved of their literatures, but we must observe those peoples from the outside, and the greater our knowledge of their cultures, the greater our awareness that we are studying the operation of minds and instincts fundamentally different from our own. [19] To be sure, we can observe their behavior and even account for it, as, *mutatis mutandis*, we study the behavior of elephants or

---

18. Most conveniently consulted in Peter's *Fragmenta historicorum Romanorum;* in the *editio minor* (Lipsiae, Teubner, 1883), pp. 292f.

19. For a clear distinction between two kinds of mentality, each of which is fundamentally incomprehensible to the other, see the epochal work of Professor William S. Haas, *The Destiny of the Mind, East and West,* New York, 1956. See also the socio-psychological study by Géryke Young, *Two Worlds, Not One,* London, 1969. The identification of two virtually antithetical types of mentality does not, of course, mean that there may not be other types, as numerous as civilizations or even more numerous. When we imagine that the minds of other races work in the same way as ours, we merely delude ourselves dangerously.

17

baboons, but we can no more establish a rapport with the inner consciousness of those people than we can with the consciousness of the animals, except by such a flight of sentimental imagination as enabled James Oliver Curwood to report so vividly the thoughts of wolves.

Given the plurality of civilizations and the biological analogy, it remained for Spengler to identify a number of discrete civilizations and postulate that each went through a life-cycle that could be defined chronologically, just as we know with fair exactitude at what age a human being will become adolescent, will reach maturity, and will become senile. The synchronisms that Spengler established between the various civilizations have been the subject of endless discussion and controversy, but we need consider here only the one of his premises on which the entire structure rests and by which that structure must stand or fall.

Spengler identifies as two entirely separate and discrete civilizations the Classical ("Apollonian"), c. 1100 B.C.—A.D. 300, and the Western ("Faustian"), c. A.D. 900—2200. These are the two for which we have the fullest information, and between them Spengler establishes some of his most brilliant synchronisms (e.g., Alexander the Great corresponds to Napoleon). Even a century ago, this dichotomy would have seemed almost mad, for everyone knew and took for granted that whatever might be true of alien cultures, our own was a continuation, or, at least, a revival of the Classical. Spengler's denial of that continuity was the most radical and startling aspect of his historical synthesis, but so great has been his overshadowing influence that it has been accepted by a majority of the many subsequent writers on the philosophy of history, of whom we may mention here only Toynbee, Raven, Bagby, and Brown.[20] The Classical, we are told, was a civilization like the .

---

20. Everyone knows the great work of Toynbee, *A Study of History,* and I trust that I need not again point out that the twelve volumes contain *two* distinguishable conceptions of the historical process, since the conceptions on which were based the first four volumes become uncertain and fluctuating in the fifth, after which his consideration of history takes a new direction, practically at right angles to the earlier one. The other works that I have cited here are less well known: Alexander Raven, *Civilisation as Divine Superman,* London, 1932; Philip Bagby, *Culture and History,* London, 1958; Lawrence A. Brown, *The Might of the West,* New York, 1963. I list these four works as particularly significant, since each

Egyptian, now dead and gone and with no organic connection with our own.

Spengler (whom Brown especially follows in this respect) supports his drastic dichotomy by impressively contrasting Graeco-Roman mathematics and technology with our own; from that contrast he deduces differences in the perception of space and time, exhibited particularly in music, and reaches the conclusion that the Classical *Weltanschauung* was essentially static, desiring and recognizing only a strictly delimited and familiar world, whereas ours is dynamic and exhibits a passionate yearning for the infinite and the unknown. One can advance various objections to the generalizations I have so curtly and inadequately summarized (e.g., is the difference in outlook really greater than that between the "classical" literature of Eighteenth-Century Europe and the Romanticism of the following era?), but the crucial point is whether the differences, which belong to the order that we must call spiritual for want of a better term, [21] are fundamental or epiphenomenal.

The fortunate preservation of vestiges of Classical culture during the Dark and Middle Ages may be explained in various ways, but our Western culture today is admittedly the product of the Renaissance, which was so named because it was from the first believed to be a rebirth of the Classical. In all the civilized nations of Europe the best minds of our race *spontaneously* turned to Graeco-Roman antiquity for models in literature, the fine arts, politics, philosophy, and the art of

---

takes its departure from Spengler and moves in a different direction. All historionomic studies after Spengler are either commentaries on his work or attempts to refute it, and a bare listing of the more important would require a dozen pages or more.

21. It should be unnecessary to state explicitly that in discussions of cultures and historical events the word 'spiritual' is used to designate the determinants of human conduct that lie between the strictly physiological and the strictly rational, and therefore implies no belief in immortal souls or the mythology of any religion or comparable superstition. It must always be borne in mind that the spiritual components of individuals and hence of societies are biological, transmitted genetically in human as in other mammals, whether or not the innate instincts fully emerge into consciousness, and whether or not they are somewhat modified by circumstances or education before they determine action.

19

living, [22] and sought to model the whole of European society on the great ages of Greece and Rome, so far as that was feasible without inciting the revolutionary violence of mass movements, which they instinctively feared. What is most significant is that their admiration and emulation was not indiscriminately directed toward the whole of the Classical in Spengler's loose use of that word as a synonym for the whole of Graeco-Roman history, but exclusively to the chronologically small part of that history which they esteemed as classical in the strict sense which they gave to that word: essentially the flowering of Athens in Greece, and of Rome in the last centuries of the Republic and the Augustan period, i.e., the periods in which the strictly pagan civilization of antiquity reached its apogee. For the great heaps of theological trash accumulated in both Greek and Latin before the fall of the Roman Empire, they had no real respect, and they likewise rejected the non-Christian works of the long decadence of the Roman Empire, except insofar as those ages of dwindling intelligence preserved fragments of, or information about, the great eras. In other words, the best minds of the Renaissance rejected the ages of Greek and Roman history in which the populations were mongrelized and the culture contaminated by the Orientals who became its representatives—and this rejection was an *instinctive* aversion, for I have found no indication that any scholar of the Renaissance was aware of the racial mutation in the populations of antiquity.

So strong was this spontaneous esteem for the great ages of pagan antiquity that it prevailed over the opposition of both

---

22. Discussions of, and disputes about, the Renaissance are innumerable. For a fair evaluation, see R.R. Bolgar, *The Classical Heritage,* Cambridge, 1954. All recent discussions of the era take their departure from Jacob Burckhardt's *The Civilization of the Renaissance in Italy* (1860), which is of great value, although it has been furiously criticized, especially by persons with ecclesiastical interests. (There are several English translations; Middlemore's, the only one I have spot-checked, is quite good.) Much of the tedious *disputaillerie* about the Renaissance could be avoided if it were remembered that most of the major Humanists held important positions in the Church or some government and therefore had to deal professionally with such matters as ecclesiatical politics and doctrines, whatever they privately believed, and also that they formed an intellectual aristocracy, had no concern for *hoi polloi* (however incomprehensible that may be to persons imbued with the mysticism about "democracy" that is in fashion at present) and, quite apart from considerations of prudence, had no wish to stir up the superstitions and blind emotions of the masses.

Church and secular rulers. The more alert ecclesiastics did not fail to perceive that the rebirth of pagan antiquity was bad for their business, but the wiser ones perceived that the intellectual enthusiasm could not be successfully repressed and elected to join what they could not defeat. Many rulers of the time were doubtless embarrassed. We can imagine the sentiments of the first Sforza, a peasant become a duke, as he watched comedies performed in Latin and pretended to appreciate humor that depended on linguistic subtleties. We owe a good phrase to the first James of England, who warned his sons that base-born men might speak better Latin, but no one could criticize the King's English. He thus differed from Lord Chesterfield, who complacently remarked to his son that gentlemen are apt to speak better Latin than professional scholars, for gentlemen study only the real classics, whereas the scholars must read large quantities of decadent stuff in search of historical information. So great, you see, was the attraction of the true classics, so great was the affinity that our race instinctively felt for the great ages of Antiquity, that for five centuries the greater part of the youth of all educated men was devoted to mastering the modalities of ancient thought so completely that they could write Latin verse and prose of classical purity and often Greek with equal facility and classical accuracy.

This devotion to the great ages of Greece and Rome produced, in spite of economic and religious considerations, a stupendous educational effort that is without precedent or parallel in the accumulated history of mankind,[23] and ended only with the fissuring of our civilization by recrudescent barbarism and cultural sabotage. All this, Spengler and Yockey would have us dismiss as "pseudo-morphosis," as a young civilization's respect for a predecessor—in sum, as an hallucination—an hallucination, furthermore, of an intensity and persistence that makes *unique* our civilization, no matter how it is explained.

---

23. It must, of course, be distinguished from such entirely different phenomena as the preservation of a sacred language (e.g. Sanskrit in India, Hebrew in Jewry), the study of a contemporary foreign language (e.g. an educated Roman's knowledge of Greek or an educated Englishman's knowledge of French), religious interest in foreign hieratic texts (e.g. the study of Pali by some Chinese Buddhists and of Hebrew by European Protestants), and the influence of exotic literature and thought, usually through translations (e.g. the great influence of Greek philosophy on the Islamic *falasifa* or the influence of Russian novelists on English writers).

My purpose here is merely to indicate a few cogent objections to the Spenglerian historionomy, not to propose solutions of the difficulties thus indicated, which would be tantamount to formulating a new philosophy of history. I turn therefore to other considerations that preclude, I think, an uncritical and merely enthusiastic acceptance of the cyclical hypothesis.

Spengler and Brown particularly insist on the deficiencies of ancient mathematics, which they both exaggerate,[24] but if there is a dominant characteristic of our civilization, it is the capacity (in good minds) for rigorously objective observation of nature and strictly rational inferences and deductions therefrom—the mentality that has made possible our science and technology. This is the type of mentality that Professor Haas, whom I mentioned above, calls 'philosophical' to distinguish it from other types, and if we look through recorded history and insist on something more than the invention of simple devices, such as wheels or bows and arrows or permanent buildings, we find the first manifestation of this mentality in the Ionian philosophers, who sought to explain the universe without invoking magic and a mythology about praeter human beings. That is the real substance of Graeco-Roman philosophy, and we should take especial notice of the New Academy, from which comes the basic method of modern science, which depends on a nice calculation of probabilities. If we look for this rational view of the world in other civilizations, we find no trace of it in the Egyptian or the Sumerian-Babylonian, for in both of these, so far as we know, the world was always thought of as the work of gods and its phenomena attributed to magic, not to the regularity of natural laws. In the Arabian ("Magian") civilization, we find only a few individuals, such as Averroës and Ibn Khaldūn, who, on the basis of a knowledge of Aristotle and other Greek authors, rise above the gross superstitions of Islam

---

24. Greek mathematics (of which a convenient conspectus may be found in B. L. van der Waerden's *Science Awakening,* New York, 1963) sufficed to produce the machine for calculating planetary motions, often called a computer, that was found in the wreckage of an ancient ship off Anticythera, and of which everyone now knows, thanks to the scribblers of wonder-books, who think it helps them prove that the earth was colonized by "astronauts." On the mathematics requisite for the construction of ancient artillery and the calculation of trajectories, see the article by Werner Soedel and Vernard Foley in the *Scientific American,* CCXL, 3 (March 1979), pp. 150-160.

and appear as mere eccentrics in a culture on which they had no influence, and we have only to read them to see how far their mentality differs from the objective use of reason that distinguishes what we may, with Haas, call the philosophical mind. In India, we find the Lokāyata, of which we know through scattered references in extant literature, but this rationalism seems to have flourished only briefly and during the period before Aryan dominance was seriously threatened, after which the 'philousian' mentality so prevailed in the conglomerate population of India that the Hindus provide Haas with his neatest example of it, and faith in the supernatural made the physical world seem nugatory and even illusory. In China, although the doctrines of Confucius and Mencius are relatively free of gross superstition, and the Fa Chia, a pragmatism confined to a ruling élite, considered society in implacably realistic terms, there is no evidence of a truly philosophical attempt to ascertain the laws of nature. We find, therefore, in our civilization a type of mentality paralleled only in Graeco-Roman antiquity, where, significantly, it is the mentality of men of our race.

The cardinal flaw in the historical theories of Spengler and Yockey is an almost perverse equivocation about the biological reality of race. Both strive to make race more or less independent of genetics, although they do not go so far as does Alexander Raven, who would reduce civilization to a "super-organic" idea. In *The Enemy of Europe* (p. 43), Yockey insists that "the idea of vertical [=linear, i.e., hereditary]race is dead. . . . The race one feels in oneself is everything, the anatomico-geographic group whence one comes means nothing," and he even deplores the racial policy of the National Socialist régime as "an enormous tragedy."[25] It is true that Yockey, following

---

25. One hears that Yockey's opinion may have been determined by awareness of his mixed Irish and Spanish ancestry, but such speculations are nugatory. A novelist can know all the inner thoughts and motivations of his characters, but when we deal with living persons, the motives of their actions are usually obvious, but an attempt to ascertain by psychological analysis the source of *rationally* expressed opinions will usually end in a quagmire of subtle hypotheses. *If* it can be shown that Yockey was in fact embarrassed by his ancestry, it will be necessary to determine the percentage of influence to be assigned to that sentiment and *also* to (a) the authority of Spengler, (b) the political doctrine of Moeller, whom I shall mention in the next note, or any one of a score of writers

Spengler, had the strange notion that the physical characteristics of race, such as the cephalic index, were determined by the landscape and soil, not by genes, in proof whereof "long-headed Jews from Sicily, and short-headed ones from Germany, produced offspring with the same average head measurement, the specifically American one." [26] Spengler was taken in by some of the propaganda for an American "melting pot" and especially by the hoax contrived by Franz Boas, a

---

connected with the National Socialist movement, (c) one or more of a hundred other books touching on this subject that Yockey may have read, (d) what he was taught in his youth and took for granted, (e) lectures that he may have heard at some time, (f) conversations with one or more respected friends, (g) veneration for writers of genius, such as Spengler and Montaigne, whose ancestry was to some extent tainted, (h) affection for respected friends of comparable ancestry, (i) consideration of the practical political problem I shall mention in the next note, (j) fear lest a scientific ethnology, recognizing a multiplicity of sub-races, would produce a hopeless multiplicity of subdivisions of the population, comparable to the jungle of sub-castes in India, as was, for example, predicted by Dr. Guido Landra when he attacked the basic National Socialist conception of race in his lectures in the University of Berlin in 1939, where, under Hitler, he enjoyed a freedom of speech that is denied to American biologists, even at Yale and Harvard, which were once respectable universities, (k) a publicist's desire to minimize potential obstacles to the European unity he wanted to promote, and (l) other possible influences that do not occur to my mind at the moment of writing.

26. *Imperium*, p. 275; the information comes from *The Decline of the West*, Vol. II, p. 119. Spengler's belief that such spurious (and inherently preposterous) data had been empirically verified was probably crucial in his thought, but there were many other influences, particularly the doctrine that a man may belong "spiritually" to a race or sub-race to which he does not belong biologically—a belief held by many of his contemporaries, notably Moeller, whose *Das Dritte Reich* (Hamburg, 1923) was a major source of National Socialism; see also H.-J. Schwierskott, *Arthur Moeller van den Bruck und der revolutionäre Nationalismus in der Weimarer Republik* (Göttingen, 1962). The urge to minimize or conceal biological and even cultural differences is related to the practical problem that has confronted every ruler and statesman since Sumerian times: the need to create a state (which is necessarily territorial) by inducing some cohesive unity among the more or less diverse peoples who are residing in that territory at the time and whom it is not expedient to expel. This was an acute problem throughout Europe, including Germany, where the proverbial differences in temperament between the typical Prussian and the typical Bavarian could seem as great as a difference between major races to a population that had, for the most part, little contact with non-Aryan races except the chamaeleon-like Jews with their racial ability to simulate the manners of other races when it is profitable to do so.

twisted little Jew, who popped into the United States, was, for undisclosed reasons, made Professor of Anthropology in Columbia University, and founded a school of fiction-writing called "social anthropology." [27] It is also true that Spengler and Yockey, unlike Raven, do not categorically deny that race in the accepted meaning of that word does determine the outlook of a people and hence the quality of their civilization, but they create some confusion by using 'race' and 'thoroughbred' to designate a high degree of excellence in individuals who, it seems, are largely the product of the soil of the region in which they reside. They simply ignore the vast amount of scientific evidence that the potentiality of every individual is unalterably determined by his heredity, although obviously his development will be affected by nutrition and other environmental factors and, of course, by sheer accident, which may terminate his life at any stage.

This attempt to minimize the biological nature of men is paradoxical in writers who not only recognize that the greater part of human conduct is determined by instincts and tropisms that are largely subconscious, but so restrict the function of reason as to make it virtually without effect on the course of history. We are told—and the proposition is illustrated by examples drawn from the history of our race—that great men, who determine events rather than chatter or write about them, have a 'tact' or instinct that enables them to make correct decisions with so little reliance on their rational powers that

---

27. A typical example is a "study" concocted by one of Boas's creations, Dr. Ruth Benedict, whose *Patterns of Culture* (1934) purported to contain an "anthropological investigation" of the Zuñi Indians, who were a model of the perfect society, uncompetitive, deeply religious, peace-loving, totally egalitarian, sexually adjusted, etc.—all this put out as an object-lesson for the vile white Americans, whose vices deprived them of such bliss. Gullible Americans put their common sense in cold storage when they saw that the preposterous tale was told by a Ph.D. from Columbia and labelled "scientific." Virtually every significant statement in the book was found to be false by responsible investigators who actually observed the Zuñi (Esther Goldfrank, Florence Hawley Ellis, J.M. Roberts, William Smith, Li An-che, Philip Farb, et al.), although they politely pretended to believe that Mrs. Benedict, Ph.D., did "inadequate field work," i.e., that she would have told the truth, had she not been incompetent, feckless, and irresponsible. I need not say that *Patterns of Culture* was cunningly adjusted to the opinions and superstitions prevalent in the 1930s and designed to benumb the minds of its readers.

they may not know why they took the action that made them victorious or successful in a given undertaking. Their strength comes, not from superior powers of cognition and cogitation, but from a faith in their own destiny. The psychological problem cannot be analyzed here,[28] but if we accept the claim that even the greatest men are basically irrational, we thereby attribute to heredity an absolute power over human conduct, of which it becomes the sole determinant, since it is beyond question that in all mammals, including men, instincts are innate and genetically transmitted. The logical conclusion to be drawn from Spengler's psychology, therefore, is that biological race is supremely important. Granting that "the race one feels in oneself" is what counts, what one feels (as distinct from what one may simulate) is genetically determined.

Yockey's denunciation of "materialistic race-thinking" does have some basis in the lamentably elementary state of our present knowledge of racial genetics, which may be compared to the state of chemical science at the death of Lavoisier. The natural laws that determine the inheritance of physiological characteristics, such as color of eyes or olfactory sensitivity, are fairly well ascertained, but we are far from being able to identify *racial* genotypes. The problem is of enormous complexity, and is further complicated by the migratory and adventurous proclivities of our own race. Everyone knows, for example, that the Chinese are Mongolians, but few know that even as relatively late as the Fourth Century there was at least one

---

28. A good example may be seen in generals who are credited with genius, such as Napoleon and George Patton, who seem to make strategic and tactical decisions by some instinctive feeling for the situation and to take risks that make their staffs turn pale, but are victorious because they either sensed or calculated the enemy's reactions more accurately than their subordinates. Before we assume that such men act by a super-rational instinct, we must be certain that what is involved is not a phenomenal power to solve extremely complex problems quickly—a power comparable in its way to the mental operations of a "lightning calculator," who performs complex arithmetical and mathematical calculations with an ease and rapidity that startle us, but who certainly does not know the answer by instinct. Hitler's decision to send troops into the Rhineland in 1936 over the protests of all his diplomats and generals, who predicted certain disaster, was once regarded as a proof of mystically intuitive powers, but we can now see that he estimated the political situation in France more accurately than his experts. Even so shrewd a psychologist as Jung was deceived by what was probably a strictly rational operation by an extraordinarily lucid mind.

Chinese Emperor (Ming) who was evidently a Nordic, having blue eyes, blond hair, and a flowing yellow beard. Even these distinctive traits are not necessarily united—everyone has seen persons with blue eyes and black hair, for example—and no one should be astonished that we find in China portraits of men in whom "the flat face is Mongoloid, but the wide open eyes are Europoid."[29] There are many hybrids and racial traits are often inextricably confused—a fact which greatly impresses thoughtless "intellectuals," who, if they had lived in the time of Lavoisier, would doubtless have clamored for legislation to forbid discrimination on the grounds that the four recognized elements, earth, air, fire, and water, are not found in a pure state, whence it follows that it is wicked to recognize differences between them and to bathe in water rather than in mud or a bonfire.

Although we can, within limits, determine the transmission and inheritance of physical traits, and although we know that intellectual capacity, as shown by intelligence tests, is genetically determined, we know virtually nothing about the biological mechanisms that transmit the almost infinitely complex elements of human consciousness and subconscious being. In certain instances, at least, the psychic elements may be independent of the strictly physiological. No anthropologist or geneticist can explain the fact that there are Jews, members of Yahweh's Master Race, who exhibit the physical characteristics of other races. The Jews in China, for example, seem to Western eyes, at least, indistinguishable from the Mongolians among whom they reside, although they are spiritually and mentally full members of the Self-Chosen People. We must assume that the Jews, who have preserved their racial identity and cohesion through so many centuries, have an empirical knowledge of genetics much greater than our own, but *our* knowledge is so limited that we can neither confirm nor disprove Dr. Alfred Nossig's terrifying boast, "A single little drop of Jewish blood influences the mentality of entire families, even through a long series of generations."[30]

---

29. The phrase is from Professor Otto Mänchen-Helfen's *The World of the Huns* (Berkeley, 1973), p. 372, where other examples of racial mixture in China in the early centuries of our era may be found.

30. Although Nossig's *Integrales Judentum* was published simultaneously in Vienna, Berlin, and New York in 1922, it is now extremely rare

There is one great difference between Spengler's concept of race and Yockey's. Although Spengler recognizes the Jews as a Magian people imbued with a Magian world-outlook and so instinctively different from us (and therefore at the limit incomprehensible to us), and although he knows that this alien body, this international nation, is today, as it was for centuries before the Christian Era, lodged in all the nations of the world that it can profitably exploit, he regards the natural antagonism between Jews and their hosts as basically not determined by biological race, but rather by the phase of civilization, the Jews representing a Magian culture that is much older than ours and now petrified. (Hence, of course, Toynbee's description of the Jews as a "fossil people," despite the absurdity of applying such a phrase to a species that is so active and powerful and, quite possibly, has a vitality much greater than our own.) Spengler asked his readers to believe that the Jews are a dwindling and disintegrating people, a negligible force in world politics and the struggle for power. I have always thought the Jews' aspersions on Spengler's memory a good example of their habitual ingratitude toward their most effective apologists.

Yockey, educated by events that Spengler did not live to see, regards the Jews as the dominant force in the world of 1952. He has very little to say, however, about their unvarying activity through all the centuries since they first appear in history, and he focuses his attention entirely on the present. We must therefore postpone consideration of it to a later section, and conclude our discussion of historical theory with notice of one crucial deficiency in both writers.

---

and has never been translated into English. Nossig gives his fellow Jews eminently practical advice on the ways by which they can most expeditiously attain the goal and purpose which, as he says, is implicit in the teachings of Moses, i.e., the formation of One World under their dominion. Recognizing that his race controls both Capitalism and Socialism, he calls for a coördinated application of both forces to put the *goyim* in their place—which, of course, will be good for the stupid animals, if they are docile. The statement I have translated occurs on p. 76, where Dr. Nossig goes on to claim that the "drop" of Jewish heredity, once implanted in an ancestor, will affect the brain cells *(Gehirnganglien)* of his descendants through many subsequent generations and thus make them susceptible to Jewish ideas of internationalism and One World. Persons of that infected heredity, therefore, are *goyim* who can readily be mobilized as auxiliaries and used to subjugate their own race and the entire globe to its destined Masters. *Horresco referens.*

It is odd that Spengler, and even odder that Yockey, has so little to say about the prime example of what they call "pseudo-morphosis," the acceptance of an alien element by a young culture, which accordingly strives to make its *Weltanschauung* conform to a pattern that is repugnant to its inner nature. As we noticed above, Spengler's dichotomy between the "Apollonian" and the "Faustian" cultures makes him consider our Renaissance an example of such a cultural delusion, but although he recognizes the "Magian" culture as totally alien to our own, he never investigates a far more startling pseudo-morphosis, the imposition of a Magian religion on a Faustian people. And of all the writers who follow the Spenglerian conception, only Lawrence Brown had the very great merit of having perceived the tragic consequences of the fact that the culture of modern Europe was, at its very beginning, infected by a Levantine religion, so that it became "a society whose inward convictions have been at hopeless variance with the outward professions the events of history have forced it to make," thus producing a spiritual tension that "has destroyed the peace of mind of every able man in the West for a thousand years."

It is true that the Christianity of the West differed drastically from all the early Christian cults, including, of course, the one that in the Fourth Century made a deal with the despotic government of the decaying Empire that was still called Roman, although the Romans, for all practical purposes, had long been extinct. What Spengler calls the Faustian soul surcharged that squalid religion with its own vision of the world, incorporating in the cult its own concepts of heroism, personal honor, chivalry, esteem of womanhood, delight in visual beauty (whether in women, in architecture, or in the mimetic arts), and love of magnificent poetry, together with the racial will-to-power—all elements which were unknown to, or expressly negated by, the holy books that Europe inherited from the mongrel proletariat of the rotting ancient world. The real scriptures of Western Christianity are not the alien Bible but the *Chanson de Roland*, *Tristan and Isolde*, the *Christias*, *Gerusalemme liberata*, *Paradise Lost*, and the many other epics and romances of a great and surpassingly beautiful tradition that ends with Tennyson's *Morte d'Arthur* and *Idylls of the*

King—any one of which would have induced apoplexy in Tertullian, Jerome, Augustine, and the other ranting or gabbling "Fathers of the Church."[31] And the religion, thus made at some points consonant with the Aryan ethos, was permitted to absorb and claim a monopoly of the antecedent and in some respects higher morality of our race, and for a millennium the cult so dominated our culture that the West was Christendom. But like the proverbial house built on the sand, the lofty and ponderous structure could not survive the collapse of its foundations.[32]

Western Christianity, unfortunately, was saddled with its Bible, which could not be discarded or ignored because it was believed to be an historical record of actual events. Indeed, it is probable that the principal reason why our ignorant ancestors accepted the religion of the dying empire they invaded and dismembered was that the religion differed from all others known to them by its simulation of historicity in its holy book, which purported to describe events that had taken place in known parts of the world at specific times and had been witnessed by many persons, including the supposed narrators. [33]

31. To anyone who has the patience and equanimity to read judiciously a fair sampling of the verbose screeds collected in the three hundred and eighty volumes of Migne's *Patrologia,* the veneration long accorded to that motley rout of shysters, crackpots, and *hallucinés* will seem unbelievable. For a concise conspectus of the character and activity of the "Fathers," see Joseph Wheless's excellent *Forgery in Christianity* (New York, 1930). Lying for the Lord is a normal exercise of piety.

32. The disintegration of a long-established tradition is always perilous to a civilized society and may be disastrous. I expressed a last hope that something could be salvaged from the ruin of the religion in a booklet, *Christianity and the Survival of the West,* written in 1969; it is now available in a second edition (with a new postscript, but with no change in the text) published in 1978 by Howard Allen Enterprises, Cape Canaveral, Florida.

33. A complementary cause was the impression produced on the invaders by the sumptuous architecture, superb engineering, beautiful literature, polished art, and elaborate social organization that had survived from earlier times in the decadent empire. There were minor causes, especially the verbal dexterity of Christian missionaries, to which some added a manual dexterity, as did St. Poppo, who used a well-known vaudeville trick to perform a miracle for Harald Blåstand ("Bluetooth"), King of Denmark, and thus bring the heathen to Christ. Charlemagne's ruthless conquest of the Saxons seemed to credulous persons evidence of the superiority of his religion rather than of the military resources of his large kingdom.

And the belief the book was a record of historical events cannot but have greatly—and tragically—affected the course of our civilization.

The Bible was an incubus of which Western Christianity could not rid itself. The collection of tales that had been thrown together at the end of the Third Century by feckless evangelists, who had been too negligent to edit out even the most glaring contradictions between or even within the pieces they selected with an eye on immediate marketing of salvation, had been made canonical by imperial decrees and pitiless persecution of the numerous Christian sects that had other gospels. [34] By the time that the cult had been accepted by most of the Nordic peoples, copies of the Latin text of "God's word" had been disseminated throughout Europe, and it was much too late to expurgate and amend the tales, let alone to assemble or compose a holy book more consonant with our racial psyche.

---

34. The Christian sect that shrewdly made a political deal with the despots of the decaying empire was one that brought with it the Jewish Old Testament, and it used the military power it thus acquired to extirpate all the competing Christian sects, including the many that rejected the Jewish compilation or logically identified Yahweh with Satan. To what extent the wily Jews actively contributed to the triumph of a sect that ensured them a privileged position in society and endless profit (plus a chance to continue their habitual wailing about "persecution") is unknown. We need not regret the suppression of the Christian sects that practiced homosexuality, promiscuity, incest, and sacred anthropophagy, but it was a disaster that the "orthodox" were able to exterminate the Marcionists, who, though less fanatical and aggressive, may have been the largest of the various sects before piety was augmented by fire and sword. Marcion, although superstitious, was sufficiently clear-headed to perceive the utter incompatibility between the Jewish book and the doctrines of even the gospels that have been included by the "orthodox" in the New Testament part of their holy book; he was also revolted by the barbarous notion that a supposedly good god would have his own son killed. There were many other sects that rejected the Jewish pretensions. The Marcionists survived underground until at least the Fifth Century, when an "orthodox" poetaster, Prudentius, laments that the government had not yet been able to butcher all of them. Had Christianity reached us in the form of Marcionism or of one of the similar sects, it would be unnecessary for some of our contemporaries to devise ingenious sophistries to argue that the protagonist of the New Testament was not a Jew. Scores of gospels that the victorious faction did not succeed in entirely destroying have come to light in the papyri, and while they give us no high opinion of the intelligence of their superstitious authors, many of them would have served our people better than the ones that were included in the "orthodox" compilation.

And there were limits to the ability of even the cleverest theologian to twist the texts into a more acceptable form, unless he went so far as to pretend that the texts do not mean what they say, but are instead a kind of cryptogram with a hidden meaning, and that God's revelation was really a kind of puzzle-contest with eternal life as the grand prize for solving his conundrums and eternal torment the penalty for submitting an incorrect answer—and that would have permitted anyone to read into the text whatever allegorical meaning or mystical *soprasenso* was suggested by his imagination or ambition. The best that could be done was to make the doctrine and practices of the religion depend, not on the embarrassing and irreconcilable texts, but on the decisions of a Vicar of God who had ecclesiastic authority over all Christendom, although even his power was straitly limited by vested interests and prevailing superstitions. This device had many shortcomings, but it made possible the development of Western Christianity.

So long as the Papacy had the political power to exterminate dissenters,[35] the religion gave Europe a needed cultural unity, but by the Sixteenth Century the Protestants became bold enough to challenge the Vicar's authority by alleging the meanings they found in selected passages of the supposed Word of God, and numerous enough to enlist the support of ambitious princes who had armies of their own. That was the beginning of the end. A century of intensive butchery produced only a conclusive demonstration that the Christians' fierce God

---

35. Heretics appeared constantly throughout the Middle Ages, but in groups small enough to be disposed of conveniently in holy bonfires, and only the Albigenses were numerous and rich enough to call for a full-scale Crusade. An interesting attempt to patch up the religion is provided by the only surviving copy of the *De duobus principiis,* which was discovered and published too recently to be mentioned in the usual handbooks. The anonymous author was repelled by the gross immorality of the Old Testament and he also saw the absurdity of the conventional Christian claim that a god who lacked either the power or the will to squelch the Devil was both omnipotent and just; in the second half of his tractate, however, he tries to salvage the portions of the New Testament that were emotionally satisfying to him. Better minds were also found during the Middle Ages, as is proved by the fame of the treatise *De tribus impostoribus,* which was attributed to Frederick II. Hohenstaufen and others who might have written it, but they were content to smile at the passionate votaries of the three impostors (Moses, Jesus, Mahomet) with equal disdain or compassion, and they prudently refrained from denouncing what Mellin de Saint-Gelays called "la créance et estude/de l'ignorante et sotte multitude."

had become senile or cynical. He had been Johnny-on-the-spot when the Jews wanted to grab the country of the Canaanites, and he had even stopped the sun in its quotidian course above the flat earth at an elevation of about thirty thousand feet—stopped it to help his Chosen Bandits slaughter all the men, slaughter all the women, slaughter all the children, slaughter all the oxen, slaughter all the sheep, and slaughter all the asses: "all these they slew with the edge of the sword." But when the Antichrist appeared in person in Rome—or in Germany—and gobbled up souls by the thousand, Yahweh didn't lift a finger or even despatch a single archangel, let alone tamper with the solar system, to help his True Believers exterminate the Catholic or Protestant Children of the Devil. At the same time, increasing knowledge of the real world made the Christian myths incredible and ridiculous. The religion slowly reverted to the proletarian squalor of its origins, despite the efforts of "conservatives" to shore-up a time-honored tradition that seemed indispensable to the preservation of a civilised society.[36]

Even at its best, however, Christianity powerfully and, indeed, immeasurably distorted our culture.

As all educated men know, Christianity is essentially a Judaized version of Zoroastrianism, as is, in fact, implied in one of the accepted legends about the nativity of its Saviour God, at which Zoroastrian priests (*Magi*) are said to have been in attendance. The Zoroastrian cult, reputedly founded by a Zarathustra, who, as is *de rigeur* for all Saviours, was born of a

---

36. *Vulgus vult decipi, ergo decipiatur,* is a Mediaeval aphorism that was doubtless repeated by many enlightened ecclesiastics before Cardinal Caraffa and by some for reasons that transcended professional interests, but only after the seismic shock of the French Revolution did concern for the maintenance of the social order become a major consideration in persuading educated men to give outward adhesion to a cult in which they could not believe. It seems impossible to determine whether, as a general rule, "revealed" religions inhibit by fear more crimes than they incite by fanaticism, but, given the state of our society in the Seventeenth Century, the celebrated Cardinal Dubois may have been right when he asserted that a god is an indispensable bogeyman that must be flourished to scare the masses into a semblance of civilized behavior. That question, however, cannot concern us here, where it is irrelevant. We are men of the West, who cannot believe, while rational, that facts can be ascertained by deciding what is most useful socially or most strongly tickles our fancy.

divinely fecundated virgin (or, what is slightly more miraculous, from several virgins simultaneously), was the archetype of all the "universal religions," of which only Toynbee seems to have perceived the importance as a force that constricts and deforms a people's native culture. It introduced some very peculiar and epochal notions that have been profoundly deleterious to all races influenced by them. We need mention only two cardinal points.

Zoroastrianism (and, of course, the Christian *rifacimento* of it) is a dualism that posits the existence of two extremely powerful gods, each of whom would be omnipotent but for the power of the other: a good god (Ahuramazda, Jehovah), who is engaged in a continuous war for supreme power with an *evil* god (Ahriman, Satan), with the odd consequence that although the good god is backed up by his presumably mighty son (Mithras, Jesus) and commands legions of doughty archangels, and the evil god can marshal legions of valiant devils, including *all* the gods previously worshipped by men, both antagonists need to recruit reënforcements from the puny race of mortals and accordingly struggle for the possession of individual souls. The cosmic conflict between the two gods is a desperate one, a holy war waged with all their resources and causing infinite devastation and suffering on earth, although, strangely enough, the result is a foregone conclusion and everyone knows that the good god will triumph in the end and spend the rest of eternity in joyously tormenting his captive adversary and all of that monarch's wickedly loyal and luckless followers.

This paradoxical and amazing dualism has infected all the thinking of our Western civilization, both religious and secular.[37] It has inspired an endless series of holy wars, not only to

---

37. It is true that today many Christians, who either do not read their holy book or read it in an emotional fog, sincerely believe that their religion is a monotheism, having been so persuaded by adroit theologians who exploit the prevalent notion that a monotheism is, for some reason, a "higher" or "purer" cult than a polytheism, thus catering to the interests of the Jews, who have claimed to be monotheists ever since they perceived, in the second and first centuries B.C., the enormous advantages of impudently claiming that their tribal deity, Yahweh, was the Providence, or *animus mundi,* of Graeco-Roman Stoicism. When the Christians began to deny the existence of Jupiter, Mars, Venus, Isis, Tanit, and all the innumerable other gods of the past, and to regard them as mere myths or illusions, they rejected the explicit testimony of the "Fathers of the

exterminate Protestants, Catholics, or other religious agents of Satan, but also, with equally frantic religiosity, to annihilate or enslave Satanically evil nations (in the United States, successively Southerners, Spaniards, [38] and Germans). I need not remark that the dualism has survived the superstitions about the supernatural from which it came and inspires ostensibly non-religious cults, as in the Marxists' holy war against the diabolically evil Capitalists or Fascists; and it goes without saying that when the zombies swarm out of the cesspools of Harvard or Yale to howl at Professor Jensen or Professor Shockley and prevent him from talking sense to such sane men as may remain in the academic ruins, the ignorant creatures feel that they are fighting the Devil and only their native cowardice prevents them from rending the learned men limb from limb in the faith that the facts of nature can thus be altered. [39] And, on the other hand, everyone can see that the missionaries who were once sent abroad to annoy the natives of Asia and Africa and "save souls" have been replaced by the far more pernicious gangs of "do-gooders," who plunder us for the benefit of "underdeveloped nations" and, in so far as they are not mere

---

Church" and of their holy book, which they thus denounced as unreliable. The religion could probably have survived that amputation, but when the Christians killed off Satan to make their religion really monotheistic, they made it intrinsically incredible. The resulting bankruptcy of the cult was wittily adumbrated by a French theologian (J. Turmel), whose urbane treatise was translated into English under the title, *The Life of the Devil* (New York, 1930), and published under a pseudonym, "Louis Coulange."

38. Some of the promoters of the Spanish-American War doubtless had the rational purpose of seizing Cuba, Puerto Rico, and other Spanish possessions for American expansion and colonization, but enthusiasm for the war was whipped up by proclaiming a *jihad*, as had been done in the unconscionable war of aggression against the Southern states. Spaniards were described as diabolic monsters of cruelty, and at least one military man attained great popularity when the press reported that he had promised to slaughter so many of the human devils that only Spanish would be spoken in Hell for the next fifty years. The prompt defeat of our hopelessly weaker opponent averted satisfaction of the Christian fanaticism and blood-lust that had been excited by the propaganda, but professions of a high moral purpose led the United States foolishly to throw away part of the spoils of the war it had won by "liberating" Cuba to make the aggression seem altruistic.

39. In England, Professor Eysenck, while lecturing on a strictly scientific topic that displeases Jews, was assaulted and severely injured by a swarm of vermin hatched out in the University of London.

racketeers, must be buoyed up by a belief that they are commending themselves to a Jehovah in whom they no longer believe.

The Zoroastrian dualism makes weak minds susceptible to hallucinations by which they identify their interests or wishes with the cause of the Good God and excite themselves with a blind and deadly hatred of their opponents or rivals (who may have the same hallucination about them) as the innately evil agents of the Bad God, to be driven by any means, fair or foul, to the perdition to which they are damned. And nothing basic is changed by replacing Ahuramazda/Jehovah with an abstraction, such as "democracy," and replacing Ahriman/Satan with an another, such as "aristocracy." [40] Ironically enough, this poisonous dualism, which came to us through the Jews, now dominates the reaction against Jewish overlordship, for most of the Jews' antagonists identify them as "the Synagogue of Satan" etc. *ad nauseam*, while those who do not usually regard the Jews as an inherently and almost praeternaturally evil people, instead of regarding them rationally as a specialized race which, being a minority among all the peoples on whom it is parasitic, has learned that its will-to-power must be advanced by cunning rather than undisguised force of its own—a race, furthermore, which quite naturally regards its own interests and purposes as just and justified by either a covenant with a deity or its own intellectual superiority, much as our ancestors felt no compunction as they took a continent away from the aborigines, confident in their own manifest superiority, although some of them were foolish enough to think that the Indians must have been inspired by the Devil to try to retain possession of their own hunting grounds. So long as our minds are clouded by the Zoroastrian myth, we shall be incapable of rational thought for our own survival.

A second epochal innovation of Zoroastrianism was the bizarre notion of religious "conversion," of which the import is

---

40. This particular form of the superstition is implicit in innumerable writings that distort history to fit some pattern of "social progress," but the reader will find both amusing and instructive an especially clear specimen, Frederic Huidekoper, *Judaism at Rome,* New York, 5th ed., 1883. That account of a struggle between the evil "aristocrats" and the pure-hearted "improvement party" (which, of course, was inspired and led by God's Race) represents, so to speak, the virus in its pure state.

clearly seen in the tradition that Zarathustra's first convert was a Turanian, i.e., a Turko-Mongolian was transformed by psychic magic into an Aryan and more than an Aryan. By the simple act of believing the stories Zoroaster told him, that alien joined the Army of God and attained an exalted position to which Aryans could attain only by believing the same stories, while Aryans who were less easily captivated by evangelical rant remained servants of Satan, the deadly foes of God, and should be exterminated as soon as possible by the Aryans, Turanians, Mongols, Semites, and others whose minds had been opened to the Gospel. The obvious effect of this superstition was to destroy awareness of the biological fact of race and replace it with a delusion that could only hasten the Aryans' racial suicide. [41]

The nonsensical notion that any anthropoid can be miraculously "converted" to "righteousness" by being made to believe the dualistic myth logically engenders a mystic yearning for "One World," in which massive slaughter of the wicked Unbelievers will force the survivors of all races to unite in worship of Jesus or Democracy and thus live in a Heaven on Earth. The fatuous dream of a potential spiritual unification accounts for the current use of the term "all mankind," which is intelligible only as parallel to such classifications as "all marsupials" or "all carnivores," with a mystical connotation that inspires unthinking awe in many of our contemporaries, and since the fantasy is, of course, biologically impossible, [42] some

41. Hastened, not initiated, because the men of our race, wherever in the world they have established themselves, cannot keep their hands off women of the native races. This lascivious fatuity, to be sure, is as universal as masculine lust, and a superior race may even regard indulgence in it as evidence of their own superiority. The great Egyptian king of the Twelfth Dynasty, Sesostris III. (Khakaure), who established border patrols to prevent the infiltration into Egypt of Nubians from conquered territory, in the very inscriptions in which he points out the racial inferiority of Blacks, boasts that he "captured their women" and "carried them off," doubtless into Egypt as slaves, not foreseeing the terrible consequences of the inevitable miscegenation.

42. No one should ever have been so credulous as to believe the claims of missionaries that they "saved souls" by transforming savages or Orientals into Christians. All that the holy men accomplished by harangues and bribery (supplemented by the incontestible superiority of our hated race which was made manifest in such things as repeating rifles and the disciplined courage of British regiments) was to induce an outward assent

childish minds, perturbed by a glimpse of reality, fester until they reach the state of the famous expert on "Mental Health," Brock Chisholm, whose diseased mind lusted for the extermination of white men so that the whole globe could be inhabited only by coffee-colored and mindless mongrels made righteous by their equality in squalor.

Belief in the psychic magic of "conversion," furthermore, opened the way for the Bolshevism that attained its fullest development in Christianity, the devastating notion that Faith —a faith that is as thoughtless and preferably as unconscious as the "faith" of a vegetable or a mustard seed—was what counted, so that an ignorant peasant, an illiterate fisherman, or the most scurvy proletarian could make himself the superior of the noblest, the bravest, and the wisest of men—and, secure in the favor of a god who so hates learning and reason that he will "make folly the wisdom of this world," the simpletons and morons, having become True Believers, can look forward to the delights of seeing, when the last have been made first, their betters suffer the most atrocious torments forever and forever. No idea, no menticidal poison, could be more effective in destroying the culture and even the sanity of the people in whom it has been injected. [43] And the poison, destructive of all social stability and hence of civilization itself, survived the mythology from which it sprang and persists today in the atheistic "Liberals" who bleat about the "underprivileged," fawn on savages, and demand an "open society" that is

to statements that the native mind was innately incapable of comprehending and translated into ideas acceptable to brains of quite different formation from ours. It was natural and inevitable that when the savages saw our race become so lunatic as to surrender its colonial possessions, the "Christianity" of those who did not at once revert to their native cults became what they had always understood it to be, a special kind of mumbo-jumbo. For a convenient survey of those developments, see *Postchristianity in Africa*, by G.C. Oosthuizen, Grand Rapids, Michigan, 1968. This "anthropological" study is the more instructive because it is written by a Christian, who naturally cannot understand the real causes of the events he describes.

43. How alien this nonsense was to the mentality of our race is shown by the fact that, professing to believe it, they promptly began to reason about the Faith and erected the vast intellectual structure of Scholasticism, "comme si raison et foi pouvaient trottiner de concert," as Maurice Garçon sardonically comments. The final result, of course, was Nominalism and the labefaction of the Mediaeval *Weltanschauung* and eventually of the alien religion that had been incorporated in it.

perpetually stirred up so that the dregs on the bottom may become the scum on the top.

Having noticed these two cardinal elements of Zoroastrianism and the religions derived from it, we need not mention others, for the vital historical question is whether this pernicious cult was Aryan in its origins or a device of aliens. To be sure, it became the religion of the Persians. It was the religion of Darius the Great, who boasted that he was an "Aryan of the Aryans" and modestly attributed his victories to the help of Ahuramazda. It was the religion of his son, Xerxes, whose mind was so blighted by fanaticism that he boasted that he had destroyed the temples on the acropolis at Athens, where the Greeks worshipped nasty devils, and had commanded the benighted Greeks to worship his One True God.[44] It is also true that all the early legends about Zarathustra state or imply that he was an Aryan, although it may be significant that his miraculous nativity is said to have occurred in many different places, and that he is always described as an itinerant prophet who was not a native of the region in which he began to proclaim his gospel and salvage men's souls. What is even more remarkable, the only name that the Zoroastrian cultists gave themselves in the time of the Persian Empire, so far as we know, was *Airyavō danghavō*, words which literally mean "the Aryan peoples." That presumptuous appellation is obviously false in an ethnic sense, for it excludes the Aryan peoples of India, who were specifically damned as the worshippers of devils, and includes the many non-Aryans who elected to be Saved and join the Elect by believing or pretending to believe Zarathustra's evangels. If the term the Magi chose for their cult was not just an impudent falsehood, it must have originated in a calculated use of *ārya* [45] in its non-racial sense, "noble, excellent": since worshippers of the good god must be good people and morally

---

44. Xerxes does not specifically mention Athens, perhaps because the name might carry an impious suggestion that God must have been taking a nap when the Greeks, though hopelessly inferior in numbers and resources, destroyed his navy and sent him scuttling back across the Hellespont, but the allusion is unmistakable. The test of his inscription (transliterated from the cuneiform into Roman characters) may conveniently be found in Professor Roland G. Kent's *Old Persian,* New Haven, 1953.

45. I give the well-known Sanskrit form, whence comes our 'Aryan'; in Avestan, the dialect of the Zoroastrian holy book, the word becomes *airya,* as in the phrase I quoted above.

superior, they could be called "the excellent people." That would make the name comparable to the famous verbal trick by which the "Fathers of the Church," in a time of military supremacy, called their motley followers "soldiers of Christ," so that non-Christians could contemptuously be called "pagans" (*pagani,* "peasants, yokels").[46]

The Zoroastrian dualism was accepted by the Aryans of Persia,[47] who vehemently repudiated their own, presumably Vedic, gods, much as Christianity was accepted by the Nordic peoples of Europe, who repudiated Odin, Thor, and their other gods as evil agents of Satan. Christianity was, of course, an Oriental cult, and the analogy makes it difficult to believe that its Zoroastrian antecedent was natively Aryan.

There are many indications that it was not. Much of the evidence is too intricate to be discussed here, and it will suffice to mention a few essentials. The name of the Saviour, however

---

46. Originally a *paganus* was an inhabitant of a rural district *(pagus)* as distinct from a townsman at a time when all prosperous landowners in the countryside were citizens of a town, so that it had about the connotation of our 'rustic.' In the later part of the First Century it acquired the meaning of 'civilian, common man' (exclusive of persons of any social distinction) and was often contrasted with *miles* ('soldier'); in the later Empire, agents of the secret police, who disguised themselves as individuals of the lower classes, went about *pagano ritu,* i.e., as 'plainclothesmen.' But under the Dominate, the status of the countryfolk *(pagani* in the first sense of the word) progressively declined to serfdom, hence the particular force of the "Fathers" propagandistic word. The trick is disguised by the Christian explanation that "pagan" beliefs lingered longest in the countryside, which does have a certain basis in fact (countryfolk, perforce, remain close to nature), but should not blind us to the origin of the religious meaning in clever propaganda.

47. It would be interesting but futile to speculate about the use of hallucinatory drugs to spread the Gospel. The Zoroastrian *haoma* has been identified by R. Gordon Wasson (*Soma, Divine Mushroom of Immortality,* The Hague, 1968) as a drink made from the *Amanita muscaria,* one of the mushrooms that are used throughout the world to produce religious experiences and visions of God. On its use when the early Christians symbolically ate the flesh of their god, see John Allegro, *The Sacred Mushroom and the Cross,* New York, 1970—a most informative study, although etymologies from the Sumerian and later languages are probably overworked. In our own time, as is well known, drugs are used by the more enterprising evangelists to induce piety in the victims they collect in colonies or fanatical bands.

it should be spelled (*Zarathŭštra, Zaratŏst, Zarataŝt,* etc.), is not readily explicable as Indo-European and may come from another language. There is reason to believe that the cult's holy book, the *Avesta* (a title which may not be Indo-European) was not composed in Persian, but was translated into a late Persian dialect from another, probably Semitic, language.[48] It is even possible that in the time of Darius the sacred language of the Zoroastrian scriptures and the liturgies recited by the Magi was Semitic, for the Persian Empire had three official languages, Old Persian, the native language of the rulers, Elamite, respected for its antiquity and still spoken at Susa, and Aramaic, the Semitic language which was most widely known throughout Persian territory and outside it, and which, accordingly, was the language commonly used by the Persians in the administration of their empire and in diplomatic correspondence with other nations. Before the extant text of the *Avesta* was written down,[49] the Greeks of the Hellenistic Age who interested themselves in the "Persian" religion found only texts in Aramaic, the language spoken by the Zoroastrian priests of their time,[50] and it is obviously possible that some of those texts

---

48. This was known to Spengler (Vol. II, p. 168), who relies on scholars in the field who are cited in the article to which he refers in a footnote. The linguistic evidence is tangled, but Avestan, the dialect of the *Avesta*, is related to Old Persian, the language of the Persian emperors, much as the various Prakrits are related to Sanskrit, and the natural inference is that Avestan is a broken-down and late form of Old Persian, rather than an early dialect of some region (Bactria?) or an hypothetical brogue of the Medes. It does resemble the decadent Persian of the last days of the Empire, which, however, is centuries earlier than the date to which most scholars (e.g. Darmesteter in the concluding part of the introduction to the third volume of his version of the *Zend-Avesta*) assign the extant text of the *Avesta.* To my mind, that is conclusive. Granting that some of the *gāthās* in the *Avesta* probably represent statements actually made by the prophet known as Zarathustra, it does not follow that the statements were made in Avestan. It is likely that many of the statements in the New Testament were actually made by one or another of the various Jesuses of whom the protagonist is a composite figure, but no one would believe that those agitators spoke in Greek to the Jewish rabble.

49. In the First Century, according to Darmesteter, whom I cited above. Other scholars would place it in the first century B.C., i.e. at the *end* of the Hellenistic Age and, of course, later than the Greek authors in question.

50. See J. Bidez & F. Cumont, *Les Mages hellenisés,* Paris, 1973 (=1938), especially pp. 35, 89-91; cf. pp. 34, 44. The English translation

were the originals, dating from the time of the Persian Empire, and not translations, as is generally supposed.

There is one significant datum which seems not to have been given the emphasis it deserves. As everyone knows, Zoroastrian priests were always called Magi, but *Magi* was not originally a word of religious meaning: it was an ethnic term that designated a certain peculiar people who lived in Media but were in some way distinct from the ordinary Medes, and during the early centuries of Zoroastrianism *only* men of that peculiar tribe could be priests and their sacred office could be transmitted *only* by hereditary descent through females.[51] That fact is as startling as though in the Roman Catholic Church the *only* word for a priest was 'Irishman,' and during the Middle Ages *only* pure-blooded Irish (i.e., having an Irish mother as well as father) could perform sacraments. The word *Magi*, I believe, creates a very strong presumption that the propagators of the religion were not Aryans.[52] It may be only a coincidence that according to a tradition in the Jews' holy book [53] which seems to have an historical basis in events that took place before the time of Zarathustra, colonies of Jews had been planted "in the cities of Media." But since forgery and imposture have always been normal Jewish devices, no weight can be given to their claim that Zarathustra was a Jew and wrote in Hebrew.[54]

---

of Cumont's *Oriental Religions* now in print dates from 1911, and is naturally less complete than his fourth edition (Paris, 1929); in the translation, he notes that the Zoroastrian texts were in Aramaic, but by an odd slip he speaks in one passage as though the Aramaic-speaking evangelists were Persians, although he must know better. This is corrected in his fourth edition.

51. Hence their famous custom of engendering offspring by sexual intercourse with their mothers or, if that was not possible, with sisters.

52. This must be distinguished, of course, from the custom, common among the Greeks, by which the priest of a local temple or shrine was a descendant of the family on whose land the sanctuary was built, and also from the formation of a caste of professional holy men, such as the Brahmanas of India.

53. 4 *Reg.* (= 2 *Kings*), 17.6 & 18.11.

54. See the texts translated from the Syriac by Bidez & Cumont, *op. cit.,* Vol. II, pp. 103-104, 129, 131, and the texts cited in their Vol. I, p. 50, nn. 3,4. At the date it was made, the Jews' claim that Zarathustra was a Jew was doubtless just a normal part of what the authors, apropos of an

The really fundamental and cogent consideration is the enormous difference between the "universal" religion and the spirit of all the certainly Aryan religions of which we know, especially the Vedic, the Greek, and Norse, which we know in detail. The discrepancy is so great that even Toynbee felt obliged to conjecture that Zarathustra (whom he accepts as an Aryan) must have been instigated by a Jew.[55]

The very idea of *evil* gods is alien and repugnant to the spirit of all authentically Aryan religions, which are never so irrational as to inject good and evil deities into a universe in which the very concepts of moral 'good' and moral 'evil' are indubitably created by human societies for their own purposes and correspond to nothing whatsoever in the world of nature. Wickedness can exist only within a given society of human beings and can be defined only in terms of the standards of morality that the society more or less instinctively applies to relationships among its own members. Only infantile minds can attribute moral iniquity to hurricanes, volcanoes, dynamite, and other natural phenomena that may be baneful to us; primitive peoples, ignorant of the causes, may superstitiously attribute such phenomena to supernatural forces and may imagine gods that are indifferent to human welfare or have been angered by some supposed offense, but so long as they have a vestige of rationality they will not imagine gods who are inherently evil and seeking to promote wickedness. A notion that species of animals (e.g. snakes, sharks, tigers) that defend themselves against us or prey on us, or that species of human beings that pursue their own advantage to our detriment (e.g. Japanese, Jews) are wicked because they obey the universal law of life is simply irrational. And when a pack of fanatics claims that all persons who do not share their superstitions are diabolically evil, they are insane, prevalent as that form of insanity may be. The Zoroastrian dualism may fairly be called the most devastating mental disease that ever became epidemic on this

impudent attempt to appropriate the Etruscans, call "la propagande juive pour imposer aux païens ses croyances" (Vol. I, p. 238), although the purpose more commonly may have been to bamboozle ignorant *goyim* by making them believe in the vast superiority of Yahweh's Master Race. The Christians naturally forged ahead in much the same way and concocted "proof" that Zarathustra had been a prophet of the advent of their Jesus; see *op. cit.*, Vol. II, pp. 118, 127, 130, 135.

55. *A Study of History*, Vol. I. p. 81, n. 1.

planet.

The Aryan religions are not infected by that black delusion.[56] Their gods, like the forces of nature, are multiple and,
as is only reasonable, are sometimes opposed to one another in
their relations with mortals. Venus and Juno may each work
against the other, just as every day the force of sexual attraction
enters into conflict with the requirement of sexual fidelity that
makes marriage an indispensable social institution. In the great
epic of our race, the *Iliad*, which deals with a war to the death
between the Achaeans and the Trojans, some of the Greek gods
favor one nation while other Greek gods favor the enemies of
the Greeks. No Greek was so irrational as to believe there was
only one god and then say "Gott mit uns! " as Christians do
when they embark on holy wars against one another. In the
Norse religion, the Aesir and Vanir are united in Asgard, but
often at odds with one another, as are the forces of nature to
which mortals are subject. The Aryan mind could never, of its
own accord, have conceived of so monstrous an inversion of
religion as appears in the mad fanaticism of the Zoroastrians,
who converted the Aryan gods of the Vedas into fiends, and of
the Christians, who converted the gracious gods of the
Graeco-Roman pantheon into malevolent devils.

The Aryans were not so foolish as to imagine that their gods
were omnipotent: their gods are far more powerful than we, but
they too are subject to Destiny, the impersonal force that is
inherent in the structure of the physical world. They were not
so credulous as to mistake the ravings of an *halluciné* or the
sophistries of a theologian for revelations of truth: they had no
gospels, and every one knew that poets and skalds were free to
invent or modify stories about the gods that might be no more
or less truthful than folktales. The Aryans did not have the
hatred of civilized life that inspires the dualists' notion of Faith,
a blind belief in certain tales by which ignorance and credulity
are exalted above learning and reason. The Aryans respected the

56. A conspectus of the basic concepts of Aryan religions may be
found in the admirably concise work of Professor Hans Günther, available
in an English version by Vivian Bird and Roger Pearson, *The Religious
Attitudes of the Indo-Europeans*, London, 1967. I am aware of the danger
that we may identify as characteristically Aryan the qualities that we, as
Aryans, admire, but a certain objectivity may be attained by considering
what is admired in the great literatures of our race.

44

gods they imagined, but with a manly self-respect also: they did not cringe and cower before celestial despots, as do races with the slave-mentality and *Sklavenmoral* of the Near East.

The Aryan spirit is innately aristocratic and heroic. Aryan man, when he is most fully Aryan, is driven by a *spiritual* passion to excel, αἰὲν ἀριστεύειν [57] —to realize, at whatever cost to himself, whatever capacity for greatness he may have within him. And while he rationally expects to find perfection in gods and men no more than in the world of physical reality, he has innately certain ideals of personal honor, fairness, and *manly* compassion that are incomprehensible to other races. [58] Both of these characteristics, however, although they are the source of all the greatness our race has attained, make Aryans vulnerable. The very superiority of men who approach our racial ideal makes it easy for a parasitic race or our own criminal elements to rouse against us the inferior's resentment of superiority and to excite envy and malice in proletarian herds, thus disrupting our society in what Ortega y Gasset calls "the revolt of the masses" and Lothrop Stoddard, more accurately, calls "the revolt of the underman." And artful appeals to our sense of fairness and compassion can excite, especially in females, the irrational sentimentality that ignores

---

57. As in *Iliad*, VI. 208, perhaps the most memorable line of our great epic, which is repeated at XI. 784.

58. An excellent work, which will enable us to see ourselves as others see us, is Maurice Samuel's *You Gentiles* (New York, 1924; recently reprinted). Jews feel only contempt for a race so mentally inferior that its men prefer to meet their enemies in a fair fight instead of stabbing them in the back when off their guard or giving them a poisoned cup under the guise of friendship. And if we consider the matter objectively, they may be right: "c'est la supériorité de ma race sur la vôtre: la vôtre mourra, la mienne durera." Farrère formulated the only biologically valid criterion of superiority. I remember an erudite Jewish professor who *could* not perceive that a chivalrous respect for valiant and honorable opponents differed from the pawkish notions about forgiveness set forth in some parts of the New-Testament medley. Apropos of the hoax about the "six million" that the Jews are using to bleed the Germans whom we conquered for them, he said, with arrogant candor, "The stupid Christians forgive enemies, but WE exact vengeance to the last drop of their blood." Whether he is correct in his confidence in his race's superiority, the future will determine—probably the near future. The other races, needless to say, also despise us for our indulgence toward them, each in terms of their own standards, and eagerly look forward to the ruin we seem determined to bring upon ourselves.

the fact that a cohesive society is an organism and, like all organisms, can live only by excreting its waste products—the grim fact that, by the unalterable laws of biology, we, like all mammals, bring to birth biological tares and misfits, which must be eliminated, if the species is not to degenerate to eventual extinction. And what the struggle for life does automatically for other mammals, our species, being capable of reason and purposeful social organization, must do deliberately—or perish.

The Christian version of the Zoroastrian dualism was Judaized, and Ahuramazda was replaced by the Jews' tribal god, Yahweh. As a result, our race lived for centuries in terror of the capricious and ferocious deity of the Old Testament, and no phrase is more common in the harangues of our holy men than *"fear* of God." Christians had to believe they were at the mercy of the supernatural monster who, for example, deliberately alienated the mind of an unnamed Egyptian king so that he would have an opportunity to afflict the whole of the obviously innocent population of Egypt with every imaginable disease, plague, and disaster, even murdering the Egyptian's children, so that his pet Jews could gloat over the torments of the *goyim,* who were evidently made so imbecile by their suffering that they permitted the Jews to "borrow" all their valuable property, gold, silver, jewels, and even wearing apparel, and then run away with the loot. Yahweh, naturally, repealed the law of gravity long enough to permit the swindlers to escape with the stolen property and to set a trap to destroy more *goyim.* And the terrible deity is credited with many similar exploits, all as vicious and immoral from every point of view, except, of course, that of the Jews who created him in their own image. And thoughtful Christians could derive little reassurance from their theologians' story that the savage god had finally repented of his blunder in picking the Jews as his pets, for a thoughtful man must quail before the appalling malevolence of the Jewish hymn of hate that closes the New Testament and is the Christians' favorite horror-story.

Thinking men were equally depressed to learn from that New Testament that Yahweh, having repented of one blunder and decided to let his erstwhile pets kill his son, bestowed his divine favors on the very dregs of a squalid, ignorant, and dirty population in Palestine to emphasize his new commands, which, quite logically, make Believing Christians dote on everything that is lowly, inferior, debased, diseased, deformed, and degenerate.

For Aryans, including, of course, the Germanic peoples who invaded the moribund Empire that had once been Roman, Christianity has been a deadly and perhaps fatal poison, a delusion that forced our people to act against the dictates of their own biological nature.[59] If ever in recorded history there was a cultural pseudo-morphosis, that was it.

---

59. Christianity was also deleterious to our race biologically, but we cannot measure or even estimate its dysgenic effect. It certainly encouraged the preservation and reproduction of the unfit, and, through both monasticism and the distribution of social rewards, it inhibited the reproduction of superior men and women. Having given the Jews a privileged position and enriched them, it facilitated Jewish penetration of our society by a common ruse: Aryan males were hooked by offering them smiling Jewesses with generous or lavish dowries; the Jewesses, although perfunctorily sprinkled with holy water, had naturally been taught by the inspiring examples of Esther and Judith that their loyalty was to their race, not to the *goy* whose bed they shared and whom they would manipulate in the interests of their kind. A Jewish strain, conceivably as potent as Dr. Nossig claimed (see note 30 above), was thus planted in many gentle, noble, and even royal families and may, as some believe, account for their decadence, both mental and physical, as frequently occurs when incompatible genetic strains are combined. But statistics on all these points are lacking, and if we had them, we should only face the impossible task of measuring what happened against what would have happened, if Europe under the Germanic peoples had adopted some other (what other?) religion or religions. Charles Renouvier's *Uchronie* (Paris, 1876) will sufficiently entertain and discourage those who *must* speculate about the incalculable.

An anonymous writer in *Instauration* (Aug. 1980) sought to explain psychologically one of the most drastic and puzzling effects of Christianity on our race and civilization. When our ancestors accepted the Magian cult, they believed themselves at the mercy of a capricious and ferocious god whom they had to appease and placate by observing absurd taboos and imposing on themselves unnatural conduct their racial instincts rejected. Thus they had a sense of guilt without consciously knowing why. By not sinning in the eyes of Yahweh, they were sinning against themselves. They were *biologically* guilty. From this inner conflict,—from the subconscious mind's reaction to the perpetual conflict between the innate nature of a healthy Aryan and the conduct his Christian or "Liberal" superstitions require of him,—comes the maddening sense of personal and racial guilt that has been for centuries and is today a black and monstrous incubus on the minds of our race. This explanation may well be right.

Revilo P. Oliver (1908-1994)

Oswald Spengler (1880-1936)

I have tried above to exhibit briefly the magnitude of the cultural distortion that is overlooked by both Spengler and Yockey, although, according to their own doctrines, it was the imposition on the Faustian soul of a Magian ideology, the product of a totally alien civilization. Spengler, however, who goes almost as far as Toynbee in regarding the Jews as a "fossil people," can be defended on the grounds that he regards the Faustian culture of the West as one that arose, around the year 900, among the dominant peoples who then lived in Europe, regardless of ethnic diversities or innate racial characteristics, and that Christianity was simply an element that entered into that culture. From that standpoint, our culture, whether for better or for worse, was as naturally and inevitably Christian as Napoleon was a Corsican. To ask what our civilization would have been like without Christianity is like asking what George Washington would have become, had he been born of different parents. Our estimate of Spengler's historionomy will therefore depend on our acceptance or rejection of (a) his conception of a culture as largely independent of biological race, and (b) his assumption that the Jews as such, have had no great influence over our history.

For Yockey, no such apology will serve. He follows Spengler, it is true, in his general doctrine of race, but he attributes to the Jews, whom he frequently designates as the "culture-distorters," a vast and decisive influence over our recent history, and since he does not claim that their baneful power is a recent phenomenon, he must logically believe that it has been exercised against us in earlier centuries. If he is to give us a philosophical comprehension of the historical process, he must explain the nature, origin, and development of that power—and obviously such an explanation must include consideration of the effects of Christianity on both our people and the Jews who, for purposes that Yockey recognizes as hostile, lived among them.

As I have said before, I come neither to praise nor to bury Yockey, but merely to evaluate his work. It is clear, I believe, that as an exegesis of historical causality, *Imperium* and, of course, its sequel are radically defective, even in terms of their own premises. They have other values. I have always believed that *Imperium* was enlightening and even inspiring reading for young men and women whose minds have not been irremediably blighted by the denaturing superstitions inculcated in the public schools. And both books are studies of politics, τὰ πολιτικὰ, in the original and proper sense of that word, not as it is used in our great ochlocracy in reference to the periodic popularity-contests between Tweedledum and Tweedledee which many Americans find as exciting as baseball games.

II

There is a modicum of truth in the frowsty verbiage about "One World" that used to excite women's clubs. It has always been obvious that there is only one earth,[1] but although an educated Roman in the first century B.C. could dream of a day when the invincible legions would add even China to the Empire,[2] he could also think of the *oecumene*, the inhabited part of the globe, as consisting, for all practical purposes, of the Roman Empire and the territories bordering on it. He was secure in the confidence that whatever happened in more distant regions, such as China and India, could have no possible effect on *his* world, except, perhaps, on the importation of rare luxuries and curiosities.

The technological achievements of our race, which made us masters of the entire globe until we succumbed to a fit of suicidal mania, did produce, around the beginning of the Nineteenth Century, "one world," in the sense that events anywhere on the planet did affect in some way the interests of

---

1. Since the very foundation of our rational thought is our perception of our place in the universe, it is worthy of note that only in 1978 did it become absolutely certain that the one earth is also unique. Fontenelle's *Entretiens sur la pluralité des mondes* in 1686 made popular the romantic fancy, which had been entertained speculatively by some Greek philosophers of Antiquity, that there were many planets that were doubtless inhabited by beings like ourselves. With the advance of astronomical knowledge, the possibilities were reduced to two planets in our solar system, Venus and Mars, and it was only when the surfaces of both had been clearly photographed that we knew how terribly alone we are in the universe. Some of our tender-minded contemporaries now console themselves with speculations about hypothetical inhabitants of hypothetical planets that may circle about some stars. Quite aside from the practical considerations that a space-craft, such as landed men on the moon, could not reach the nearest star in less than 700,000 years, this is sheer phantasy. As was concisely stated by the distinguished Australian biologist, Sir John C. Eccles, "there is no evidence that life started more than once" in the entire universe, and "the chances of rational beings existing elsewhere in the universe are so remote as to be out of the question." This fact, as significant in its way as the Copernican revolution, will profoundly affect our whole Weltanschauung in coming decades.

2. E.g., Lucan, I. 19.

the great colonial empires of Britain, France, and Spain and might vitally concern some of the other Aryan nations, such as Germany and the United States. The peoples of other races were merely raw material; they occupied their territories on our sufferance, either because it would not be economically profitable for us to dispossess them or because the reciprocal jealousies of the colonial powers made a war between Aryan nations the price of annexing China or Morocco. And since our race seemed to be healthy, it was only reasonable to foresee that, with our continued progress and expansion, the lower races would, in the course of nature, become extinct.[3]

Until 1914, no fact was more obvious than that the power-structure of the world, after the decline of Spain, depended on the three great nations of Europe, Britain, France, and Germany, with two outlying states, Russia and the United States, available as auxiliaries to one or the other of the three. It is true that beneath this structure there was a disquieting fact: seventy years before, Benjamin D'Israeli had emphatically warned Europeans that race was the basis of civilization, that "there is only one thing that makes a race, and that is blood," that all the nations of Europe were covertly under the control of the Jews, and that the "destructive principle," which was being used stealthily to undermine our civilization, was "developing entirely under the auspices of the Jews."[4] Only a very

3. Charles Darwin to W. Graham, 3 July 1881: "Remember what risk the nations of Europe ran, not so many centuries ago, of being overwhelmed by the Turks, and how ridiculous such an idea now is! The more civilised so-called Caucasian Races have beaten the Turkish hollow in the struggle for existence. Looking to the world at no very distant date, what an endless number of the lower races will have been eliminated by the higher civilised races throughout the world."

4. *Coningsby* (1844) and *Endymion* (1880) are novels, but, as D'Israeli (who changed his name to Disraeli) explained in a preface to the former, they are political discourses put into the form which "offered the best chance of influencing public opinion." The same views were expressed in many of his speeches, both in and outside of Parliament. Some persons, notably Douglas Reed in his last and posthumous book, *The Controversy of Zion* (Durban, South Africa, 1978; available from Liberty Bell Publications), believe that D'Israeli, who professed to be a Christian, was sincerely trying to warn his contemporaries in Britain of the menace that would eventually destroy them. Others note that he always received massive support from the Jews in England and elsewhere, and especially from the Rothschilds when he made his dramatic gesture of buying control

few members of our race were sufficiently alert to understand what he had told them in the clearest possible terms. And thirty years before 1914, Friedrich Nietzsche had clearly foreseen that Europe faced "a long series of catastrophes" and "wars such as the world has not yet seen," had perceived that our civilization was suffering from a degenerative disease of both intellect and will, and had identified the deadly infection as a superstition that the Jews had devised and disseminated to poison our minds and souls.[5] Only a few men of philosophical intellect understood him. Not only the masses, of whom rational thought for the future is not to be expected, but almost all of the persons who thought of themselves as an aristocracy or a learned elite were sunk in an euphoric complacency, believing in an effortless and automatic "progress" and the Jewish economic system in which money is the only value of human life.

In 1914, our civilization was worm-eaten at the core, but its brightly glittering surface concealed the corruption within from superficial eyes. It was taken for granted that the globe had become one world, the world of which the Aryan nations were the undisputed masters, while all the lesser races already were, or soon would become, merely the subject inhabitants of their

---

of the Suez Canal and then selling it to Great Britain when the British government could raise the money. He may have told the truth about race as a calculated gambit, feeling certain that the British were too stupid to understand. He was not in any sense a defector from his race, which he described as the true "aristocracy of the world," but he courteously told his British hosts that their race could aspire to equality with his. He thus inspired the absurd myth of "British Israĕl," the preposterous notion that the British (but not other Aryans) were the Israelites of the "Old Testament" and should reunite with their fellow Jews to rule the world. Even those who believe that D'Israeli assimilated, rather than simulated, British culture have to admit that he, who became the Earl of Beaconsfield in the British (!) peerage and Prime Minister to Queen Victoria, opened the way to power for the most vicious of England's resident enemies. See below, pp 66f., and the analysis of his political activities by Rudolf Craemer, *Benjamin Disraeli* (Hamburg, 1940).

'5. *Also sprach Zarathustra* was published in 1883-84, and *Zur Genealogie der Moral,* the most incisive of the later works, appeared in 1887. Note that Nietzsche, like all of his contemporaries, took it for granted that the world belonged to the European race, which was menaced only by the rotting of its own moral fibre, not by external enemies. He was, of course, right at that time. For a suggestive discussion of the folly that led to the suicide of Europe, see the work by Luis Díez del Corral that is available in H.V. Livermore's excellent translation, *The Rape of Europe* (London, 1959).

colonial possessions. This reasonable conception of the world's unity oddly survived the catastrophies that followed and it conditioned unthinking mentalities to accept the preposterous notions of current propaganda for "One World," which is couched in endless gabble that is designed to conceal the fact that it is to be a globe under the absolute and ruthless dominion of the Jews—a globe on which our race, if not exterminated, will be the most degraded and abject of all.

The apparent unity of the globe when it was under the dominion of our race depended, as must all rule, on military power, but it was so contentedly accepted by the other races in the various colonies because our power was proof of a biological superiority that was evident in the discipline of our troops and the courage, intelligence, and moral integrity of our men.[6] It was therefore a function of a biological unity that was only belatedly perceived by our people, and even then only by the few men who were able and willing to study the hidden foundations on which the imposing structure of power really rested, notably the Comte de Gobineau and Vacher de Lapouge. The reality of race was generally overlooked because men took the innate superiority of Europeans so for granted that they thought it unnecessary to mention it and instead concentrated their attention on the rivalries and antagonisms that divided the great powers of Europe, assuming that a shift in the balance of power in Europe would automatically be a shift in power over the entire globe. Ignoring D'Israeli's blunt statement that "language and religion do not make a race," men generally thought in geographic terms: Europe was a region with odd prolongations to Canada, Australia, the United States, and other lands possessed by a European people.

It is not easy to determine when our people first became

---

6. General Hilton, in his *Imperial Obituary* (Devon, Britons, 1968), remarks on the very significant fact that during the Pax Britannica an English gentleman, if he ran short of funds anywhere in the world, could borrow money from a native shopkeeper or man of means without difficulty, since there was never doubt about his absolute integrity and hence the certainty of repayment. When he was in Tibet, a region seldom visited by outsiders, the abbot of a Buddhist monastery unhesitatingly lent him 700 rupees—a large sum for the time and place—although his only security was trust in a British gentleman's honor. General Hilton's analysis of the causes of Great Britain's suicide is one of the most important documents of our time.

54

aware that Europe was inhabited by men who differed generically from the inhabitants of other parts of the world. The perception seems to have evolved slowly from the effective unity of Europe created by the preservation of Latin as the common language of educated men, which, in turn, depended on the religious unity of Western Christianity. A very clear statement of it appears in a discourse by Pope Urban II in 1095, reported by William of Malmsbury.[7] Urban regarded the Germanic peoples of France as a "race chosen and loved by God," but he recognized European unity by saying, in substance: "There are three continents, of which *we* live in what is by far the smallest, while Asia and Africa are inhabited by *our* enemies. Even the small part of the world that we possess is under attack by our enemies, who now occupy Spain and the Balearic Isles. We must strike back and subdue them before they destroy us." We, in other words, are Christendom, and it is significant that while Urban recognizes the Byzantines as Christians and asserts the propriety of aiding them against the Turks, he does not think of them as European: they are foreigners who fortunately practice what is much the same religion. In short then, Lawrence Brown is right when, in his *Might of the West*, he defines the West as composed of the descendants of the peoples who were Catholics in the Middle Ages.

With negligible exceptions, all the inhabitants of Europe thus defined were Aryans, comprising Nordic, Alpine, and Mediterranean subraces with a slight Dinaric admixture in some places.[8] The leadership throughout Europe (even, e.g., in Italy)

---

7. William's *Gesta regum Anglorum,* written before 1120, was edited by William Stubbs (London, 1887-89). My quotation is a condensed paraphrase of the relevant part of Urban's discourse, which was long and dealt with many other matters. Frederic Duncalf, in his part of Volume I of *A History of the Crusades* (edited by M. W. Baldwin, University of Wisconsin, 1969), observes (p. 220) that William relied on contemporaries who had heard Urban speak, but he oddly omits mention of Urban's appeal to defend Europe against its enemies by taking the offensive; he concentrates on the strictly religious and economic parts of the speeches by which Urban inspired the First Crusade.

8. The clearest and most concise exposition of the basic differences between races and subraces that I have seen is Roger Pearson's booklet *Race & Civilisation* (London, 1966).

was mostly Nordic. The differences between the subraces, although slight when compared to the great differences that distinguish Aryans from all other races, impeded a consciousness of racial unity at a time when Europe was truly international (and, to be exact, there were no nations in the modern sense, the territories being divided according to the rulers who were sovereign within them). The great contribution of the Church was that it transcended all territorial boundaries and gave all educated men a common language and common culture. They could move freely throughout Europe. William of Occam, the great Nominalist, studied at Oxford, taught in Paris, and spent the later part of his life in Pisa. The abbots of Monte Cassino in its great days came from Germany. One could multiply at great length examples of internationalism *within Europe* during the Middle Ages.

The Renaissance did not diminish, indeed, it strengthened, the awareness of the spiritual chasm that divided Europe from the rest of the globe. When the Reformation sundered the continent politically, its cultural unity was maintained by the *Respublica litterarum*, the European community of educated men who rose above the religious fanaticism of the masses and were largely independent of the various ecclesiastical organizations. They shared a culture based on the great Aryan literature and thought of Antiquity. From Spitzbergen to Palermo, every man who could consider himself literate had at least read Vergil, Horace, and Ovid, Cicero, and Livy, and read Homer, Plutarch, Lucian, and the Planudean anthology in Latin translations, if his education had not been sufficient to make him at home in Greek, while men who could claim to be learned had read far more extensively in both of the learned languages. Latin of Classic quality was the language of scholarship and of international communication until it was partly supplanted by French in the Eighteenth Century. Although original writing in Latin, both prose and verse, and translation into Latin from the modern vernaculars gradually but steadily declined thereafter and has all but ceased today, a knowledge of our race's great classics, read in the original texts, was expected of all educated men before the onset of recrudescent barbarism that followed the First World War; and cultured men of our race remained aware of their common bond.

For this bond there has been no real replacement. When

Thomas Arnold, in 1830, asserted that a "happy peace" had "taught every civilized country of Europe" that it was "disgraceful" not to be well acquainted with the languages and literatures of all the others, he meant that educated men must acquire (in addition to competence in Latin and Greek) fluency in French, Italian, German, and English; he not only failed to explain why countries in which Spanish, Portuguese, Norwegian, Swedish, Dutch, etc. were spoken were not civilized, but he proposed an educational standard to which few could attain. Today, English or recognizable imitations of it seems to be becoming a universal language, spoken and written not only by our people but also by Asiatics and even some Congoids, thus obfuscating its racial quality, since a Japanese may artificially compose better English than many Germans, who must struggle against the many deceptive similarities between it and their native tongue. In the United States, and to varying degrees in other white nations, literature is no longer taught in any language in the public schools, having been supplanted by contemporary gabble chosen for its virulence as a poison for adolescent minds. The real sciences are not an effective bond since our research and our technology can be successfully imitated and even adopted by Russians, Japanese, Chinese, and Semites, thus producing an illusion of universality that seems to support Jewish propaganda for "One World," in which we are to be but one of the subject races.

After the catastrophe of 1945, our race's fatuity became so great that the bond between once-great Britain and the British overseas in Canada, South Africa, Australia, and New Zealand was progressively broken, and Europe has become a merely geographical term. Politically, Europe has become less than it was in the Middle Ages, for treason and lunacy went so far in 1945 as to deliver a large part of it to its Soviet enemies. But nevertheless, the peoples of what remains of Mediaevel Christendom are perforce bound together by a common interest, whether they know it or not, and, as Yockey demonstrated in both *Imperium* and *The Enemy of Europe*, they will ineluctably share a common fate. At the very best, no nation of what remains of the old Europe can hope to escape that future, except that some one nation may be given the privilege that the cannibals accorded to the white captain when they promised to eat him last. One hears that the Irish are particularly encouraged by such a prospect.

That some Europeans are aware of the unity thus forced on them is shown by a few small organizations, such as "Jeune Europe" and *Nation Europa*, which the Jews still tolerate. The only political expression of this unity is the "Common Market," to which most of the European nations, including Britain, have adhered, but that is obviously a device to frustrate an effective unity by opening all the nations to a deadly influx of their racial enemies in the guise of "workers" or "refugees," while forcing Britain into hostility toward the British in Australia and New Zealand and thus applying to those countries economic pressure to facilitate the work of their own traitors, who yearn to submerge the white population in a flood of their Oriental enemies. It is not by any means a coincidence that the "President" of the "European Parliament" is Simone Veil, a Jewess who was gassed and cremated by the awful Germans, but obviously rose from the dead, as God's Race seems able to do on occasion, and is probably still collecting from the Germans for her temporary decease.

The Enemy of Europe presents us with a double problem. To criticize Yockey's work, we must, naturally, consider the situation in 1949, when he published *The Proclamation of London*, a small booklet in which he anticipated in print part of what he said more fully in the book which he had already written, although it was not published until 1953.[9] To assess

---

9. On the circumstances of the publication of *The Enemy of Europe*, see above, pp. 1f. *The Proclamation of London* was issued anonymously as a manifesto of the "European Liberation Front," in which Yockey was associated with several patriotic Englishmen, notably Peter Huxley-Blythe, the author of *The East Came West* (Caldwell, Idaho, 1964), a very important book, which I reviewed in *American Opinion*, May 1966. What is probably the most trenchant writing attributed to the Liberation Front is a brief article, "The Real Culprit," reprinted in *The Liberty Bell*, March 1981, pp. 53-56. The anonymous author claims to be over seventy years old; neither the style nor the argument is Yockey's, and the article was obviously written after 1970, i.e., at least nine years after his death and twenty years after the Front founded by Yockey disintegrated for a variety of reasons that must be left to his future biographer. It is clear, however, that the programme of his Liberation Front, set forth on the back cover of the *Proclamation*, was injudiciously candid and too drastic for the time and place. The integration of Britain into a single sovereign European state was a proposal that startled Britons who remembered that for a time their nation had seemed to stand alone against the continent, and in addition the manifesto called for the "immediate expulsion of all

the relevance of his work to our plight today, we must naturally take account of all the misfortunes that have come upon us in the past thirty years.

In 1949, Yockey claimed that "throughout all Europe there is stirring today . . . the Idea of the Imperium of Europe, the permanent and perfect union of the peoples and nations of Europe." There was little or no evidence that such an idea was "stirring" anywhere in Europe when Yockey wrote, but unless he wrote to create what he pretended was already in existence, he did sense the coming of the general sentiment for unity that did emerge a few years later and was, by one of our enemies' standard techniques, captured and aborted in the "Common Market."

In 1949, what was left of shattered Europe was only beginning to recover from trauma. Everywhere there were grim ruins left by the suicidal insanity that had culminated only four years before, and it would be another decade before the most conspicuous scars of the war were effaced or covered up. The moral damage was greater and more lasting. Men were still appalled and benumbed by the frightful demonstration of how thin and fragile was the veneer of Western civilization—by the revelation of what treachery, barbarity, and inhumanity the supposedly Anglo-Saxon nations, Britain and the United States, were capable when they ran amok to please the Jews. There were, to be sure, some highly intelligent men who had been able

---

Jews and other parasitic aliens from the soil of Europe," a demand which it would not have been feasible to carry out at once and startling to a nation that had just ruined itself to punish its racial brethren in Germany for insubordination to God's Race, even though the policy of exporting Jews from Europe was entirely in accord with Zionist propaganda for the establishment of a "Jewish homeland," which many naive persons took seriously. The programme of the Front, furthermore, included some economic demands, especially "the abolition of all unearned income," which (at least in the bald statement) contravened the innate instincts of Aryans, who (when not diseased) insist on a man's right to transmit property to his descendants. That demand, which must have seemed Bolshevik to most Englishmen, was exploited by Jewish propaganda that called Yockey a Communist. The *Proclamation* states that it was being simultaneously published in German, Spanish, French, Italian, and Flemish, but I have not seen or heard of a copy in any of those languages. When the *Proclamation* was reprinted by the Nordland Press in 1970, the editor knew of only three surviving copies of the original booklet. It is now available from Liberty Bell Publications.

to observe objectively the Götterdämmerung. Perhaps the most remarkable book that Yockey could have (but, so far as I know, had not) read, since it was published before 1949, was Peter H. Nicoll's *Britain's Blunder*.[10] It is a book that should encourage everyone who has not despaired of the powers of the Aryan mind, for its author, a singularly courageous Scot, had retained the lucidity and perspicacity of his intellect while living in Britain, where the population had been virtually crazed by the lies injected into their minds for many years by their great War Criminals, in collaboration with the Jews, to pep up the cattle they were stampeding to the slaughter. Although Mr. Nicoll, naturally, did not have access to much information that was then kept secret, he saw the essentials of the disaster with a clarity that still arouses our admiration.

Another judicious observer of the European catastrophe was Prince Sturdza of Romania, who had the great advantage of being able to view events with relative detachment from his post as Ambassador in Berlin. His sagacious analysis of the plight of Europe, *La Bête sans nom: enquête sur les responsibilités*, written in September 1942, was published in 1944 and, of course, before the terrible conclusion of the Jews' Crusade. [11]

---

10. *Britain's Blunder* was published by its author, *s.l.&a.* [1948] and copies of it have been made extremely rare; it has been recently reprinted, again *s.l.&a.*, and copies are available from various dealers in books that have not been given the Kosher seal of approval. It is a slender volume of 140 pages, which its valiant author later expanded, with the assistance of the distinguished American historian, Harry Elmer Barnes, to a book of about 600 pages. This, however, is available only in a German translation, *Englands Krieg gegen Deutschland* (Tübingen, 1963). I assume, but do not know, that the Jews still permit the German publisher (Grabert) to sell copies of the book.

11. *La Bête sans nom* was published at Copenhagen (Les Nouvelles Éditions Diplomatiques) in 1944 under the pseudonym "Charpeleu" and in an edition of 2000 copies. Copies of it have now been made extremely rare. Prince Sturdza, before going to Berlin as Ambassador, had been Foreign Minister of Romania, a small nation that was necessarily a pawn in the great game for world dominion, but one which, it is possible, was the key pawn that determined subsequent moves on the board. He, a most judicious and dispassionate observer, believes that the *coup d'état* and murders carried out by King Carol and his Jewish leman in 1938 impelled Hitler to negotiate a "non-aggression" treaty with the Soviet as a desperate expedient to avoid the war that the Jews' stooges in Britain and the United States were working so hard to force on Germany. (See *Suicide of Europe*,

Although Prince Sturdza wrote before the tragic end, a judicious reader could extrapolate from his analysis of the causes and reach, after 1945, essentially the conclusions that its eminent author set forth in print much later in a book which he, who could write a fluid and lucid French, mistakenly wrote in Romanian,[12] and which is now generally available only in an English translation, drastically censored to please the Jews, that was made and published by the Birch business under the title, *The Suicide of Europe*.[13]

The two books I have mentioned represent the best European thought around 1949, which, needless to say, was confined to a few men of extraordinary lucidity and perspicacity, and certainly did not represent the sentiments of the masses of stunned and befuddled victims of the war, whether in England or anywhere on the continent. What immediately concerns us here is the virtual despair of the authors. Nicoll concluded that "the general consequences of the most lamentable and perhaps the most unnecessary war in modern history" were "the destruction of Europe, the ruin of her greatest nation, the enthronement of brutal tyranny" and the "decadence of Britain as a great power," which had become an American base and would be, "in years to come . . . subjected to the appalling fate to which Hiroshima and Nagasaki were condemned." The

---

pp. 122-4). Hitler's decision, made on the advice of his General Staff and, no doubt, the infamous traitor, Admiral Canaris, may have been a military blunder, as Prince Sturdza believes; it was certainly a blunder from the standpoint of Hitler's desire to avert a war with England and France, for it made it possible for the Jews to generate "world opinion" that National Socialism and Communism were essentially the same thing, and it is extremely doubtful that the War Criminals could have driven the British and Americans to an attack on Germany without the confusion caused by that spurious "allian˒ ."

12. *Rômania şi sfârşitul Europei: amintir din ţara pierdută* (Madrid, 1966).

13. Boston (Western Islands), 1968. The translation and publication was subsidized by an American lady, who said she did not know how drastically the text was censored. For a few examples of the censor's alterations, see Warren B. Heath's introduction to the English version of Bacu's *The Anti-Humans* (Englewood, Colorado, 1971; now available from Liberty Bell Publications).

instigators of the British attack on Germany had effectively "destroyed the classical Christian ,civilization of all Europe," and while Nicoll does not deny that there may be some hope of a new civilization to replace what was destroyed, he can see only a vague and tenuous hope for a far distant future. Prince Sturdza's conclusions are stated in the title of his later book: the result of Jewish instigation was simply the Suicide of Europe, which, for all practical purposes, became what India was in the Eighteenth Century when Britain and France were contending for mastery: Europe had become a territory on which would be fought battles to determine whose colony it would become. Such hope as Prince Sturdza permitted himself was that the American people might someday have a government that would act in their own interests.

The contrast between these views and the optimism of the *Proclamation* is obvious, and the expressed confidence in the proximate formation of an European Imperium must have been an example of wishful thinking. In *The Enemy of Europe* Yockey is much more realistic. He explicitly recognizes (p. 86) that "since Europe has no power, the question is: How is power to be obtained? " Europe *as a whole* has only a choice of enemies. Its only chance of regaining power depends on adroit political manoeuvering.

In that sense, the European unity that Yockey recognized is an unalterable fact, whether or not the various European populations know it. It is simply a consequence of the Suicide of Europe and the invention of high-altitude bombers and ballistic missiles. It is a consequence of the British-American innovation of total war against civilian populations. A war, for example, between France and Germany or between Britain and France is now, for all practical purposes, inconceivable, although people talk about an odd anachronism called a 'limited war,' in which both sides agree to use only some of the available weapons and thus, in effect, make the 'war' a kind of sporting contest, a large-scale football game.

Despite much babbling and squawking now fashionable, a 'limited' war can be only border skirmishing or a feint to test an enemy's resolution, a mere preliminary to a *real* war.[14]

_____

14. It is true that Western nations at one time observed certain moral

Given the small extent of their territories and the concentration of their populations, a real war between Britain and France, for example, could be only the equivalent of the situation that was once much debated by theorists of the code of honor, a duel to be fought with pistols at arm's length. At the present time, the only powers that could fight a real war are the United States and the two that it created for the destruction of civilization, Soviet Russia and China.

Yockey, therefore, was right: the nations of Europe can no longer be independent of each other, however unpleasant that fact may be. If either England or France were occupied by a major power, the other would be helpless. And all the nations of Europe, concentrated in a relatively small and densely settled territory between the Soviet and the United States, are equally vulnerable and will necessarily share the same fate. Thus Europe, *nolens volens*, is a single political entity.

OVERSEAS EUROPE

When Yockey speaks of Europe's colonies, he is thinking of the territories outside Europe inhabited by our race, essentially Canada, Australia, New Zealand, South Africa, and the United States, of which the latter, in continuing revolt, so to speak, against the mother country, had become its most dangerous enemy. He does not consider separately the future of the others. When Britain attacked Germany in 1939, she was able to count on the whole-hearted support of the English who lived overseas. Everyone knows, of course, that she can no longer do so. If she were attacked today by any nation—the United States,

---

restraints in war, but since these were repudiated and abrogated by the British and Americans, it is idle to dream of restoring them in the foreseeable future. See F.J.P. Veale, *Advance to Barbarism* (2d edition, Appleton, Wisconsin, 1953; 3d edition, New York, 1968). (I have not seen the first edition, published in England in 1948; I probably should have mentioned it when I referred to Nicoll's book above.) — I need not remark that the 'limited war' in Vietnam was merely a device to kill white Americans, oppress American taxpayers, and further disgrace the United States. It was not in any sense a real war: the eventual defeat of the Americans was agreed on in advance, though probably not in writing. The importation into the United States of a horde of Mongolian enemies as "refugees" was probably not a part of the original plan and seems to have been added only when opportunity offered to afflict the American boobs yet further.

the Soviet, France, Sweden, Ireland—she would find that she had not only kicked South Africa into independence, but has so alienated the three other former dominions that she can hope for no more than a few platitudes in the local newspapers and, if events give an opportunity for them, kindly obituaries. There is no indication that Yockey foresaw this development.

In 1949, Europe still had extensive possessions overseas. The British not only entertained strange illusions about what they called their Commonwealth and the consequences of their folly in forcing "self-government" on their former subjects of other races, but Britain still possessed very extensive territories in Asia and Africa, and even some in the Western Hemisphere, as crown colonies of which she had not yet been stripped by the traitors in her government. France possessed Indo-China until it was taken from her by American treachery[15] and Communist China, which the Americans had created by stabbing their Chinese allies in the back. France considered Algeria a part of "metropolitan" France. In addition to the numerous minor possessions, she owned Madagascar and half of the Dark Continent north of the British Union of South Africa, while the rest of the territories of the savages were divided between Britain, Belgium, Portugal, and Spain, and the colonies that had been taken from Italy were booty that in a sane world Britain and France would have divided between them. And although the United States had set up a kind of vaudeville show called the "United Nations" to disguise a little its subservience to its enemies in the Soviet and further the subjugation of the American people, there was in 1949 no apparent reason why

---

15. The nerve center of Communist agitation among the natives was evidently the American embassy, in which inflammatory bulletins urging the natives to get rid of the nasty white men were printed on the embassy's presses. So far as one can determine from the conflicting reports, the Americans promised military aid to the French, should the Chinese invasion become formidable, and then broke their promise at the last minute when the situation at Dienbienphu became critical, thus producing the delightful massacre of the French troops, which had been hopelessly outnumbered by a fresh invasion from China. Americans who dote on Mongoloids naturally reck nothing of the American lives that were squandered in Vietnam, but they should try to calculate the total of all the precious yellow lives that were lost in Annam, Cochin China ("South Vietnam"), Cambodia, Laos, and Tonkin ("North Vietnam") as a direct result of the American's racial and diplomatic betrayal of the French to promote lovely "anti-colonialism."

the European nations, which had not yet realized that they had defeated themselves as catastrophically as they defeated Germany in 1945, should not have retained and ruled their colonial empires.

It is true that in 1949 our race was already showing alarming symptoms of a kind of epidemic lunacy called "anti-colonialism," which was supposedly derived from the prating of a shyster named Woodrow Wilson, whom the Jews had installed as President of the United States in preparation for the First World War.[16] A bigot who had peddled an ostensibly secular theology under the name of "political science," Wilson, when he used the United States to exacerbate the war in Europe and prevent a reasonable peace, had devised a mysticism called "the self-determination of peoples," which, like "theosophy" and "spiritualism," had a great appeal to minds that had been weakened by Christian superstitions. And, oddly enough, Great Britain, which had the most to lose by self-mortification, was the first Western nation to take a morbid pleasure in harming itself.[17] Incidentally, sentimentalists should note that the

---

16. On the training of Wilson by the Jews, who boasted that their satrap, Baruch, "leading him like [sic] one would a poodle on a string," taught Fido to sit up and bark ideals for political bonbons, see Colonel Curtis B. Dall's *F.D.R.* (2d ed., Washington, D.C. 1970), especially pp. 134-38. Wilson seems not to have been entirely devoid of conscience, for he is reported to have lamented, "I have ruined my country!" before his mind broke down in 1919, perhaps under the strain of realizing that he, a supreme egotist, had been merely a *fantoche* in the hands of his masters. His insanity was, of course, concealed from the American boobs, whose government continued to be conducted in his name until 1921. He partly recovered his reason before his death in 1924, but left, so far as is known, no confessions. His election to the presidency in 1912 was, of course, contrived by stimulating the vanity of Theodore Roosevelt and inciting him to form the "Progressive Party" and thus split the Republican vote and punish William Howard Taft for his lack of alacrity in kowtowing to the Jews. As Colonel Dall notes, the Jews laughed over their manipulation of Theodore Roosevelt, their "other candidate" for control of the United States.

17. The psychopathology of masochism would require a separate treatise. Such mental alienation appears in various races, usually as a concomitant of religious mania, but may take a peculiar form in Aryans, beginning with the notion of *tapas* that appears in India not long after the Aryan conquest and also in the Norse myth of Odin's hanging of himself on the world-tree. The hallucination is, of course, the basis of Christian

Western nations that contracted a kind of contagious epilepsy and had masochistic fits in which they forced "self-determination" on their colonies, invariably inflicted great suffering and enormous loss of life on the subjects whom they "liberated."

In 1949, Great Britain had already begun to destroy herself, and although some mental and moral deficiency in the English must be regarded as the primary cause, it could be argued that the fatal folly was a consequence of the initial blunder that was made when D'Israeli was injected into the British peerage. A Jew named Samuel, who showed his contempt for the English by assuming the illustrious Norman name of Montagu, so enriched himself by his depredations in banking and international finance that his friend, King Edward VII, ennobled him with the good Anglo-Saxon name of Baron Swaythling. (*Si quid sentiunt Manes*, the ghost of the first King Edward, who had tried to run the Jews out of England in 1290, must have gibbered in fury at the act of his namesake.) The "British" Baron's son became Secretary of State for India in 1917 and worked, sometimes slyly, sometimes almost openly, to undermine British rule in India and to arouse among the natives discontent that could be used as a pretext for further sabotage of the Empire. In collaboration with Viscount Chelmsford, who

austerities, appearing in most tales about saints, and particularly conspicuous in Seventeenth-Century Spain, where normally intelligent men had fits in which they lashed their backs with whips weighted with lead until the blood from their excoriated flesh flowed down over their trousers. They imagined that Jesus, if he happened to be watching, would be pleased to see them torture themselves. The same hallucinations are epidemic today in a holy conspiracy called Opus Dei, which was used by "our" C.I.A. to undermine and eventually capture the government of General Franco in Spain, for the members of that Catholic sect regularly torture themselves by wearing sharp-pointed chains next to their flesh and flogging themselves with lead-loaded whips, confident that Jesus will be so pleased that he will assign them specially luxurious quarters in the best apartment house in Heaven and make them members of his own exclusive club. Incredible as it may seem, men who appear outwardly sane secretly indulge in such masochistic perversions. A Catholic Irishman, John Roche, a professor of the History of Science(!) with a doctoral degree from Oxford (!), was bewitched by Opus Dei when he was an undergraduate in an Irish college and acquired an addiction to self-torment that he compared to addiction to narcotics. He did God's Work by torturing himself for fourteen years (and doubtless serving the conspiracy in other ways), and he experienced "withdrawal symptoms" after he came to his senses. See his confession in the *Sunday Times* (London), 18 January 1981, p. 15. Even now, however, he has not guessed that the godly Opus Dei is partly or entirely financed by the C.I.A.

was closely tied by marriage to the Goldmans and may have had Jewish genes himself, and who became Viceroy of India in 1916, "Montagu" prepared in the name of the King's government an official and astounding report on India—astounding because its authors were not attainted for high treason. The crucial section of the long and rambling document is cited by General Hilton in his *Imperial Obituary*. The report bewailed the deplorable fact that 95% of all the peoples of India were happily content under British rule and hoped for its continuance. It was therefore England's duty, the titled saboteurs said, to "bring about the most radical revolution" in India to enable the 5% of malcontents to terrorize and suppress the "pathetically contented" 95% and thus prepare India for "nationhood," i.e., for perpetual rioting, the venomous racial animosities that always accompany multi-racial societies that are not under foreign rule, large-scale massacres, savage atrocities, and contemptuous hatred of white men.

The work of dismembering the British Empire was carried on by a Jew residing in England, Rufus Isaacs, who was rewarded for his involvement in the malodorous Marconi scandal[18] by being successively created Baron, Viscount, Earl, and finally Marquess of Reading, Lord Chief Justice (!) of England, and Viceroy of India, where he made a feint of maintaining British rule while sapping its foundations. [19] His fellow tribesmen ran

18. A typical financial operation carried out by artfully depressing the value of Marconi stock in both England and the United States to induce its owners to sell for a fraction of its worth and then artfully inflating its value to sell it to the public for more than it was worth. It involved the bribery of the Chancellor of the Exchequer, an unprincipled opportunist named Lloyd George, by the common device of "selling" him at depressed prices stock for which he would not be expected to pay until it greatly increased in value (it soared suddenly to twelve times its former price). English newspapers that were still in English hands sometimes caricatured Lloyd George as a little boy travelling under the escort of his two Jewish tutors, Isaacs and Samuel.

19. See the inadvertent admissions in the laudatory biography by H. Montgomery Hyde, *Lord Reading* (London, 1967), Chapter 8. For example, he censured and forced the resignation of General Dyer for having restored order in Amritsar after a mob killed five Englishmen, beat an Englishwoman almost to death, looted banks, and otherwise exhibited their idealistic aspirations. The fact that General Dyer had been publicly thanked by the decent Sikhs, who bestowed on him the highest honor in their power, merely proved the need for the "radical revolution" that

interference for him in England by a standard ploy, using their increasing control of the English press to publicize shrill protests that he was "brutally" failing to truckle sufficiently to the "aspirations" of babbling babus, whose minds had been stuffed with "democratic" verbiage in British schools. And so, in 1947, the British ignominiously retreated from their largest colonial possession, and the Hindus and Moslems promptly began to massacre each other on a scale that brought joy to the hearts of the apostles of "self-determination." And the "Republic of India" and Pakistan were created as enemies of our race and civilization.

Yockey certainly understood that the "successful Indian Mutiny in 1947," as he called it in the *Proclamation*, was a consequence of the First World War, which was itself suicidal and an effect of the "Culture-disease" spread by the Jews, but he does not remark on the curious circumstance that the British retreat from India had been conducted, not by Englishmen, but by aliens with British titles. He comments on the fatal decadence of the British aristocracy and upper class,[20] which he attributed correctly to a spiritual decay, but, perhaps in keeping with the racial theory we noticed above, he does not ask the drastic and fearful question, How British are the

---

would teach them "nationhood" and perpetual violence. Another trick was a loud campaign to end "racial discrimination," an infallible means of stirring up trouble and inciting other races to hate ours.

20. General Hilton (*op. cit.*), writing from an entirely different standpoint, also attributes some part of the responsibility for the loss of the Empire to the dilution and demoralization of the upper classes by "democracy" and Jewish ethics. The subject races respected gentlemen (cf. note 6 above), but not the bounders who gradually replaced them in an age in which a Lloyd George could become the King's Prime Minister and harbor several Jews in his Cabinet. The General could have mentioned the most flagrant instance of which I have heard. Around 1925, a certain Charles Arthur, who probably could not have attained a commission in the army before 1914 and certainly could not have held it long, was a Captain in His Majesty's Army and was appointed by His Majesty's Government *Aide-de-Camp* to Prince Hari Singh, son and heir presumptive of the Maharaja of Kashmir. The up-to-date young captain enlisted several accomplices and worked the old badger-game on the naïf young prince, whom they successfully blackmailed for the astonishing sum of 125,000 pounds sterling. Their enterprise would have remained unknown, had not Captain Arthur and one or more of his accomplices forged an endorsement on a cheque to cheat the "outraged husband" of his share of the loot.

68

British? It is a crucial question that admits of no precise answer, and discussion of it would require an inordinately long excursus. (Cf. note 27 below.)

THE HEARTLAND

For Yockey, both kinds of colonies have only a secondary importance. The attitudes and cultural vitality of Europeans who have established themselves in other continents are determined by the power and vitality of their mother country. European dominion over other races is merely an epiphenomenon, a measure of a European nation's power, a salutary reminder that, as he tells us, power can be maintained only by increasing it.

We return, therefore, to the fundamental fact that new weapons have imposed on Europe a necessary unity. He is aware, of course, of the impediments to such a union: the ethnic differences that seem small only when our race is compared to other races; the corresponding differences in traditions and temperament, producing what Jacques Rivière described as discordant nervous rhythms; and the diversity of languages, perhaps the most troublesome barrier of all and one that grows higher, as the major languages deteriorate with the decline of education in the several countries. So great are the differences within Europe that the eminent historian, Geoffrey Barraclough,[21] denies that "European unity" ever existed in the past or the present, rejects all claims for a "common western European tradition," and sees no cultural force that can create "bonds (or potential bonds) of unity between England and France (for example) or France and Spain." Very well, but later in his book he foresees that in the future "the war of 1939-45 will appear . . . as the decisive conflict in which Europe, committing suicide, surrendered mastery to the coloured peoples." So, in the end, he sees, as does Yockey, a unity imposed on Europe by a common destiny, by the natural and implacable hatred that the other races feel for our own—races that both the Soviet and the United States, in an effective partnership, are inciting and arming against our homeland.

21. Geoffrey Barraclough, *History in a Changing World* (Oxford, 1955), pp. 43, 183.

Yockey urged Europeans to consider the grim realities of the plight they brought upon themselves by their insane and suicidal war for the Jews. He told them bluntly that they must not permit themselves to be narcotized by the endless drivel about "peaceful solutions," "world peace," "one world," and the rest of the gabble to which weak minds are addicted as to opium or cocaine. If they are to have a future, they must deal with both the aliens that drove them to suicide and their own tares, which he, using a German idiom, calls the "Michael stratum."

It is a regrettable but undeniable fact that the great mass of the population is interested only in present comfort and gross satisfactions; unwilling to take thought for their class, their nation, or their race and incapable of taking such thought anyway; materialists in Yockey's sense of that word (which has nothing to do with philosophical thought, from which they would instinctively flee as owls from the light) and craving only animal satisfactions, although they frequently have fits of religiosity or hypocritically affect a concern for their "fellow man," if such concern is in vogue and profitable. They are proletarians, regardless of income; they are by nature *Untermenschen*, the more pernicious the greater their incomes or the higher the positions to which they have climbed in a governmental or industrial bureaucracy. Theirs is the ochlocracy for which the United States made the world safe, while making the world unsafe for civilization. They are, however, a necessary part—a very large part—of every population, and the first task of a statesman is to control that mass in the interest of a civilization it cannot understand.

Yockey reminded Europeans that the only political reality is power, military power, not the twittering of idealists and "Liberals" as they hop from perch to perch on a tree of which they cannot see the roots or understand the life. And he suggested the means whereby Europe might regain at least some of the power that it had insanely thrown away to please its enemies.

THE NUTCRACKER

Yockey saw Europe as lying, temporarily helpless, between two overwhelmingly powerful antagonists, so that the only choice left to it was a choice between its two enemies, which were fortunately enemies of each other. His thesis depended, therefore, on his belief that the Soviet Empire and the United States were irreconcilable forces. And since the United States was obviously an instrumentality of the Jews, that meant that the Jews had lost control of Russia. Yockey thus proposed a solution to a problem that has been earnestly, sometimes furiously, and in the end inconclusively debated ever since, so that it remains the most urgent problem that is immediately before us. On the truth or falsity of Yockey's solution will depend our foreseeable future.

We are confronted by a total lack of trustworthy data. *All* of our information concerning conditions inside Russia comes from either Soviet or Jewish sources and is therefore mendacious except insofar as it may, through inadvertence or coincidence, contain some elements of fact. Russia—I speak of Russia because the rest of the vast Soviet Empire is merely its appanage—is, on even the most hopeful assumption, in the hands of men who have mastered the techniques of misinformation and disinformation, and who have virtually absolute and total control over all significant news concerning events in their empire, except what may come through Jewish sources. To be sure, a considerable number of men have defected from the Soviet and found asylum in Western nations, but for each of them we must first try to determine whether or not he is, as some of them undoubtedly are, a Soviet or Jewish agent, sent to increase our perplexity and confusion by providing a superficially different variety of misinformation and disinformation. If we have satisfied ourselves of his *bona fides*, we have the even more difficult problem of determining whether his reports are misleading because his knowledge of the facts is limited and inadequate, or because he has made his report serve his own resentments or ambitions, or because he conceals some part of the truth to avoid offending the Jews or a corrupt and perfidious government that could at any time return him to Soviet territory and a terrible death.

Our dilemma may be illustrated by a trivial bit of news from Russia, chosen at random. The press recently reported that Brezhnev was being treated by a wonderful "psychic healer," whose photograph shows her to be a not unattractive young woman, white but certainly not Aryan. She is said to have a luxurious apartment in Moscow, complete with servants, to travel in a limousine, complete with chauffeur, and to dress expensively and elegantly.

Our press is apt to be truthful in reporting trivial matters, if one allows for the journalists' normal sensationalism. If the "psychic healer" were said to be ministering to a British Prime Minister or an American President, we would suppose that he either

(1) was in fact suffering from some psychosomatic malady, or

(2) had found a neat way to maintain a mistress in style.

But the news is about the Soviet President and came through a censorship that is vigilant about even trivialities. So we have to consider other possible explanations:

(3) Brezhnev has become senile and feeble-minded, and the rulers of the Soviet are preparing us for his replacement.

(4) Brezhnev's sickness is political, and we are being prepared for his removal by sudden death or forced retirement into obscurity.

(5) The mention of Brezhnev is merely a trick to secure wide publicity for a story concocted by Russian experts in psychological warfare to further the epidemic of superstition and irrationality that is reducing the American masses to imbecility and thus hastening the national paralysis. This interpretation is supported by the inclusion in the story of a statement from a Russian physician, who certifies the miraculous cures accomplished by the witch's "laying on of hands." The story therefore fits neatly into the long series of stories that have been coming out of the Soviet in recent years to make credulous persons believe that Russian "scientists" are making wonderful discoveries about "extrasensory perception," "telepathy," "psi-power," and other occult hocus-pocus.

(6) The story was manufactured by the Jews for the same purpose. As everyone knows, their press and boob-tubes in the United States are making a concerted effort to induce hallucinations in the masses by lustily advertising the charlatans, thaumaturges, astrologers, "psychics," evangelists, and other swindlers who are so lucratively preying on the ignorant and simple-minded.

(7) There is the last possibility that this and other hokum about "psychic" marvels in Russia, instead of being acts of psychological warfare, more or less accurately reflect a wave of

occult superstition in the Soviet that is tolerated either because (a) the rulers think it provides harmless amusement for the masses, or (b) the régime is actually disintegrating and cannot shore up the official Marxian religion. The latter hypothesis will please those who wish to attribute recent disorders in Poland to Russian weakness, and the perennial hopefuls who never tire of assuring us that there is a craving for "freedom" in Russia and that a proletarian revolution there is sure to break out any moment since 1947.

The story about the "psychic healer" is, of course, too trivial to be of interest other than as an example of the kind of questions that we must ask ourselves about every bit of seemingly significant news that comes out of Russia, a territory that is enclosed by a censorship as efficient as the famous border that prevents unauthorized escapes from Soviet territory. No one can be really certain of what goes on behind that barrier. The most brazen lying is commonplace even when there is no official censorship. There is no greater intercourse between two nations than that between Britain and the United States, and thousands of Britons are visiting or travelling in this country at any given time. But nevertheless one of the leading newspapers in London, *The Observer*, on 8 March 1981 carried a scare-head in large type: "Shadow of Terror Falls on U.S. Jews," and feeble-minded Englishmen were invited to believe that all of the millions of God's Race in this country were cowering in dread of the moment when the American "Nazis" will start popping them into gas chambers and reducing them to holy ashes.

We have been assured so many times that the Jews were losing or had lost control of Russia and the Soviet! The first wave of such hopeful thinking came when Bronstein, alias Trotsky, scuttled out of Russia, having purportedly lost a power-struggle with Dzhugashvili, alias Stalin. One consequence was that the misfits, crackpots, overgrown infants, and mattoids that formed the Communist Parties in civilized countries split into "Trotskyites" and "Stalinists," who quarrelled as furiously as did the Christian Homoousians and Homoeousians. The net result, however, was to accelerate and amplify the diffusion of Communist propaganda, and in the late 1930s the weekly periodical, *Time*, which was then still largely in American hands, suggested that Bronstein and Dzhugashvili were really coöperating in staging a performance for the suckers. The subsequent murder of Bronstein in Mexico proves nothing, for by that time (1940) he had become an embarrassment and impediment to "Stalin," who needed to reunite his stooges and dupes in the United States in preparation for the day when the American cattle would be stampeded into Europe. The view expressed by *Time* is not widely held now, but it has never been conclusively refuted.

After Trotsky's exodus from the new Holy Land in 1929, the next onset of propaganda that the Jews were losing control of their Soviet colony came with the "purge trials" of 1936-37, in which a passel of "Old Bolsheviks," most of them Jews, were spectacularly prosecuted and liquidated by Stalin's subordinates, most of them Jews. The trials were a shock to Westerners who naïvely believed no hair on the head of a Jew could be harmed in a country controlled by his fellow tribesmen, forgetting how savagely Jews slew one another in struggles for power within their race, e.g., when Jesus and Onias slugged it out for the office of High Priest in 170-169 B.C., or the otherwise unrecorded occasion around A.D. 30 that provided the corpses which proved to horrified archaeologists that Jewish ingenuity had found a way to increase even the torments of crucifixion for fellow Jews who were mutinous. No one yet has convincingly explained why Stalin preferred to stage a grandiose show for the civilized world instead of having the selected "Old Bolsheviks" quietly disposed of in convenient lime-pits.

Yockey, however, was convinced by a smaller show in Prague and, as he tells at the beginning of *The Enemy of Europe*, he revised its text in 1952 to take into account an event that he had foreseen in 1948. He discussed it in greater detail in an essay, "What is Behind the Hanging of the Eleven Jews in Prague? " It was clearly written for publication by his European Liberation Front, but, so far as I know, never printed. [22]

Yockey marshals his arguments effectively. When Stalin joined the Jewish Crusade Against Europe, he appealed to Russian nationalism and patriotism to encourage his armies and

---

22. It may have appeared in the short-lived periodical, *The Frontfighter*, of which I have seen only one number. I have photostats of a typewritten copy. It is reproduced in Appendix II below.

peoples. That is one of the few verifiable facts before us, but we remember that our great War Criminal used American patriotism to pep up the livestock that he was sending to Europe to slaughter and be slaughtered for Yahweh's Master Race. For that matter, the cannon-fodder were told that wicked Hitler planned to invade the United States, and there were nincompoops so ignorant of military and naval logistics that they believed it. On the other hand, it was Germany's purpose to destroy the Soviet, so there was a genuine basis for Stalin's appeal to his subjects.

It is undoubtedly true that the Slavs feel a deep racial antipathy to the Jews and would gladly purge their territory of them. The question, however, is whether they are or will become sufficiently intelligent and strong to indulge that desire in defiance of the rest of the world, whom the Jews would infallibly incite against them.

It is probably true that the Jews planned to obtain a monopoly of atomic weapons by having them made the exclusive property of the silly vaudeville show in New York City called the "United Nations," which was simply a flimsy screen for their age-old dream of "One World" under their rule.[23] If so, Russia's insistence on using American and British knowledge to equip herself with the feared weapons disappointed them. To that extent, at least, Stalin acted as a Russian Czar, not as a stooge for the Jews.

Yockey believed that the "cold war," proclaimed by the Jews' half-English stooge, Churchill, on a visit to the United States, was really an attempt by the Jews to encircle Russia, rather than a convenient pretext to get more Americans killed, in Korea and elsewhere, and to pump more blood out of the veins of American taxpayers to flush down sewers in Asia and to subsidize, under the guise of "foreign aid," the Communist conquest of one nation after another. It must be remembered

23. It would seem that the Jews lost interest in the farce, which now serves to provide, at the expense of American taxpayers, a luxurious life in New Jerusalem-on-the-Hudson for diplomatic riff-raff and savages, whose endless jabbering is as significant as that which may be heard at the monkey house in Bronx Park. Muzzy-headed American women still fancy that the babble has meaning, but the Jews are too intelligent to pay attention to it and probably do not even laugh when some idler calls for a "resolution" against their world-capital in Palestine.

that at the time Yockey wrote, the rodomontade manufactured in Washington sounded more convincing than it does now in retrospect, and that the "cold war" did excite intelligent Americans with a hope that they could force their government to action in conformity with its endless jabbering about "saving the Free World."

Yockey also took seriously the Yiddish yelping about "anti-Semitism" in Russia, which may have been no more than a ploy to deaden the hostility toward Russia felt by Americans who still hoped that their nation would someday act in its own interests. It must not be forgotten that the Americans who were most hostile to the Soviet were precisely the ones who would be mollified by reports that the Russians were shaking off their Jewish masters. [24]

Yockey also noticed that in the United States a pair of Jews, the Rosenbergs, were falsely accused of treason (for they had been strictly loyal to their race) and thrown to the wolves—to appease the Americans who resented the betrayal of their own country by Roosevelt and his successors, and also to facilitate the escape of other spies and saboteurs who had been caught in the act.

Yockey therefore concluded that the "treason trials in Bohemia" were "an *unmistakable* turning point" and, despite the official piffle in both Russian and Jewish sources, marked an "undeniable reshaping of the world-situation." The fact that "the Russian leadership is killing Jews for treason to Russia" was nothing less than "a war-declaration by Russia on the Jewish-American leadership." Stalin, who, Yockey recognizes, "had been pro-Jewish in his inner- and outer-policy" for thirty-five years, had at last taken the part of Russia against international Jewry, who had to abandon their hopes that they

---

24. A good example is Commander S. M. Riis, a veteran of Naval Intelligence, who was stationed in Russia at the time of the Jewish take-over of that country in 1917-18. In his old age, he succeeded in boarding the ship that had brought Kruschchev to the United States; he conversed with agents of the N.K.V.D. disguised as simple Russian sailors and was assured that Kruschchev was a "real Russian" who was kicking out the alien invaders. Believing that the Jews had at last lost control, he was greatly encouraged. See his *Karl Marx, Master of Deceit* (New York, Speller, 1962).

could "replace the Stalin régime." Yockey could not foresee that Stalin would die a year later in circumstances that gave rise to rumors that the Jews had at last succeeded in poisoning him.

To the end of his life, Yockey remained convinced that a war between the Jews' United States and the Soviet was inevitable. That conviction was the basis of his last essay, written shortly before his death in 1960. Its cover is reproduced here on the following page.

I do not know whether Yockey saw and approved the vividly symbolical painting, in the manner of Salvador Dali, that is reproduced on that cover or the date that is set beneath it. If he did set the date, 1975, he was in good company, as I shall remark later.

The World in Flames is a concise and lucidly logical conspectus of the situation in 1960, cogent if one accepts the premise that the Russians had liberated themselves from the Jews. On that assumption, the relentless expansion of Soviet power and the establishment of a Soviet outpost in Cuba, at the very doors of the United States, represented a series of defeats for the international race.

Yockey's analysis of the military situation is still valid. The Americans, if they are driven to fight the Soviet, will rely on ballistic missiles, but cannot win a war, since, even if they had an effective army, it could not mount an invasion of Soviet territory with the enormous number of ground troops necessary to occupy it, and Europeans cannot be induced to fight again for the American-Jewish symbiosis. Russia will use ballistic missiles, but cannot win the war by occupying the United States, since the logistic problem of transporting armies across the Atlantic or Pacific is one she cannot solve.

American missiles can inflict a certain amount of damage on a few cities, etc., but Russia is relatively invulnerable to such attacks because she is not really urbanized, her important installations are scattered throughout her vast territory, and her essentially agrarian people have the high morale of imperialism and will not be dismayed by such destruction and losses as it may be possible to inflict on them. Russian missiles, produced by German scientists and technicians and therefore more accurate and effective, will be directed at American cities, the

THE WORLD IN FLAMES

AN ESTIMATE OF THE WORLD SITUATION

By Francis Parker Yockey (Ulick Varange)

Porta Capitolina Americana   1975 A. D.

Le Blanc Publications

destruction of which will not only paralyze the nation militarily, but will dismay a population already demoralized by peace-lubbers, fatuous females, and youth made derelict and cowardly by the rotting of our culture. The blasting of a few cities will make the panic-stricken rabble eager to surrender. (Yockey probably did not know that Washington was even then making studies of "strategic surrender" in the event of hostilities.)

When the United States surrenders, as it must and will, the situation will be drastically changed. Yockey notes that the British, a relatively civilized people much given to prating about their moral superiority and to the vapid idealism of humanitarians, having obtained the support of Americans crazed by a holy war, induced the Germans to surrender in November 1918, and then, by an act of unprecedented treachery, blockaded the helpless Germans for the express purpose of killing civilians, and did in fact starve to death a million Germans before lifting the blockade in July 1919. Now the Russians are barbarians and have never talked nonsense about the "sanctity of human life" and similar vaporings of sentimentalists. Their leaders, furthermore, are realists and have never shown the slightest inclination to imagine that treaties are more than pieces of soiled paper. Even if the United States does not surrender unconditionally (that would be poetic justice!), the Russians will not be obligated by such terms as they may have granted on paper to spare themselves unnecessary effort. In all probability, therefore, they will proceed, after the surrender, to annihilate forever the United States as a possible source of future trouble. They will, of course, immediately destroy all of the country's remaining industrial capacity. What is uncertain is whether they will elect (a) to occupy the territory with troops, reduce its population by starvation or shooting them as may seem the more entertaining, and spare the rest for use as serfs, at least until the land can be colonized by Russians, a virile and growing people; or (b) to reduce the territory to a lifeless and uninhabitable desert.

Yockey, writing in 1960, believed that the inevitable war might be precipitated at any time and would certainly begin no later than 1975, the date given on the cover of his booklet. He obviously miscalculated, but so did men with access to the secret information accumulated by what was left of American

Intelligence services. It was also in 1960 that an American Colonel in Military Intelligence, who had extensive experience during the Korean "War" and had maintained, after his retirement, close connections with the C.I.A., privately assured me that the war was inevitable, that the United States would be quickly vanquished, and that the country would be occupied by Russian troops, who would systematically exterminate all Americans suspected of intelligence and self-respect. That, he was certain, would happen by 1970 at the latest. His calculations thus allowed a shorter term than Yockey's, whose major thesis he did not accept. He believed that when the Russians invaded this country, the Jews would joyously coöperate with them, as they had done everywhere in Europe. He also believed that the Russians would therefore minimize damage to New York City and other Jewish enclaves in the United States.

Other miscalculations, made at the time by men whose experience and knowledge qualified them to judge, gave approximately the same result, with only a difference of a few years in the terminal date. It would take many pages to recapitulate the evidence and logical deductions on which the various estimates were based, and many more to inquire why the expected war did not occur. It will suffice to have made it clear that Yockey, an observer without access to secret information, was no more in error than experienced men who had the great advantage of knowing facts that were concealed from the public.

THE PARADOX

Yockey was aware of the major objection to his analysis: If the Jews had lost control of Russia, how did it happen that the United States, which saved the Soviet in 1941-45,[25] continued

---

25. In his essay on the hanging of the eleven Jews in Prague, Yockey mentioned a small part of what America, at the behest of its Jewish masters, gave to the Soviet: 14,795 airplanes, 375,883 trucks, and 7,056 tanks. He seems not to have known that the Soviet was also supplied with both the technical information and the materials necessary for the manufacture of atomic bombs. In *The World in Flames,* he does comment on the thoroughness and ubiquity of Soviet espionage in the United States, in contrast to the nugatory efforts of American Intelligence to penetrate Russia, but he seems not to have asked himself to what extent Soviet espionage depended on Jews in its service and on coöperation with the Jewish espionage system, admittedly by far the best in the world.

to facilitate the expansion of Russian power? I cannot do better than quote his answer:

Russian "successes"—except for its German-made rockets—are all the gift of the Washington régime. Jewish-American political stupidity is invincible. But the power-gifts which the Washington régime has made to Russia are not explicable entirely by simple stupidity, simple incapacity. There is the further factor at work that the Zionist Washington régime is on both sides of most power-questions in the world. Its sole firm stand is its fundamental anti-German position: Germany must be destroyed, its young men must be slaughtered. In Algeria, Washington is with both sides: it is with the French Government, as its "ally": it is with the rebels by virtue of its world-program of "freedom" for everybody. In Egypt, the Washington régime told Palestine, England and France to attack, and when Russia rose, it told them to stop. It was, within a week, anti-Nasser and pro-Nasser. It occupied Lebanon, then evacuated it. It held back Chiang when, from his island, he would have attacked China, with whom the Washington régime was then at war. It defended South Korea, but helped the Chinese maintain their supply line to the front. During the Chinese War in Korea, it made war and negotiated peace at the same time, for years. In Cuba, it forbade the exportation of arms to the loyal Batista and thus helped Fidel Castro; now it is committed to the overthrow of Castro.

It is a psychological riddle, decipherable only thus: the Zionists have two minds, which function independently. As Jews, they are committed to the destruction of Western Civilization, and in this they sympathize with Russia, with China, with Japan, with the Arabs, and as such they anathematize Germany, which is the mind and heart of the Western Civilization. As custodians of the United States, they must half-heartedly retain at least the technical and political domination of that Civilization even while destroying its soul and meaning. In a word, they are working simultaneously for and against the Western Civilization. Quite obviously, they are thus doing more damage than conferring benefit. . . . .

Thus the newspaper tag of "East versus West" is

meaningless. It is East versus East, with the West supplying the lives and treasure for destruction.

The foregoing analysis is, of course, open to question. Was there ever any change in the policy actually pursued by the government in Washington, as distinct from blatting by Presidents and the like to keep the boobs confused? Was not that policy consistently and uniformly directed to ensuring the maximum disgrace and loss to the Americans and to making them take slow and unperceived steps toward their eventual liquidation? The commitment "to the overthrow of Castro" of which Yockey speaks was, of course, just a spoonful of paregoric for the grown-up moppets. Most recently, as everyone knows, the United States delivered to Castro another possession, Nicaragua.

Yockey's attribution of schizophrenia to the Jews is, of course, subject to the basic consideration that we can never understand their mentality: we can only observe the actions of a race generically different from our own and accumulate data which will enable us to say, statistically, that in a given situation the racial collectivity will react in a specific way. It is always hazardous and usually or invariably wrong to describe their conduct or motives in terms of our psychology and morality. What would be schizophrenia in an Aryan or group of Aryans, for example, is such by contrast with the normal mentality of our race. If it is characteristic of another race, it cannot be anomaly in that race, and what seems abnormal to us must be normal in it. Yockey, however, is right in that those who believe that the Jews no longer control Russia must postulate that their racial mentality functions in a way that is incomprehensible in terms of our standards of rationality.

By far the most thorough, objective, and cogent presentation of the case for the view that the Russians have attained at least a measure of independence is found in Wilmot Robertson's *The Dispossessed Majority* and its pendant, *Ventilations.* [26] He has

26. *The Dispossessed Majority* (Cape Canaveral, Florida, 1972), pp. 451-465, cf. pp. 346-353. *Ventilations* (ibidem, 1973), pp. 9-17. The publisher, Howard Allen Enterprises, announces that completely revised editions, printed from newly set type, of both books will be published in the autumn of 1981.

assembled all the usual data, and almost every datum is open to doubt. Statistics and statements from Russian and Jewish sources represent what their authors thought it expedient for us to believe at the given time, and the Jews notoriously conceal, so far as possible, their actual numbers in each country they have infiltrated. When we are told, for example, that the percentage of Jewish deputies in the Supreme Soviet dropped from 41.1% to 0.25% between 1939 and 1958, we wonder whether the source is Russian or Jewish; if it is an estimate made by a European, it must be largely based on personal names, and the ingenuity of Jews in masquerading under native names and otherwise concealing their race is notorious, and we have the further and insoluble question of the genetic effects of a tincture of Jewish blood in any individual's ancestry. [27] Furthermore, if the persons holding office are demonstrably non-Jewish, they may nevertheless be mere puppets manipulated from behind the scenes by Jews through wives, financial or political pressure, or deeply implanted superstitions.

---

27. See above, p. 27, note 30. If Dr. Nossig is right about the genetic peculiarity of his race, that opens possibilities far more drastic and terrible than any thus far glimpsed or imagined by even the most vehement anti-Jewish writers. With the exception of a few noble families that have kept archives—it is said that there are in Britain two families that can trace their ancestry back to 1066 with certainty—the genealogical records of most individuals, even those who have attained some prominence, seldom go back more than a very few generations without the help of fantasy, and they quickly reach the point at which ancestors, especially females, are mere names. The names of Jews fall into three categories, viz.: (1) authentically Jewish names, e.g., Isaac, Jesus, Nathan; (2) Western names that have become distinctively Jewish, e.g., Rosenthal, Finkelstein, Oppenheimer; and (3) distinctively Aryan names assumed to conceal the individual's race, e.g., Montagu, Stewart, Brown. Resort to such disguises is an inveterate Jewish habit, probably dating from the time at which the race first developed its techniques for penetrating nations of *goyim*. And usually when the bearers of such names are not our contemporaries, the deceit can be detected only through the indiscretion of the Jews themselves. For example, the exemplary myth of Esther in its fuller text, preserved in the Septuagint, is warranted "authentic" (!) by pious Jews, and the names given are Dositheos, who is identified as a Jewish priest and Levite, his son, Ptolemaios (= Ptolemy), and the latter's son, Lysimachos. All are good Greek names; the first, we happen to know, was frequently assumed by Jews and so might suggest some suspicions; the second is, of course, the name of the famous Macedonian dynasty; and the third is the honored name of a number of distinguished Greeks. If we saw the names out of the context, we should never doubt but that Ptolemy and Lysimachus were of pure Greek ancestry and, of course, Aryans.

The cumulative effect of the data taken together is impressive, but it seems to us inconceivable that the Jews, having taken over the whole government of Russia in their Bolshevik revolution[28] and always conscious of their secret and vigilant antagonism toward the races that show a tendency to be less than perfectly docile, could ever have permitted themselves to lose a mastery attained with such long and persistent labor and intrigue. (Note that we instinctively credit the Jews as a race with an order of intelligence higher than that of Aryans, and think them exempt from the fatuity that led our race to throw away its power and revel in its own degradation and impotence.) The only plausible explanation is Robertson's.

This explanation rests on two premises:

(1) The Jews have a racial genius for infiltration, subversion, revolution, and destruction.

(2) Their race is devoid of ability to organize and direct a viable society, whatever its type and whatever the political theory on which it is based. Having created chaos, the Jews can themselves survive in it only by enlisting the managerial talent of another race, commonly selecting administrators from the surviving (lower class) population of the nation they have just

---

28. Aryan observers who were on the scene in Russia at the time of the Bolshevik take-over assure us that fully 85% of the Bolsheviks in positions of authority were Jews, and we know that the most important of them were sent into Russia from Switzerland by the stupid Germans (who were resorting to what could be described as a species of germ-warfare, probably at the suggestion of Jews high in Kaiser Wilhelm's government) and by Woodrow Wilson, who insisted that the British escort to Russia a shipload of venomous vermin from the East Side of New York City. A secret report to the U.S. State Department in 1919 (released from classification as secret in September 1960) lists the thirty foremost Bolshevik leaders, and identifies twenty-nine of them as Jews and one as a "Russian." That one "Russian" exception was Ulyanov, alias Lenin, who, as is universally admitted, was a mongrel of mixed Jewish and Tatar (Turko-Mongolian) ancestry and without a drop of Russian blood. It is nugatory to inquire anxiously about details and to wonder, for example, whether the real name of "Zinoviev" was Apfelbaum. It would not really matter if all the official heads had been Russians, for credit for the operation must go to its architects. St. Paul's in London is the work of Sir Christopher Wren and the mansion that now houses the Thomas Publishing Co. in Springfield, Illinois, is the work of Frank Lloyd Wright. The identity and race of the stone masons who worked on the former, and of the bricklayers who worked on the latter structure is irrelevant, as is the race of their various foremen.

destroyed.

The first of these propositions is beyond question. It is verified by all history, for no nation deeply penetrated by Jews has long survived. It corresponds, furthermore, to their racial psyche, as frankly stated by some highly intelligent and remarkably candid members of the race, as, for example, by Samuel Roth in *Jews Must Live*[29] and by the eminent Maurice Samuel, [30] in his oft-quoted avowal:

We Jews, the destroyers, will remain the destroyers for ever. *Nothing* that you will do will meet our needs and

29. Roth's *Jews Must Live* (New York, Golden Hind Press, 1934) has—for obvious reasons—disappeared from most or all libraries and become extremely rare. It is a book of 319 pages, including the frontispiece, etc.; about half of it was reprinted, Birmingham, Alabama, 1964, and is available from Liberty Bell Publications. Roth's is by far the most complete description of the quotidian behavior of the great mass of ordinary Jews in business and social relations, and we all owe him gratitude for his honesty and admiration for his courage. Relevant here is the reaction of Jews when the lowly Aryans try to have a club or a hotel or a residential district of their own. The Jews yell about "discrimination" and by bluster and, if need be, secret financial pressure, force their way in, but when they have made it squalid and hideous with their vulgarity, they abandon it and flock back to their own colonies, preferably leaving the Aryan owners bankrupt and dispossessed. Such conduct would show malice in an Aryan, but, if we are objective, we must attribute it to the impulsion of a racial instinct that operates as automatically and as subconsciously as an uncorrupted Aryan's instinctive admiration of certain forms of beauty.

There is an interesting analogy in the behavior of the Jews in ancient Alexandria, where a huge swarm of them, estimated at one million, took over a large part of the city and made it their vast and opulent ghetto, into which no Aryan, naturally, wanted to go. Not content with that, they perpetually swarmed through the rest of the city and were moved by their "righteousness" to break up the Greeks' theatrical performances and athletic contests, harassing the *goyim* until they finally lost patience, whereupon the Jews rushed wailing to the reigning Ptolemy or Roman governor, complaining of "anti-Semitism" and "persecution," and often, through the intrigues and financial power of wealthy and ostensibly civilized Jews, obtaining some punishment of the "intolerant" Greek population. Since the Jews, so far as is known, reaped no profits from these events and some of their rabble were injured or killed in the riots they provoked almost regularly every few years, their harassment of the Aryans must have been instinctive, rather than the result of some conscious plan or conspiracy.

30. See above, p. 45. The reprint is available from Liberty Bell Publications.

demands. We will forever destroy because we need a world of our own.

One could corroborate Samuel's statement by citing hundreds of Jewish writings, ancient and modern. An example from the early years of the Christian Era is one of the great Jewish hoaxes, the forged Sibylline Oracles, [31] which were disseminated (naturally with a forged certification that they were authentically Greek) to demoralize and subvert Graeco-Roman civilization by exciting dismaying apprehensions among the ignorant and credulous. No Aryan, I imagine, can read them without being appalled by the nihilistic lusts and venomous hatred of civilization that inspire them. A recent writer has cited, as an example of the innate nihilism of the Jewish soul,

the Jewish apocalypse that the Fathers of the Church selected for inclusion in their appendix to the "Old Testament." That wild phantasmagoria describes in loving detail all the disasters and torments with which Jesus will afflict and destroy the civilized peoples of the earth when he returns in glory from the clouds with a squad of sadistic angels. One should note the characteristic provision that *goyim* are not to be merely killed outright: they are to be made to suffer agonies for five months first. But what

31. There are adequate editions, under the title *Oracula Sibyllina*, by A. Rzach (Vienna, 1891) and J. Geffcken (Leipzig, 1902, reprinted 1967). I have not seen the edition by A. Kurfess, *Sibyllinische Weissagungen* (München, 1951), which is said to contain a German translation. Some portions of the collection have been translated into English in various discussions of early Christianity, but I know of no complete translation of the long and miscellaneous collection. If there were one, persons whose minds are saturated with apocalyptic nonsense would undoubtedly find in it wonderful "prophecies" of the election of Reagan, the Jews' terrorism in Lebanon, and perhaps the latest increase in postal rates.— A few old Greek reports of oracular statements are inserted here and there in the collection of forgeries to lend an air of authenticity to the hoax, of which the aim was to throw a scare into ignorant and weak-minded *goyim*, although some items encourage them to hope for a savior of some kind who will make all the earth his kingdom, with brotherhood and oodles of "world peace" for everyone, by teaching the wicked to venerate the living "Sons of the Great God." It is usually difficult to date the various hariolations, but it seems that the earliest forgeries in the collection were perpetrated by Jews in Egypt during the Ptolemaic period: see John J. Collins, *The Sibylline Oracles of Egyptian Judaism* (Society of Biblical Literature, 1974).

Lloyd Graham has properly called the "diabolical savagery" of the Jew God is not satisfied with exterminating all the *goyim* with every kind of torture a lurid imagination could invent. He destroys the land, the mountains, the sea, the whole earth; he destroys the sun and moon; and he rolls up the heavens like a scroll, presumably including even the most remote galaxies . . . . *Everything* is annihilated. And all for the sake of Jesus's pets, an elite of 144,000 male Jews who despise women. For these, to be sure, he creates a New Jerusalem, in which they will loaf happily for a thousand years. [32]

One can only stand aghast at the ferocity of that lust to annihilate the whole universe!

Robertson's second proposition is less patently true, but it may be significant that in the apocalypse we have just mentioned, when the New Jersusalem is lowered *en bloc* from the newly-created sky, it is minutely described with what Frank Harris called "the insane Jew greed, which finds a sensual delight in mention of gold and silver, and diamonds and pearls and rubies," but there is no practical provision for the Chosen Few of the Chosen People who are to spend the next thousand years in it. We may assume that they will be miraculously supplied with food and raiment, perhaps by hard-working angels, and can spend part of their time in swilling down food and drink; but the noble males will have no nasty females around, and we can only guess whether they will find succedaneous amusements. For the rest, they evidently will have nothing to occupy their idle hands and vacant minds—for a thousand years! It looks as though the author of the wild hariolation was intent only on the glorious destruction of the whole universe, and gave no thought to organization of the society that was to follow.

Jewish mythology has much to say about kingdoms and an empire of Solomon in the stolen land of Canaan, but archaeological data is too scanty to permit reconstruction of the historical basis for those tales. It is fairly certain, however, that when the wealthy Jews in Babylon betrayed the city to Cyrus the Great, the only non-Jew whom they ever called their christ, they made a deal with him for special privileges in his empire,

---

32. Ralph Perier in *Liberty Bell,* August 1980, p. 20.

for that is securely established by the Elephantine papyri.[33] The privileges seem to have included the establishment of a religious capital in Jerusalem, and a Biblical book called *Esdras (Ezra)* and Josephus[34] give us a vivid description of the great caravan of rich Jews who set out from Babylon, their chariots loaded with gold and silver, with thousands of their *goy* slaves trudging along behind, while hundreds of slave musicians went ahead, so that the caravan travelled "to the music of harps and flutes and the clashing of cymbals," while the majority of Jews, who preferred to stay with business in Babylon, rejoiced and made merry. And when the immigrants reached Jerusalem, they began to dispossess the natives and kick them around, and they cunningly made their new Temple a fortress, as Herod was to do much later.

Under Persian protection, the Jews enjoyed autonomy, taxing and oppressing the hapless natives of Palestine (including the Samaritans, the native Jews, who vainly appealed to Persian justice), but when we hear next of them,[35] the high priest, John, murdered Jesus, his brother, right in the inner sancturary of the temple, evidently as part of a civil disturbance so great

---

33. Edited by A. Cowley, *Aramaic Papyri of the Fifth Century B.C.* (Oxford, 1923). The Jews of Elephantine, who thought of themselves as perfectly orthodox and seem to have been so regarded by the newly-established Temple in Jerusalem, recognized as the chief of their gods one whom they called YW (probably pronounced *Yu'*, a form that became *Ia* in the Septuagint) or YWH (thought to have been pronounced *Ya'u*) and provided him with a female consort, 'NT (probably identical with the Ugaritic—Canaanite goddess 'Anath). In the first century B.C., therefore, the Jews had not yet generally adopted the henotheism which appears in most of the "Old Testament," which they converted into monotheism when they came into contact with Graeco-Roman Stoicism and saw how expedient it would be to kidnap the Stoics' Providence (*animus mundi*). Of course, the erudite Bezalel Porten, in his *Archives from Elephantine* (University of California, 1968), labors mightily and learnedly to disclaim the early polytheism of the orthodox Jews, once (p. 175) even going so far as to suggest that the magnanimous Jews subsidized the worship of the gods of Arameans in Elephantine as a "goodwill gesture"!

34. *Antiq. Iud.*, XI,i-v.1-183. There is an excellent edition and translation of this work by H. St.J. Thackery, completed by Ralph Marcus, in the Loeb Library. Needless to say, the decrees of Cyrus and Darius quoted in the Biblical book and (with variations) by Josephus are forgeries.

35. *Antiq. Iud.*, XI,vii,297 sqq.

that the local Persian governor had to intervene to restore order—and he, of course, was cursed for his pains, ostensibly because he wanted to peek into the sanctuary, where the Jews kept something they did not want *goyim* to see. [36] A spot of murder in the sanctuary did not seem worth noticing to the Jews of John's faction, for he was undisturbed in the exercise of his pious office.

John was succeeded by his two sons, who seem to have shared the high priesthood until one brother decided to knock the other out on the grounds that he was married to a Samaritan bitch instead of a nice orthodox Jewess, and that started another smouldering civil war. And so it goes, on and on, endlessly, with the Jews in Palestine unable to keep peace among themselves; with their various factions appealing to the Seleucid Greeks or the Romans to restore order in favor of one faction, while all factions are seemingly united in hatred of the civilized but useful *goyim,* whom they try to play off against each other through elaborate intrigues; and with the distracted *goyim* unable to protect the Jews who are friendly to them and are accordingly murdered stealthily by *sicarii,* experts in the art of plunging daggers into a man's back when he is off his guard.

In contrast to the perpetual disorders and outbreaks in Judaea, where the Jews enjoyed a local autonomy, the majority of the Jews, scattered in enclaves throughout the civilized world (with the largest concentration of them probably in Babylon) and thus directly under the laws of the nations in which they

36. What the secret was is not known. The soldiers of Pompey reported they had seen in the sanctuary a statue of Yahweh with an ass's head. They are unreliable witnesses, of course, but there is some uncertain corroboration of their report, and such theriomorphic gods were normal in Egypt, whence the Jews claimed to have come. We cannot affirm that the soldiers were right, but what we must do is avoid the knee-jerk reflexes of most historians, who ignore this and all comparable evidence because they *know* that God's Holy People wouldn't do nothin' wrong. The Jews' talk about the strict piety of their race is a hoax, and false even after they appropriated the monotheism of the Stoics. For a brief summary of some recent archaeological evidence, see the *Scientific American,* CCXXVIII #1 (Jan. 1973), pp. 80-87. It is uncertain whether the Jews who worshipped Helios and Apollo in their synagogues in the Third Century (A.D.) identified Yahweh with those gods or added them to their ceremonies to ingratiate themselves with the "pagans" among whom they were living.

had lodged themselves, seem to have lived in comparative peace with each other and with their hosts, except on the rare occasions on which there was an opportunity to betray a city to invaders or on which a self-appointed christ incited the Jewish rabble to insane outbreaks and massacres of the hated *goyim.*

After A.D. 70, the only autonomous or independent Jewish state that we can take into consideration is modern "Israël." [37] As everyone knows, the Jews extorted the Balfour Declaration from Britain as the price for stampeding American cattle into Europe in 1917, but since the English seemed to have had some scruple about betraying their Arab allies, the Jewish terrorists had to blow up and ambush quite a few stupid *goyim* before their new Zion was established formally in 1948 and God's People could start oppressing, kicking, and butchering the natives. [38] On this artificial "nation," which is, of course,

---

37. Not all Jews in Palestine followed the christ who caught the dozing Greeks and Romans off their guard in 132 and had great success in slaughtering them, but since the Romans were so bigoted that they disapproved of his cleverness, his ephemeral kingdom was quickly reduced to guerrilla bands hiding in the hills, and the christ never really governed any of the territory he claimed.— The Jews did infiltrate and take over the kingdom of the Khazars in the Eighth Century, but too little is known about its internal government to permit us to use it as an example. (Incidentally, the Khazar-theory, so dear to Christians who want to eat their cookie and have it too, will have to be abandoned, if we accept the elaborate haematological study by Professor A. E. Mourant and his assistants, *The Genetics of the Jews* (Oxford, 1978). His results show that the Jews, despite the great differences in physical appearance, form a single hybrid race, having an infusion of at least 5% to 10% of Negroid blood, wherever in the world they have taken up residence.)— The old Jewish colony in India claims to have penetrated that sub-continent before 175 B.C., since it did not observe the five great Jewish festivals, all of which (despite fabricated claims to greater antiquity) were instituted after that date. Whether or not those Jews reached India so early, it is certain that they never formed a state of their own: see Schifra Strizower, *The Bene Israel of Bombay* (Oxford, 1971).— Arthur J. Zuckerman's long treatise, *A Jewish Princedom in Feudal France, 768-900* (Columbia University, 1972), was based on tortuous inferences from illusory evidence, and his mighty Jewish realm in southern France and northern Spain was only a figment of his own imagination; see the review by Professor Bernard Bachrach in the *American Historical Review*, LXXVIII (1973), pp. 1440-41.

38. One wonders whether the British would have been so prejudiced as to become vexed, if the Jews had blown up their Parliament while it was in session. The first bomb planted in the building failed to explode and the

supported by double taxation[39] of the world's beasts of burden in the United States, see Robertson's comments on it. It has its internal stresses, of which some reports are permitted to reach us, and is obviously held together only by its policy of steadily encroaching on the Semitic peoples around it and expanding its ill-gotten territory with military equipment donated by the American boobs. Living on money from the *goyim* and terroristic aggression, "Israël" is certainly no proof that the Jews have the ability to organize and govern a state of their own.

There is much to be said for Robertson's analysis, and we would accept his conclusion that the Russians have at last emancipated themselves—but reason revolts.

It is true that the Jews, who have always to be "persecuted" to conceal the extent of their actual control and power, are now screeching about "aunt-eye-see-mites" in Russia, but every few days we see the photographs of our real rulers, Kissinger, Armand Hammer, and others of the tribe, cuddling with Brezhnev and other real or supposed masters of Russia; American bankers are eager to supply the Soviet with seemingly unlimited quantities of the counterfeit currency manufactured by the Federal Reserve; and American farmers toil in their fields to supply the Soviets with all the grain and other foodstuffs they want. That, of course, may be just more of the looting to which the American serfs are accustomed. What really matters is the Jews' apparent satisfaction at the results of their sabotage of our armed forces. Since Yockey wrote, our Army has become what he foresaw. Demoralized by the operations carried out in Korea and Vietnam to kill and maim as many young Americans as possible while arranging defeats that would show the world how crazy and contemptible Americans are,[40] our remaining

Jewish High Command cancelled its orders before a second could be placed; see Avner, *Memoirs of an Assassin* (New York, 1960) pp. 104-121. His organization of "freedom fighters," he says (p. 64), operated on the principle that "an Englishman would always be a filthy Goy, who could be killed for that reason alone."

39. "Double taxation" because, in addition to the enormous subsidies that are openly and secretly sent to "Israel" by the Americans' government, the vast sums that are "privately" remitted by Jews residing in the United States are also taken from the American people. No one *dares* to protest.

40. It will be remembered that an American officer was even tried by

military officers are cynically trying to "stick it out" until they can retire on large pensions after twenty years. They are replaced by Jews, mulattos, and uniformed bureaucrats, whose notion of fighting is intriguing for promotion. If we look at our "fighting men," we see a motley horde of louts, perverts, females, and savages sullenly awaiting the day when they can put the hated "honkies" in their place. Do you really think that with that rabble the United States could defeat and occupy Ireland? For that matter, could our ground troops occupy Cuba?

Russia now has the largest and most modern navy in the world. Our navy, far inferior in equipment, sports mulatto Admirals who strut around in ostentatiously slovenly attire and lord it over their white underlings, who try to conceal their resentment at the degradation imposed on them. The British officers who inspected the *Nimitz,* our largest carrier, were amazed to discover that parts of the great ship are "off limits" to white officers so that the savages won't kill them. The *Nimitz* is not a warship; it is a floating slum, on which, as a recent accident showed, the multi-racial warriors can't stay off drugs long enough to perform a perfunctory naval exercise. One hears that on some of our smaller carriers that still have white officers in command, it is thought that the white crew could "get rid of the niggers" and get the ship into fighting trim.

Since the operation of aircraft requires skill and intelligence, our obsolete bombers and comparatively few modern fighting planes could be relied upon, barring sabotage by multi-racial ground crews commanded by such ornaments as a Jewess Major General. But the failure of the maladroit attempt to rescue the "hostages" that we had cravenly abandoned in Iran naturally suggested doubts as to our capabilities even in the air, although

court-martial and imprisoned for having killed some of the enemy in Vietnam. The court-martial was held by our Army in slavish and shameful obedience to the outcries of journalistic pimps whose employers were engaged in a concerted effort further to demoralize our armed forces, and the campaign involved downright lying about the conditions of warfare in Indo-China. For an understanding of what war is like in such territory with such a population, see William Wilson's *The L. B. J. Brigade* (Los Angeles, Apocalypse, 1966). The essential point is that the Vietnamese are *naturally* and by instinct as barbarous and treacherous as the crazed British and Americans *made* themselves when they repudiated all the canons of our civilization in the Jews' Crusade Against Europe.

the ineptitude may have been ordered in Washington. In the event of a war with the Soviet, we could sacrifice our air force and inflict a small or moderate amount of damage.

As for intercontinental ballistic missiles, the chances are that we are now inferior to the Russians, while our country, as Yockey pointed out, is far more vulnerable than theirs.

At the time of writing, it looks as though the Jews intended to order the Americans to clear the way for a Jewish advance and occupation of the Semitic countries around "Israël." We could undoubtedly destroy the oil fields of Saudi Arabia and thus augment the fake "energy crisis" that is now used to chevy the boobs, and we could create by bombing from the air chaos in the other Semitic or partly Semitic countries—unless Russia intervened. That would mean a war with the Soviet, and, incidentally, if there were such a war, the Russians would certainly have to indulge, in sheer self-defence, their natural racial antipathy to Jews—all of the three million or more of them now in Soviet territory.

Since Yockey wrote, there has been one major alteration in the situation. The natural and inevitable racial hostility between the Russians, who are largely Aryan, and the Mongolian Chinese has evidently converted their original coöperation into active enmity. It is possible that fear of a Chinese invasion would deter the Russians from intervention in the Middle East, but we do not know enough about conditions inside both of the empires that we created as our powerful enemies to calculate the chances of that. The most that we can say is that it does not now seem likely that the Russians would abandon a strategically important part of the globe to Zion. And if they do not, that means war with the Jews' vassals, the United States.

In the event of such a war, the stooge in the White House could utter platitudes and talk about "saving the world for democracy," but there is no slightest indication of a will to fight in a nation—if it still is a nation[41]—that has long been

---

41. In the continuous avalanche of books, most of them worthless and many worse than worthless, that vertiginously descends from the presses these days, the few important works are buried in the mass and often carried to oblivion unnoticed, but I hope no one has overlooked the

lousy with peace-lubbers and the like. The Russians would have all the advantages of a first strike, and could inflict some spectacular damage on our cities, and, as Yockey predicted, our rabble would immediately clamor for surrender and start a furious civil war, if Washington even hesitated to put into effect its cherished plans for a "strategic" capitulation.

The only alternative is the remote possibility that the United States has some really horrendous secret weapon which has not been betrayed to the Soviet, but that possibility is very remote.

So with all this before us, we are asked to believe that the Russians have become independent? Preposterous! With the example of Germany before us, we all know how terrible is the vengeance that Yahweh's Master Race inflicts on insubordinate *goyim*. If the Jews had been defied by the Russians, our armed forces would be drastically purged and every able-bodied white American below 40 would be conscripted and trained for the coming war. The Jews and their lackeys in all the media of communication would be frantically pumping a factitiously patriotic sludge in the faces of the boobs. Our holy men would be yelling in their pulpits about our Christian duty to smite the Antichrist in Moscow and help an omnipotent god who obviously cannot help himself. Our automobile plants would be again converted to the production of airplanes and tanks; and all our laboratories would be filled with "crash programmes" to devise more effective missiles and counter-missiles.

You have only to look around you to see how absurd is a suggestion that the Jews' supremacy has been threatened in the

---

sagacious analysis of our society by Professor Andrew Hacker, *The End of the American Era* (New York, 1970). He concludes that the United States has become nothing more than a geographical area, inhabited by incompatible races and individuals who, rootless and bewildered, no longer have a common culture or even a common interest. "What was once a nation," he says, "has become simply an aggregation of self-centered individuals." Our civilization—Aryan civilization, although he does not use that naughty word—has been so eroded and rotted that the American majority has lost all cohesion and has become merely a colluvies of miniature minorities, each composed of no more than half a dozen persons with a common purpose. Therefore, he concludes, "Our history as a nation has reached its end," and we have reached "a juncture at which it becomes pointless to call for rehabilitation or renewal." The only question now is the exact date and form of the final catastrophe. I wish I could refute that conclusion.

Soviet! It's simply unreasonable!

So we say, but we do not know. My only point here is that if the Jews no longer control the Soviet, the only explanation is the one advanced by Yockey and Robertson. Although they differ in their psychological analysis, they agree that the explanation must be some mental peculiarity in Yahweh's Sons that impels them to conduct that would be irrational and insanely improvident in an Aryan.

THE THIRD SIDE OF THE COIN

We have, I think, followed Yockey and Robertson in drawing logical conclusions from the evidence before us. But all of our evidence—what we are told and what we are not told—comes from either Russian or Jewish sources. We do not have even a simple choice between stories told by two habitual liars, for when they disagree, both may still be lying, each in his own interest. And the world's masters of deceit are wily and subtle.

When travelling carnivals toured our country, the yokels were regularly fleeced by what was known as the shell game, which had many variations. In one variation, the sucker was led to believe that he had been given, inadvertently, a glimpse of the obverse of a coin and so could confidently bet on what would appear on the reverse when the shell was lifted, but, of course, when the coin was exposed, one with a different reverse had been substituted by a bit of prestidigitation.

When we ponder the Soviet enigma, one possibility always occurs to us, that internal rot within the empire may have gone much farther than we have been permitted to suspect by our sources—may have gone so far that what seems a monolithic state has some inner and hidden weakness great enough to affect its foreign policy. That speculative conjecture, however, we have always dismissed as gratuitous, since there was no plausible evidence to support it.

The periodical called *Fortune*, in its issue for 29 June 1981, published an astonishing article, entitled "Russia's Underground Millionaires," by a Jew, Konstantin Simis, formerly a Soviet lawyer and official in the Ministry of Justice, who says that in 1977, when the manuscript of a book that is to be published in this country was found in his apartment, he was invited to leave Russia and join his son, a professor in an American university.

According to this article, the Soviet is as rotten politically as the United States, although, of course, there are superficial differences. Corruption within the Communist Party we naturally take for granted, but here we are told of massive corruption of the Communist administration by bribery from outsiders, almost all of them Jews. There are distinct analogies to the almost universal political corruption that was established in this country in 1917 by the crackpots and mutton-heads who tried to prohibit our people from drinking alcoholic beverages.

We are told that there functions efficiently within the Soviet an enormous black market with its own factories, its own distribution-system, and its own retail outlets, operating comfortably by virtually wholesale bribery of Communist managers and police, and operated by capitalists, almost all of them Jews, who accumulate what are large fortunes by any standard and store their surplus wealth in gold, jewels, and other things that are intrinsically valuable. A typical entrepreneur, who was arrested, through some mischance, by the Secret Police, was found to have in his possession such valuables to the amount of 350,000,000 rubles, which, at current exchange, would equal $546,000,000.

This great *essor* of Jewish enterprise, according to the author, began "in the mid-1930s" with such talented entrepreneurs and masqueraders as Isaac Bach, who, while officially only a supervisor in a small workshop and paid as such by the state, was secretly a capitalist worth some $135,720,000, "owning at least a dozen factories manufacturing underwear, souvenirs, and notions, and operating a network of stores in all the republics of the Soviet Union." Such surreptitious business flourished, it should be noted, while Lazar Moseevich Kaganovich was Stalin's Deputy Premier in charge of industry, and naturally continued to flourish under his successor in that office, Benjamin Dimshitz, another Jew.[41a] And it has now

41a. Dimshitz (or Dymshits) is the only Soviet official of very high rank whom Wilmot Robertson (*op. cit.*, p. 456, n. 16) recognizes as a Jew. It's evidently a matter of the right man in the right place. What is extremely curious is that he is not even mentioned in the list published by *Candour*, to which I shall refer in note 48. below.

reached the high financial level shown by the one example mentioned above, which, we are given to understand, was not at all extraordinary, except that the apostle of free enterprise either neglected to bribe all the officers of the Secret Police concerned or was rashly careless in some way that made it too awkward for them to cover up for them.

The commercial activities of those energetic Jewish business men interest us only because they are all categorically prohibited by Soviet law, which provides for the guilty minimum penalties of years of imprisonment in slave labor camps. It necessarily flourishes through a vast system of pay-offs and the like [42] that would do credit to the genius for organization shown by American politicians. There are "tens of thousands of such factories" owned by capitalists of the black market, but almost all of them are actually state factories, operated by managers appointed by the Communist government, who fulfill their quotas and then turn to production for the capitalists, using, of course, the machinery provided by the state, their working staff, and sometimes materials provided by the state, although the production for the black market is usually of better quality and uses better materials. The manager must be given his cut, of course, and so must the workmen, who are often employed on overtime. All government inspectors must be bribed, and so must all local agents of the Secret Police, especially those in the branch that is expressly charged with policing industry. Much of the raw material must be obtained from nominally state establishments, with, of course, a corresponding round of cuts and bribes. The retail outlets are, for the most part, state stores which handle black-market goods surreptitiously, and so managers and bookkeepers and clerks must be given their cuts and massive bribery must keep inspectors and agents of the police in line. And, of course, it is necessary to put the fix on the bureaucrats who preside over the inspectors and agents. In short, the Communist empire must be a seething mass of political corruption. And after all such

42. When Franklin Roosevelt was gabbling about the "Four Freedoms" to entertain the boobs during the Jewish Crusade Against Europe, knowledgeable "New Dealers" defined the Four Freedoms as the rake-off, the pay-off, the shakedown, and the fix. There are technical differences between these four aspects of government in a "democracy," but we need not define them here.

business expenses, the promoters reap huge profits and become enormously wealthy.

The "tens of thousands of factories," we are told, are chiefly in Moscow, Odessa, Riga, Tiflis, and other major cities in which are concentrated the Jews now in Russia—some three million of them, according to Jewish sources, who are now being "discriminated against" by the Soviet, it not being explained why they are only half as numerous as the Jews who were "discriminated against" by the Czarist régime, under which they owned half the industry of Russia. We may assume that free enterprise is providing good incomes for a large part of the three million, perhaps most of them in one way or another.

Despite the massive bribery of Communist officials, something more is required for this vast clandestine business, which must be conducted without written records, and in which sums that may amount to hundreds of thousands of rubles exchange hands without documents of any kind or witnesses, "in an atmosphere of complete trust," such as could never exist among legitimate business men in this country. The explanation is given by the author: it is "the sense of national identity among Jewish underground businessmen," who may not be eager to migrate to their race's capital in Palestine, but "feel a blood relationship with it" and contribute money (in American currency!) to it. If the commercial honesty that is dictated by a sense of racial solidarity, which Aryans can only envy as they reflect with shame on the egotistic venality and financial opportunism of their own people, is reinforced by Jewish racial courts, the *kahal*, which some anti-Jewish writers allege to be secretly maintained in Jewish colonies, the writer gives no hint of them. [42a]

42a. Jews vehemently deny the existence of the *kahal* and denounce as "anti-Semitic" the Jew, Jacob Brafmann, who wrote the most extensive and detailed description of the quasi-religious racial courts. His work has been translated into German, with a learned commentary by Dr. Siegfried Passarge, *Das Buch vom Kahal,* 2 vols., Leipzig, 1928. See also the work of the Argentine writer, Hugo Wast, whose essay and novel, *El Kahal,* is also published in Mexico (Editorial Diana, 6th edition, 1964). Wast describes the operation of the Jewish tribunal in modern Argentina, and says "El Kahal es un soberano invisible y absoluto," which regulates the entire life of Jews, "comercio, política, religión, vida privada en sus detalles más minuciosos." He says that the disciplinary powers are vested in a secret tribunal, *Beth Din,* which, I gather, operates with the summary

One limitation on the felicity of Jewish capitalists in Russia is the need to observe some discretion in public display of their wealth, since too much ostentation has brought some of them to the attention of Communist authorities not on their payroll, with sad results. Prudent financiers limit their public expenditures to what they can pretend was legitimate income, e.g., from winning tickets in a state lottery, and amass their wealth in gold, jewels, and similar articles they can easily hide. Foreign money can be obtained, but would have no advantage in Russia. We may guess that the Rockefeller banks in Russia probably assist capitalists to transfer abroad holdings that they can enjoy when it pleases them to "defect" from Russia. The author suggests that the vast investments in gold and jewels, if not made for a miser's satisfaction in mere possession, may perhaps be held in anticipation of "the downfall of the Soviet régime."

If we accept Simi's account of the vast wealth of Soviet Jewry and the pervasive corruption of Soviet government in all its functions, including the Secret Police, it will be obvious that the ingenuity, secrecy, and bribery that maintains the capitalists' clandestine businesses could also promote a secret and formidable revolutionary underground, capable of striking suddenly and perhaps decisively. And that will alter all our estimates of the probable future of the Soviet and of its capacity to wage a major war. We accordingly wonder whether some credence may not be due to some reports about efficient and ostensibly Christian "undergrounds" in the Soviet. The reports once put out so industriously by evangelists who pretended to solicit funds for such organizations can be dismissed as mere sucker-bait, but, if Simis is right, such organizations could exist. [42b]

---

powers and secrecy of the Westphalian Vehmgerichte of the Thirteenth to Sixteenth Centuries, which will be familiar to many readers from the description, doubtless with romantic amplification, in Sir Walter Scott's *Anne of Geierstein.* The supreme *kahal* of the Jews, with jurisdiction over all colonies of the international race, sits in New York City, according to Wast. American attorneys who have handled litigation between Jews who have tried to swindle each other are certain no *kahal* is now in operation, but notice an odd convention in such matters, e.g., a bitterly resentful and injured Jew will not denounce his adversary for smuggling or fraud in income-tax reports, although he has proof in his possession.

42b. If we believe Paul R. Vaulin, *The Regiment of Kitezh* (Mobile, Alabama, 1977), Russia is now honeycombed by a formidable conspiracy

We can neither affirm nor deny the accuracy of Simi's story. If that number of *Fortune* has reached Russia, his report has probably been denounced in *Pravda* as an "outrageous Fascist lie" and perhaps even as "anti-Semitic," with many "proofs" of its spuriousness; if it hasn't been, it will be, at least when his book is published. All that we can do is say that the story is amazing, and put it down as another question mark around the enigma.

AT THE WAILING WALL

We must grant that the evidence for the Jews' supposed loss of authority in Russia is meager and unsubstantial. Self-appointed "Kremlinologists" (!) expound to us the intentions behind certain Soviet policies, but mind-reading is always a hazardous business. It is true, for example, that Russia has supplied some weapons to the Semitic and largely Semitic countries that are menaced by the Jews' constant aggression and implacable hatred. (The Arabs and their allies, by the way, have always to pay cash to the Soviet, while the Jews have only to requisition all the equipment they want from their American serfs.) We are told that Russia clearly intends to impede the plan, of which the Jews openly boast, to make Jerusalem the capital from which Yahweh's Race will rule the whole world; but, for aught we know to the contrary, the subtle minds of Russia's rulers may be cozening the Arabs and planning eventually to betray them, as the Americans, for example, betrayed Chiang Kai-check.

The nominally American government in Washington is in a fever of anxiety over the supposed plight of the three millions of the

of Christians, who have penetrated the Soviet bureaucracy and even the Secret Police, having placed or enlisted secret agents in strategic posts, and counting on exciting a revolt of "a quarter of a billion [Russian]men" when the time comes. Two colleagues of the author on the faculty of the University of South Alabama certify that the narrative "describes actual events," was written by "an American agent" who was dropped by parachute into Soviet territory in May 1972, and was copied from his manuscript, which "was smuggled out of the USSR by an American student." They further certify that Satan prevented the publication of the book by a commercial publisher, so that it had to be published privately "without the permission of Satan." If there is any truth to the story, the Soviet Secret Police have become hopelessly inefficient and stupid. There is an implication that the Christians' god keeps the conspiracy invisible to Communist eyes, and it would seem that Satan hasn't been able to wake up the Politburo.

Self-Chosen People in Soviet territory, and claims to be squandering American resources as bribes to the Russians to increase the privileges granted to Jews (but no other race), in the hope that soon the whole three millions will follow the 200,000 who have recently flown from the Soviet and, after touching ground in Israel, flocked into the United States, except for a minority, who, after getting a whiff of their tribesmen in Israel, promptly flew back to their Soviet homes.[43] One cannot be impressed by the ostensible reasons for a policy of which the net result is further to augment American subsidies to the Soviet while simultaneously augmenting the saturation of our country with Jews.

The other evidence is much noise and very few facts, all of them no better than the facts on which are based the Jews' assurance to the British that in the United States the wicked "Neo-Nazis" are on the very verge of stuffing ten or twenty millions of God's persecuted darlings into crematoria. [44] The cause of the Jews' terror is, admittedly, the fact that a dozen Americans have had the awful audacity to investigate a rather grandiose, but typical, Jewish hoax and expose its absurdity. [45]

---

43. It is true that the Russians do not seem eager to welcome them back. *The Daily World,* 8 January 1979, reported that 300 Jews, who had left the Soviet, fled to Italy after they had a good look at the ant-heap in Israel. They were appealing to the "United Nations," evidently in the hope that the clowns in that circus would intercede and obtain for them permission to return home.

44. See above, p. 73.

45. On the hoax about the "six million Jews" who are said to have been exterminated in Germany before they migrated to the United States and a few other lands and began to collect for their deaths from the Germany they had ruined, the pioneer work was that of Paul Rassinier, who had been himself an inmate of a German concentration camp and later spent years in touring Europe vainly in search of someone who had actually seen one of the famous "gas chambers," for which the basis, of course, was only the Germans' attempts to control with disinfectants the epidemics of typhus brought into the camps by Jews and their body lice. See Rassinier's *Le mensonge d'Ulysse* (Paris, 1950) and its sequels, *Ulysse trahi par les siens* (Paris, 1961), *Le véritable procès Eichmann* (Paris, 1962), and *Le drame des Juifs européens* (Paris, 1961). An English translation of the last of these was published by Steppingstones, Silver Spring, Maryland, 1975, which issued in the following year a translation of the book on the Eichmann trial (which Rassinier had originally intended to entitle aptly, "Les maître-chanteurs de Nuremberg"), now published by

What the British may be stupid enough to believe, I do not know, but the imminence of a real "holocaust" in the United States will be considered unlikely by the hapless Americans, who cringe before the Jewish Terror; who see the homes of men who dare disbelieve the hoax besieged by mobs of Jews screaming for their blood and threatening to burn them and their families in their houses; who know that Presidents and Vice Presidents of the United States who dared mutter *in private* some lack of reverence for Jews were hounded from their office and forced to resign; who know that no business man dares offend our masters, not even by subscribing to a journal that does not have kosher approval, for even if it comes to a postoffice box under an assumed name, the spies will learn his identity and the Jews stealthily or openly will destroy his business and perhaps his family . . . It would be idle to go on enumerating what is known by everyone who ventures to raise his eyes and look about him. My point is that Americans should know that the fact that Professor Butz has not yet been murdered and all copies of his book destroyed by the F.B.I. is not satisfactory proof that the United States is persecuting the People of God. And it may not be amiss to consider Jewish lamentations about Russia with critical intelligence rather than

the Historical Review Press, Chapel Ascote, Ladbroke, Southam, Warwickshire. I understand that translations of Rassinier's several books are assembled in *Debunking the Genocide Myth,* published by the Institute for Historical Review, Torrance, California. The fullest and most systematic demolition of the infamous hoax, which has been used to extort forty billion dollars or more from the helpless people of Germany, is the masterly work by Professor Arthur R. Butz, *The Hoax of the Twentieth Century,* published by the Historical Review Press, *s.a.* (1976), and available from Liberty Bell Publications; an American edition is published by the Institute for Historical Review in California. An especially notable work in German is *Der Auschwitz Mythos* (Tübingen, Grabert, 1979; available from Liberty Bell Publications) by Judge Wilhelm Stäglich, who thus brought on himself pseudo-legal vengeance by the Jews' puppet government in Bonn, which tried to make him penniless and did succeed in depriving him of half of his meager income. The author of a smaller volume on the same subject is now in prison in Germany for having dared to contradict God's Master Race. A very useful and handsomely illustrated book is William N. Grimstad's *The Six Million Reconsidered, s.l.&a.* (1977), which has been reprinted by the Historical Review Press in England and in the United States by the Institute for Historical Review. Perhaps the most noteworthy aspect of the "six million" hoax is the hoaxers' contempt for the simple-minded Aryans: they did not take the trouble to make their various fictions plausible or consistent. The point, of course, is that Aryans must be so trained that their minds will freeze and all thought stop whenever one of God's People speaks to the curs.

faith.

One bit of evidence adduced by Wilmot Robertson is the publication by the Ukrainian Academy of Science (in 1963) of a book that spoke of Jews without reverence, and he adds that the Soviet authorities did not suppress the book until after "world opinion," as manufactured by Jewish journalists, began to howl. The suppression, however, does not satisfy the Jews, who now wax indignant that its Satanic author was, after a time, permitted to return to his employment, instead of being liquidated or starved to death.[46]

Although as late as 1979 the Jews were still assuring themselves in some of their racial publications that their tribe was flourishing in the Soviet and that 400,000 of them ensconsed in Moscow alone were joyful,[47] they are now telling themselves in their own publications, as well as in "our" press (which they own or otherwise control) that the international people are being "persecuted" by the vile Russians, in whose country they have chosen to reside. The volume of this propaganda is enormous, and it would be a waste of time to notice slight differences in the pitch of what is just one unending screech, but, if we dare be so evil as to look at a few specimens intelligently, we may derive some hints from them.

A yell by Kevin Klose in the *Washington Post*, 15 July 1979, headed "Soviet Jews are Fearful of Rising Anti-Semitism," brings us the shocking news that many more Russians are now being given positions in the Russian universities and other "institutions of higher learning where Jews have traditionally

---

46. See, e.g., the article by Dr. Spier that I cite below.

47. A clever twist in propaganda was used by Aaron Vergelis, editor of the periodical in Yiddish that is lavishly financed by the Soviet. In his tour of this country in January 1979, he assured his Jewish audiences from coast to coast that "Soviet Jews are building a new and happy life in their *[sic!]* multi-national homeland," and that propaganda that the Jews are not living high on the hog in the Soviet is really a form of "anti-Semitism" spread by "anti-Communists" to incite hostility to the Soviet and to encourage the nasty "anti-Semitic" elements in the United States. "Anti-Sovietism," he proclaimed with Talmudic subtlety, "is the greatest anti-Semitism." His speeches were widely reported in the frankly Jewish press and summarized in the *Daily World,* 30 January 1979.

excelled." A book published in only five hundred copies "calls Zionism 'the worst form of fascism' "—a statement which should be good for a laugh even in Russia. Another, of which 45,000 copies were printed, "alleges that 'Zionist centers' control Western media." One gathers that Russians should not be told of the Jews' virtually total dominion over the press and boob-tubes of the United States, Britain, France, and other Western nations. Chief among the horrors that are giving the three million Jews in Russia nervous palpitations are two letters one or more diabolic Russians may have produced on a mimeograph and are clandestinely circulating to some "members of the Moscow intelligentsia." One of these horrid letters declares that "both in the U.S. Senate and the Central Committee of the Communist Party there is a powerful Zionist lobby." Americans know about the Senate and the rest of "their" government in Washington, where, according to the press on 26 July, Reagan, "personally ordered" everyone to cease and desist from criticizing the Jews' terrorist bombing of Lebanon and slaughter of the Semites who don't understand that the Jews have a right to their homes and lives—acts which some misguided men thought tactless at the very time that the United States was about to rush another big shipment of our best weapons to Israel, for which Reagan has "a very special affection." We wonder, however, whether the mimeographed letter was as accurate about Russia as about the country that once was ours. A second letter, furtively typewritten and copied on a mimeograph, says that Brezhnev's wife is a Jewess—as everyone in and out of Russia has long known—and that there are only three "real Russians" among thirteen members of the ruling Politburo. There is no claim that the second statement is not equally true, but Klose reports a rumor that "Russophiles," persons so wicked that they love their own country, expecting that Brezhnev will soon depart from this world, are manoeuvering "within secret 'higher circles' of the [Communist] party . . . to heighten traditional Russian antagonisms and force Jews from such positions of power and influence as they now hold." Just as though God's People didn't have a prescriptive right to "power and influence" over the lower races!

What interests us is the claim, in the mimeographed sheet that is being clandestinely passed around to a few Russians, that the Russians have only three representatives in the Politburo. The journal founded by the late A.K. Chesterton, *Candour*, published in its issue for Nov.-Dec.1978 a list, obtained from Russian sources, of the members of the Politburo. This shows twenty-one men besides Brezhnev, and the score is: Russians, 6; race unascertained, 1; Jews, 14, including the Minister of Defence, the Minister of Foreign Affairs, the Chief of the Secret Police, and two others, who are among "the most powerful men in the USSR."[48] Date and place of birth are given and the real names of the Jews, most of whom operate under aliases in public, as is their custom. *Candour's* informant adds that "90% of the Soviet Ambassadors are Jews," and lists twelve examples. Since I am unfortunately deprived of the revelations from on high that enable so many in the "right wing" to *know* whatever they want to believe, I cannot affirm either the accuracy or inaccuracy of the list in *Candour*, but if the list contains no more than a fair percentage of truth, it would seem that the international race has prematurely rushed to its Wailing Wall, perhaps from sheer force of habit.

TOD UND VERKLÄRUNG

The most nearly sober of the current lamentations is a long article by Ruben Ainsztein in the well-known and widely influential British periodical, *New Statesman.* On the cover of the issue for 18 December 1978, where it is illustrated by a photographic montage that shows the evil face of Hitler behind the evil face of Stalin, the article is entitled, "Soviet Union Today: Anti-semitism Institutionalized," but above the article itself appears the apocalyptic title, "The End of Marxism-Leninism." The author naturally does not miss a chance to reiterate the Jews' great "Holocaust" hoax, and he assures us that "Only Stalin's [mysterious!] death saved the Jews who had survived Hitler's Final Solution from annihilation." He then speaks of the awful book that Robertson mentioned, but without quite telling us that it was suppressed in 1963. His featured evidence, however, is a confidential memorandum to certain committees

---

48. It is odd that *Candour* and the clandestine mimeographed sheet that scares the Jews in Russia agree only on Kosygin as a loyal Russian. *Candour's* source had no information about Romanov, and, what is most remarkable, Suslov, who is one of the three "real Russians" on the mimeographed sheet, is identified in *Candour* as a Jew, born in 1902 in the principal city of Azerbaijan, whose real name is Suess and who is the principal representative in Russia of the B'nai B'rith that operates in the United States and watches over the Aryan sheep. Cf. note 41a above.

in the Communist Party, allegedly written by Valery Nikolaye-
vich Yemelyanov, and presumably typewritten or mimeographed, of which Jewish agents were able to filch part in
January 1977. [49]   In that memorandum Yemelyanov reportedly not only said unkind things about the sacrosanct race, but
even proposed the formation of an international organization to
unite civilized men of the West to oppose and perhaps avert the
consolidation of Jewish control over the entire planet.

I naturally cannot tell whether Yemelyanov did indeed
express such evil thoughts, but I note that in a long article in
the *Jewish Chronicle* (London), 25 July 1980, Dr. Howard
Spier complacently remarks that the "paranoid" Professor
Yemelyanov had been fired from his academic position and
incarcerated in a "psychiatric hospital." [50] That sounds to me
as though the Children of God still had influence in the Soviet
Union, but it does not prevent Dr. Spier from chattering with
fear about the likelihood of pogroms because, although "overt
antisemitism" is not feasible in Russia today, there are Russians
who regret that it is not and who even dare to write articles
with "racial overtones," which are "thinly disguised antisemitism" and therefore offensive to Yahweh's Master Race.

Among the innumerable shrieks of the Jewish Banshee, none
is better written or more coherent than Robert Wistrich's article
on the wickedness of Stalin in the *Jewish Chronicle*, 22
February 1980. Like Ainsztein, Wistrich identifies Stalin as the
serpent who appeared in the Soviet Eden and, after beguiling
the Slavic Eve by justly equating disrespect for Jews with

---

49. Further information about the memorandum that Yemelyanov
hoped to keep confidential is given in a despatch from Jerusalem published
in the *Daily Telegraph,* Britain's largest conservative newspaper, on 9
March 1978. One of the Ministers in the Israeli government moaned that
the stolen memorandum was "an all-out declaration of war against the
Jews" by the one man who wrote it.

50. Poor Yemelyanov must have been released from the madhouse
after Spier wrote, for a few lines in the Spanish press in January 1981
reported that he had been arrested and imprisoned for "racism,"
presumably shortly before. Since Yemelyanov is, so far as we know, the
only man in the Soviet Union who has dared to suggest (in a confidential
memorandum) actual opposition to the Jews, it may be assumed that if he
were publicly crucified, the three million tribesmen in Soviet territory,
who are now quaking with terror, could sleep o' nights.

cannibalism and making it punishable by death, finally gave effect to the evil thoughts he had secretly harbored in his black soul for a long time and slyly sold her the deadly apple of patriotism. The article is noteworthy for the relative absence of the usual hysteria and for its author's respect for logic, and especially because it identifies, as did Yockey, the hanging of the eleven Jews in Prague as the turning point of Stalin's policy: "for the first time, antisemitism and anti-Zionism openly fused." The trials in Prague were a first step toward "Stalin's own Final Solution of the Jewish question—mass deportations to Siberia .... The plan was foiled *[sic!]*" by the opportune death of Stalin. Stalin's policy was reversed, he is now discredited, and his monuments "have been pulled down," but the terrible thing is that "Stalin's heirs . . . studiously avoided mentioning antisemitism in the catalogue of his crimes." And that means, oh horrors! that we "must reckon with the return of the pogrom traditions of the Tsarist State under a thin veneer of Marxist-Leninist verbiage."

Two of the best articles, which I have mentioned, and numerous others assert that Stalin intended in his own mind to solve Russia's Jewish problem by either transporting the aliens to Siberia, as Wistrich says, or by exterminating them, as Ainsztein claims, presumably by finding engineers and chemists who could overcome the practical obstacles to constructing and operating "gas chambers," such as are celebrated in the Jews' great hoax about the "six million."[51] The evidence that Stalin had *in petto* a plan to become the Antichrist[52] is both meager

---

51. The choice of this number may have some special significance. In the early years of this century, and especially during the administration of President Taft, American busybodies were a-twitter over the supposed plight of the *six million* dear Jews who were "imprisoned" in Czarist Russia because they preferred not to leave it.

52. It must be remembered that the term 'antichrist' does not specifically refer to the christ called Jesus who is the hero of the "New Testament." A christ is, of course, a divinely-appointed King of the Jews, who will lead his race to a solution of the Gentile problem by exterminating Aryans and the like, except for some who may be spared for slavery. The apocalyptic fantasies of the Jews call for the appearance of an 'antichrist,' i.e., a particularly disrespectful and wicked *goy*, before the appearance of the real christ, who will put the lower races in their place. An 'antichrist,' therefore, is a powerful adversary of the Jews, except, of course, in Christian terminology.

and in conflict with all of his career before he was seventy-three, but we must remember that Dzhugashvili began his career as a theological student and doubtless acquired early the arts of dissimulation and hypocrisy, in which he must have perfected himself. There can be no doubt but that he was a highly intelligent man, so it is out of the question that he could ever have taken seriously the Marxist religion, which he used to manipulate the misfits, simpletons, idealists, and other crackpots over whom he climbed to power, and to outwit his fellow thugs.[53] So talented a man could have concealed even from Jews his opinion of them, but it is also possible that he, like Luther and many other men, trusted the Jews during the greater part of his career and changed his mind only late in life.

The best proof that Stalin was or became inimical to the Self-Chosen People is that a pack of Jewish physicians tried to poison him a few weeks before he died suddenly, reportedly of a "cerebral haemorrhage." They would not have done so without good reason. It is true that some persons believe the story that the physicians were innocent, but they do so on the usual grounds that Jews are "righteous" people, and without reflecting that nothing could be more righteous than killing *goyim* that get in the way of God's Own. As all Christians well know, that is the lesson that is taught throughout the "Old Testament," which seems such an appalling record of crime to persons who read it without Faith.[54] The virtually infinite

---

53. It goes without saying that Communist leaders do not believe in Communism. An acute young American, Duane Thorin, who had been intensively interrogated while a prisoner, stated the facts concisely in *A Ride to Panmunjom* (Chicago, Regnery, 1956): "Intellects that failed to see through the falsities of communism were so arrested that they were of only limited use in the totalitarian state." Czeslaw Milosz in *The Captive Mind* (New York, 1953) devotes a chapter to the practice of *ketman* by the more intelligent Communist professionals as they jostle for places on the ladder: like Moslem and Christian theologians, they feign a belief in the orthodox doctrine of their sect and try to catch each other out by devising Talmudic quibbles as traps to obtain admissions that will justify a charge of heresy.

54. Christians, I understand, find especially edifying the tale that is told about Moses in *Exodus,* 2.11-15,19; 4.19-20. Seeing an Egyptian treat a Jew harshly, Moses found an opportunity to catch the *goy* alone and, after looking all around to make sure no one could see them, rubbed him out, probably by stealing up behind him and stabbing him in the back. Moses hid the body in the sand, but when he found that someone had seen him after all and would turn stool-pigeon, his chutzpah failed him and he took it on the lam across the border into a foreign country, where, passing

superiority of their race is taken for granted and openly avowed by Jews today.[55] The Holy People, for example, did not hesitate to boast over the French radio of their cleverness in poisoning a thousand German officers by slyly putting arsenic in the bread they baked for them.[56] And, as everyone knows, Begin, who is now dropping bombs on the civilian population of Lebanon in preparation for conquest and annexation of that helpless country, early distinguished himself by his efficiency in killing *goyim*, such as the English men, women, and children whom he blew up by planting a bomb in their hotel. For such valiant deeds he is sometimes criticized adversely by "aunt-eye-see-mights," who do not understand that his victims were just English pigs and probably should have been butchered anyway.[57]

The heroic physicians, like the Lopez who was the personal physician of Queen Elizabeth I and tried to poison her, were caught, but we shall never know whether they had colleagues who were more successful. It is, of course, not unusual for men of Stalin's age to die of natural causes, but a sudden death that occurs so soon after an unsuccessful attempt at assassination,

---

himself off as an Egyptian, he lay low for many years until God came to his hide-out and told him the heat was off in Egypt and the cops were no longer looking for him.

55. According to the press, Dr. Michael Wyschogrod, Professor of Philosophy in the City University of New York, frankly told a conference sponsored by the National Conference of Christians and Jews that there was a vast difference between harming a Jew and killing *goyim*, because "what happens to the Jewish people is not quite the same" as what happens to other people in that there is "an element of the divine" in Jewish history that makes it special. He admitted that "humanists" and other irreligious persons would think the racial distinction "a scandal," but that is because they do not "grasp the uniqueness of Jewish history." Dr. Wyschogrod also told his audience what makes that uniqueness: the fact that a Jew is always a detached limb of his race and only secondarily an individual. "I am first a member of the Jewish people," he declared, "and only secondarily Michael Wyschogrod." That, of course, is something an Aryan can never understand, for while he may feel a loyalty to, or a duty towards, a class or nation, he can do so only *as an individual,* and even the strongest effort of the imagination will not enable him to think of himself as having the relation to his race that a member of his body bears to him. The conference was reported in *The Christian News,* 30 April 1981, p. 15.

56. See the *Toronto Daily Star,* 9 March 1968.

57. Cf. note 38 above.

and occurs so opportunely—should we say providentially? —for a man's deadly enemies will always arouse suspicions.

When a great monarch dies, there is always a bitter struggle for power among the *diadochi*, and from what we know of Communists and given the impossibility of dividing the empire, we may be certain that the contest in Russia was especially vicious, but the essential facts concerning it remain secret. Eventually Krushchev, whatever his antecedents,[58] came out on top, having pleased his henchmen by vituperating the man who had saved Russia, the Soviet, and Communism from the German invasion. In 1961, he ejected ignominiously from its tomb the body of the architect of Russia's position as a world-power, had his monuments and memorials destroyed, and even carried post-mortem hatred so far as to change the name of Stalingrad, the site of Russia's most celebrated victory. Such spitting on a national hero and the sheer fury of the posthumous vengeance taken on him, must have had a deeper motive than a mere courting of popularity among the serfs, as sometimes happens in "democratic" countries. In fact, the vitriolic denunciation of Stalin for "tyranny" was a somewhat hazardous gambit, since it might encourage discontent with that tyranny, which was continued with only superficial changes. What the motive was, however, we cannot determine: it may have been known only to the inner circle of the Politburo and must remain an enigma for us.

In sum, then, the evidence before us warrants the conclusion that for a period of about six months—from early November 1952 until 5 March 1953—Dzhugashvili-Stalin openly showed a certain hostility toward the Jews that he had doubtless meditated for some time before putting it into practice.[59] It is reasonable to conjecture that he may have intended or wished

---

58. I refuse to debate the vexed question whether or not Kruschchev was really a Jew masquerading as a Slav. The evidence on both sides of the question is suspect.

59. The earlier stages of the affair that reached its climax with the hanging of the eleven Jews in Prague are uncertain. The most important of these Jews, Rudolf [nice Germanic name, Gothic hrôth-wulfs!] Slánsky, was arrested on a charge of treason on 27 November 1951, but the Czech executive who had formally ordered the arrest, Kópriva, was himself arrested on 23 January 1952, thus producing a neat confusion to keep everyone puzzled.

to put into practice the stated principles of Zionism. During those six months or more, the Jews seem to have lost the power to control Russian policy, and it may be they did not subsequently recover their dominance over it.[60] There is evidence that Russians are now permitted to occupy in the universities and bureaucracy positions that Jews want.

For the rest, we can only note that there is not the slightest indication that the present régime in Russia intends to accept the theory of Zionism, as it would surely do, if it wished to rid its territory of Jews. Hitler, to be sure, accepted Zionism and made great efforts to foster it, and the Jews will never forgive him for having taken them at their word, but nevertheless a régime that is really anti-Jewish would not overlook the enormous advantage it would obtain by officially supporting Zionism.[61]

---

60. By far the most complete and objective treatment of the whole question known to me is the late Andrey Diky's *Jews in Russia and in the USSR, s.l.&a* [1978?]. When I last heard, copies could be obtained from L. Volovlikoff, P.O. Box 8082, Ottawa, Ontario. This work is based on Russian and Ukrainian sources not generally available, especially periodicals, and its author makes every effort to be fair and more than fair to the Jews, giving them the benefit of every doubt. In an appendix, pp. 297-319, the author lists the officials of the eleven principal organs of the Soviet government from 1932 to 1939. Here are the totals: Jews, 447; non-Jews, 68; race undetermined, 34.

61. As we all know—or should know—the premise on which the Zionist movement was founded, and on the basis of which support for it (including the Balfour Declaration) was solicited, was that Jews and Europeans represent incompatible races and cultures, and that the presence of the aliens in Europe will always result in irremediable tension and animosities, to the distress of all concerned. The only solution, therefore, was the creation of a "homeland" to which all Jews could emigrate and in which they could form a nation that would have a geographic unity corresponding to its spiritual unity. See the writings of the founder of Zionism, Theodor Herzl, in his *Tagebücher* (Berlin, 1922-23) and the passages that were suppressed in the German edition but restored by Marvin Lowenthal in his translation of excerpts (New York, 1956). Herzl's diaries record his negotiations with various European monarchs and prime ministers and his reactions to their attitudes, and I can find in his writings no indication that he was not sincere in his purpose. He did obtain from the British government in 1903 the offer of East Africa as the desired homeland, and was bitterly disappointed when the Jewish Congress rejected the offer. As is well known, the National Socialist government of Germany made great efforts to obtain a homeland for the Jews in Palestine, Madagascar, and in a large part of the territory of the

We are here interested in Yockey. From the foregoing it will appear that he, more alert and perspicacious than other observers, was right in his analysis of the situation in Europe and the world in 1948-52, when he wrote *The Enemy of Europe.* He did not foresee the sudden death of Stalin, and it can be argued that if Stalin had survived for a lustrum after 1953, Yockey's prognosis would have been fully verified and the history of Europe and of the entire world would have taken a far different direction.

Yockey did not live to witness the official denigration and vilification of Stalin that began in 1961. You may wish to determine in your own mind what conclusions he would have drawn from that astonishing reversal of Russian propaganda, and whether or not he would have revised *The Enemy of Europe* to take it into account

THE DYING AND THE DEAD

If Yockey had not been hounded to death by the Jews and were alive today, would he take again, without variation, the oath he took in 1946 when he left Wiesbaden, where he could no longer endure the obscene spectacle of the foul murders that the Americans were committing to please the Jews?

I will go from one end to the other of my beloved Europe. I know well that I shall be going only to a churchyard, but I know, too, that the churchyard is dear, very dear, to me. Beloved dead lie buried there. Every stone over them, every bomb-crater containing the pulverized bones of these dead, tell me of a life once so ardently lived, so passionate a belief in its own achievements, its own truth, its own battles, its own knowledge, that I know, even now I know, that I shall fall down and kiss those stones, those endless ruins, this blood-drenched, sacred earth, and weep.

---

former Russian Empire; these efforts were successively frustrated by Great Britain, France, and the defeat of Germany in 1945.— It is faintly amusing that Kevin Klose, in the article about "Anti-Semitism" in the Soviet that I mentioned above, lists a report that when the Russians grant exit visas to the Jews who wish to emigrate, they maliciously give preference to the ones who will head for the United States instead of remaining in the national ghetto, where they could enjoy "family [i.e., racial] reunification."

But I surely also know that then, despite a convulsive rage at the perpetrators of this crime, I will again stand erect over this European graveyard and swear the solemn oath that to my last breath I will fight tooth and nail against those who attempted, in vain to be sure, to destroy the cradle of our Western Culture, with its unmatched accomplishments, with its deeds unique in the annals of Humanity. This, I, Francis Yockey, do solemnly swear!

Do men die of broken hearts?

The physical scars of the Suicide of the West have been effaced. The ruins have been replaced by restorations or new structures that often do not show the grotesquely anti-human vulgarity of Jewish art. The intellectual and spiritual devastation, however, not only remains but grows apace. It reminds us of H. G. Wells' anticipation of nuclear warfare: the atomic bombs he imagined produced a steady chain-reaction, so that their craters constantly grew larger and spread wider, gnawing away the countryside, mile after mile. Or perhaps a better analogy would be an endemic disease that slowly but steadily destroys a dwindling and dying race.

Even a cursory survey of Europe today would require a volume, but we may permit ourselves a few hurried glimpses.

In Germany, the Jews did not insist on their original plan, set forth in Theodore Kaufman's *Germany Must Perish!*,[62] that

---

62. Newark, New Jersey, 1941; reprinted *s.l.&a.*, and available from Liberty Bell Publications. Kaufman's book is an excellent and most instructive specimen of Jewish thinking. He wrote before his tribe had invented the Holohoax, and so he can only scream that the Germans are militaristic and have produced such awfully wicked philosophers as Nietzsche; that makes them "an execrable people" and they must be exterminated, one and all. He prides himself on his tender heart, which makes him recommend that instead of having all the Germans massacred at once, the survivors, men, women, and children, should be herded together and sexually mutilated by surgeons (he even computes how many will be needed for the godly work) so that they cannot reproduce their damned species. In *Schuld und Schicksal* (Munich, 1962), J. G. Burg, a Jew who was born in Germany and lived throughout the war in Germany or adjacent territories, believes that Kaufman's book was part of a concerted effort by the Jews' master minds to exasperate the Germans and thus incite pogroms to help create "world opinion" for a war against Germany and for dispossession of the inhabitants of Palestine in favor of the Jews,

after their Huns had overwhelmed Germany, the surviving Germans would all be surgically sterilized to ensure the prompt extermination of a nation that had offended the Sons of the Covenant. That Final Solution might have seemed objectionable to "an-tie-see-mites." So the good work was entrusted, in Germany as in other Aryan nations, to the demoralizing and disintegrating effects of what Yockey calls "culture-distortion": "democracy" (i.e., government by organized crime), "education" (i.e., sabotage of children's minds), usury, financial piracy, drug-addiction, promiscuity, miscegenation, mongrelization, promotion of superstition and irrationality, and the other blessings Americans now enjoy. That is working very well in Germany. A statistician has calculated that if all things continue as they now are, in ninety years the only living Germans will be senescent and past the age of reproduction.

In Germany, as in other Western nations, the Jews are resorting to pseudo-legal terrorism as well as mob violence to enforce belief in their "Holocaust" hoax, and they are more or less committed to the slovenly version of the tale that they used as a pretext for the obscene and savage murders committed by the British and Americans at Nuremberg. That fiction was an improvement on earlier versions,[63] but it relied principally on the perjury of a German traitor who had been an American spy

and Burg supports his conclusion with photographic reproductions of documents in German and Yiddish. He quotes (p. 72) Chaim Weizmann as having said *in 1934*, "I would much rather see the *annihilation of the Jews in Germany* than failure to make Israel a land for the Jews." Weizmann (who became the first president of "Israël" when it was finally established in 1948) in October 1934 mobilized Jewish pressure on the British government to make Britain frustrate Hitler's proposal that Jews who wished to leave Germany should be permitted to go to Palestine or whithersoever they wished, taking with them one thousand *pounds sterling* and goods to the value of 20,000 marks, the remainder of their holdings (if any) to be paid for in regular installments over a period of years. Several subsequent efforts by Hitler to help the Zionists attain their professed goal were frustrated by Britain and her allies, obviously in obedience to Jewish commands. It was the failure so to exasperate the Germans that they would resort to pogroms that made it necessary to invent the "Holocaust" hoax. It is noteworthy that, with the exception of Burg and a very few others, the Jews do not seem to regard as immoral the efforts of Weizmann and other Elders of Jewry to procure the "annihilation of the Jews in Germany," who numbered about 500,000; presumably the sacrifice of those Jews would have been "good for the Jewish people," and that is all that matters.

63. According to the *Courrier du Continent,* a valuable little bulletin

throughout the war, and was so carelessly contrived that it could not resist critical examination.[64] Since the exposure of the great hoax, there has been a belated attempt to produce "witnesses," who, I estimate, are as numerous as the individuals, many of them Aryans, who have reported their vacations aboard "flying saucers" or their confabulations with little green or cerise men from Mars or elsewhere. The principal burden of the attempts to enforce belief in the incredible, however, is the doctrine that it is an "insult to the Jewish people" to disbelieve whatever they choose to tell the lower races.

We should not err, as do so many anti-Jewish writers, by interpreting this Jewish terrorism in terms of our own mentality and so regarding it as a consciously evil fraud. As several Jews told the National Conference of Christians and Jews, "normal [i.e. Aryan] ethical standards" are "irrelevant" in such matters.[65] I do not profess to understand the Jewish mentality, but it may be that one aspect of it was revealed by Professor Eric Goldman of Princeton University, if he was correctly quoted as contending that history is a "weapon" to be employed for "determining people's ideas and attitudes," and that a respectable historian has a "responsibility . . . for making sure that he writes history in such a way as will bring about the kind of action

published at Lausanne, in its issue for May 1981, a delightful early version of the "Holocaust" hoax was given by a Jew residing in Sweden, Dr. Stefan Szende, in a book published at Zurich in 1944. According to this version, hundreds of thousands of Jews were exterminated by the cruel Germans at Belzec (a small town about twenty-eight miles south-southeast of Lublin), where the Germans had constructed a vast underground installation, including huge halls, built entirely of metal, with floors that could be raised or lowered by machinery. Each floor was a triumph of engineering, so large that several thousands of dear Jews could be packed on it, nude, at one time. The elevator then descended until the Jews were immersed in water to their waists, when a powerful electric current was introduced into the water, electrocuting them instantly. Then the elevator went up to a station at which a further application of electricity incinerated and presumably vaporized all the thousands of corpses, and the machine was ready for a new batch of several thousand. Presumably this version was thought too complimentary to the Germans' famous talent for engineering and applied science, just as the claims that Germans had exterminated 40,000,000 or 12,000,000 Jews were considered a bit hazardous mathematically and the figure was reduced to the 6,000,000 in the current version.

64. See the works cited in note 45 *supra.*

65. Reported in *The Christian News;* see note 55 *supra.*

that he wants." Professor Goldman even made the frightening claim that his equation of history with propaganda was the view of "most historians [!]."[66] One can imagine no more total contrast to the Aryan conception of history as an effort to recover, as accurately as possible, the absolute truth about what actually happened: Von Ranke's famous standard of a perfectly objective description of the past *wie es eigentlich gewesen wäre*, and James Harvey Robinson's addendum that history should also determine objectively, if possible, *wie es eigentlich geworden wäre*. It is quite possible that to the Jewish mentality what actually happened appears completely irrelevant, and our interest in ascertaining historical truth may seem to be just another odd manifestation of our mental inferiority. The only thing that matters is what you can make your subjects believe, including, perhaps, the mass of your own race. To us, that seems reprehensible deception, but it is quite possible that to the Jewish mentality "truth" *is* whatever is good for God's People.[67] That may be why Jewish forgeries and hoaxes seem to us so amazingly careless, and we wonder why their contrivers

---

66. Goldman is quoted by Professor James J. Martin in his section of the impressive biographical monument, *Harry Elmer Barnes* (Colorado Springs, Myles, 1968), p. 241. That Goldman may be right about the majority of persons who now call themselves historians is suggested by the fact that the once-respected American Historical Association, which turns a penny now and then by renting out its membership list, crawled on its yellow belly in abasement and apology when it found it had rented the list to the Institute for Historical Review in Torrance, California, which wickedly conducts historical research that does not bear the Kosher seal of approval.

67. This attitude carries over, of course, into the Judaic religions, such as Christianity with its ostentatious repudiation of the "wisdom of this world" and its exaltation of the believing nitwit above rational and learned seekers of the truth. A good example is Augustine, who must have known that he was lying (by "pagan" standards, at least) when he assured his open-mouthed congregation that he, as a missionary, had saved the souls of a whole nation of Africans, who had eyes in their chests and mouths where a man's neck would be but no heads, organs for which good Christians would presumably have no use. The same spirit appears in the numerous ecclesiastics who, during the Middle Ages, equipped a cathedral, monastery, or church with one of the many foreskins clipped from the infant Jesus when he was circumcized or a bottle of the Virgin Mary's milk or another Holy Shroud. The contriver of the imposture could tell himself, perhaps sincerely, that he was helping save the souls of many yokels by stimulating the tourist trade and augmenting his revenues.

disdained the relatively small amount of work that would have been required to make their fabrication consistent and plausible: to them it seemed apodictic that people *ought* to believe what is good for the Jewish people without thinking about it. The tales in the "Old Testament," for example, are attempts to simulate an historical record, but it seems never to have occured to the rabbis to make them internally consistent and less absurd. [68] And the nonchalance appears today. When Professor Butz's masterly exposure of the Jews' Holy Hoax about the Germans was first published, Jews residing in the United States and holding professorships in American universities, who must surely have learned from observation of their *goy* colleagues what we consider to be the academic standards of integrity, began at once to denounce as "an infamous lie" a book of which they had never even seen a copy, and did so without even taking the trouble to ascertain its title, which they gave as *"The Fabrication of a Hoax"* or *"The Holocaust Never Happened,"* and urging that such disgrace to the academic profession be "rooted out" and presumably exterminated. The venomous hatred is, of course, only natural, but what is significant is that the learned professors did not take the two minutes of time for a phone call by which they could have learned the title of the book they were denouncing so hysterically. To us simple-minded Aryans, that seems amazing.

---

68. It is true that when the "Old-Testament" tales, in the form that they had around the beginning of the first century B.C., were translated from Hebrew and Aramaic into the *koine* dialect of Greek, thus forming the Septuagint, the translators did make some superficial efforts to clean up some absurdities in addition to converting the stories to monotheism. For example, the author of the myth about Esther gave the stupid Persian king the name of Assuerus or Ahasuerus or something like that, a purely fictional and non-Persian name. The translators made him Artaxerxes, which was safe enough, since there were three Persian monarchs of that name, who ruled between 484 and 337 B.C., and that sounded plausible to persons who had no real knowledge of Persian history. In the story of God's unsuccessfull attempt to murder Moses (*Exod.* 4.24), the translators reflected that it was undignified for the creator of Heaven and Earth to be lurking about a desert inn, and they accordingly made the terrorist "an agent of the Lord," which is certainly less grotesque. The Hebrew text underwent some censorship after the Septuagint was made; for example, in the tale of Esther there were several deletions, including the passage in which Esther explains to Yahweh how repugnant to a Jewess is coitus with an uncircumcized man, although, of course, she remains faithful to her duty to manipulate in the interests of her race the *goy* whom she has attracted sexually.

The continuous rewriting of history, so graphically described in George Orwell's *1984*, may seem to the racial mentality of Jews no more than a common-sense provision for ensuring "social justice" and the like. For example, a Jew recently wrote a book to prove that no tribe of savages ever practiced anthropophagy: all stories of cannibalism, except in a few cases of acute hunger (e.g., the Donner Party in California), were invented by the nasty "race prejudice" of the swinish Aryans. [69] I don't know whether that claim is important for Jewish purposes, but if it is, it is surely a proof of the evils of "racism" that it isn't feasible as yet to have all books of history and ethnology that mention cannibals dumped down a "memory hole" into ever-burning incinerators in all the libraries of the world. So far as I know, this attitude toward historical facts has never been systematically investigated, but Samuel Roth, the eminent and courageous Jew to whom we owe so much, touches on it in his references to the "Old Testament." [70] But, I repeat, we must not be misled by the emotional binges of writers who hate Jews and cannot consider the problem objectively. Whatever tampering with facts may seem to us, we must remember that to the Jews it is simply an expression of their righteousness, however little we may be able to comprehend such an attitude. It is strictly comparable to the mentalities, equally alien and mysterious to us, that Professor Haas studied in his fundamental *Destiny of the Mind.* [71]

So much has to be said in explanation of the recent imposition of righteousness in Germany. The puppet government in Bonn has ordered its courts to find that it is a criminal offense to doubt even the most impossible parts of the Holohoax, on the grounds that such doubt "denies to every Jew the respect to which he is entitled." [72] Men are now serving long

---

69. Professor W. Arens, *The Man-Eating Myth* (Oxford University [!],1980).

70. See note 29. Roth discussed the expurgations and falsifications of the stories on pp. 25-51, 57-62 of his book. These chapters and part of a chapter were omitted in the reprint to avoid sending Christian holy men into fits.

71. See above, p. 17, n. 19.

72. The decision of the German Supreme Court is quoted in the Jews' "intellectual" periodical, *Patterns of Prejudice,* January 1980, pp. 32f. The

prison sentences for having dared to express such doubts, and recently the Bonn government's Thought Police raided the homes of almost 500 Germans who were suspected of having in their possession books, pamphlets, or leaflets of which the Master Race disapproves. It is also a criminal offense in Germany to doubt the "authenticity" of "Anne Frank's Diary," a hoax contrived with such contempt for the Aryan mind that it contains such blatant internal contradictions that it could not impose on any reader who has even a modicum of critical intelligence.[73] And the exercise of normal intelligence is a criminal offense even though the Bonn government's own criminological laboratory reported that the manuscript was written throughout in the hand of a single author, who made many of his revisions with a pen that had not been manufactured before the supposed "martyrdom" of the young Jewess who is supposed to have written it. And there are rumors that the Jews are demanding that all mail that comes into Germany be opened and censored, lest some vile correspondent abroad say something that might start ratiocination in the *dumm Kopf* of a cringing German. Such is the plight of Germany today.

The British have not yet sunk so low, but one has misgivings for the future. They destroyed their empire, sacrificed the lives of 357,000 persons, permanently depleting their racial vitality through the loss of much of their best blood, and inflicted painful and often irremediable wounds on 370,000 more; they disrupted their society and demoralized their whole population; and they impoverished themselves and their descendants, perhaps forever. All this they did to punish the Germans for having wanted to have a country of their own, and I wonder whether many Englishmen expected gratitude from the Jews. If they did, what were their sentiments when they read recently in William R. Perl's *The Four Front War* that among the dastardly persecutors of God's Race the vile British are second only to the

---

article goes on to demand more stringent legislation in Germany to "plug the loopholes" in existing laws and make certain that Aryan curs do not even think improper thoughts.

73. If you want to make sure that you didn't overlook any of the ridiculous contradictions in the yarn, see Ditlieb Felderer's incisive booklet, *Anne Frank's Diary* (Torrance, California, Institute for Historical Review, 1979).

vile Germans? Maurice Samuel was right: *nothing* that Aryans *can* do will ever satisfy his insatiable race.

Americans, remembering the old British tradition of gentlemen, are wont to assume that British politicians must be somehow morally superior to the gangsters of the great syndicate of organized crime that rules the United States. That is a mistake: the only difference is that the subordinate gangs, which stage competition on the lower levels, are called "Conservative" and "Labor," instead of "Republican" and "Democratic." Their activities correspond, even in detail, to the treason and looting that James Farrell has clearly described in his new book, *The Judas Syndrome*. [74]

The British, no less than the other Aryan nations, are driven by the death-wish that has been so deeply and perhaps ineradicably implanted in their subconscious minds. Not content with liquidating their empire, they began to import into their already overcrowded and overpopulated island hordes of anthropoid vermin from all over the world, from black savages to turban-wearing Asiatics. Any rational man could have predicted from the very first the inevitable consequence of the wholesale importation of racial enemies, but now, as well-organized mobs, directed by portable radios, surge through large quarters of British cities, burning and looting and killing, the Anglo-Saxon and Celtic boobs are astonished and listen, open-mouthed, to their governmental betrayers as they chatter about "unemployment" and, with almost incredible effrontery, claim that there are no "racial overtones" to race riots. The solution, of course, will be to surfeit the vermin with yet more blood sucked from the veins of the tax-paying serfs, who do not seem even to remember that they once had a country of their own. No one, so far as I have heard, has even dared to suggest

---

74. San Francisco, Fulton-Hall, 1980. The author skirts warily around the edges of the race problem, but he does consider the sheer insanity of importing into our overpopulated land ever growing hordes of black savages, mestizos from Puerto Rico, Cuba, and Mexico, and Mongoloids from southeast Asia in the guise of "refugees." The obvious result will necessarily be a situation like that described in Jean Raspail's "chilling novel about the end of the white world," *The Camp of the Saints*, of which the English translation, published by Scribner's in 1975, had so large a sale that it is now out-of-print in both cloth-bound and paperback editions. (Guess why!).

what should be obvious even to schoolboys: the architects of the policy that imported the racial enemies and the loud-mouthed holy men and "humanitarians" who approved and endorsed that policy are either (a) conscious traitors, who intended the consequences of their acts, or (b) so feckless and feeble-minded that they must henceforth be excluded from influencing national policy in any way.

Traitors have imposed on the befuddled British a "Race Relations Act" to make certain that the white population, which is being dispossessed, does not openly resent the hordes of alien invaders. Englishmen are now in prison for having been so bold as to assert that their race is fit to live. And although the British, who are still a majority on what was once their island, are harassed by economic pressures and deafened by the clamor of their dervishes and the rest of the rabble of world-improvers, their bovine acceptance of their degradation makes one wonder whether the imprisoned men were not mistaken in the belief they expressed. Christians, of course, must be expected to obey the command of the Jew they worship: "Love *your* enemies and slaughter *mine*" (*Luke* 6.27 & 19.27). But Christians are a minority in Britain, estimated by competent observers at less than one-fifth of the white population. What of the other minority that should be dominant, the intellectually superior minority that has enjoyed the incomparable advantages of the British public schools and of Oxford or Cambridge? They evince no more comprehension of reality than the religious. The gods first make mad those whom they would destroy. And we can only behold with painful catharsis the tragedy of a nation which once had an empire on which the sun never set, and which, in Herculean madness, reduced itself to a mass of frightened sheep, huddled together on a small island on which the sun will someday set for the last time.

The "Race Relations Act," to be sure, has some loopholes, and Englishmen who hire competent solicitors expert in such matters can still make some appeal to facts and reason without going to gaol, although, of course, they expose themselves to surreptitious chastisement. The Jews, needless to say, are agitating for legislation to "plug the loopholes" in the existing tyranny.

As mere specimens of the English way of life today, we may note the following. The Jews burned the printing establishment in Uckfield, Sussex, that had been printing magazines and books that do not bear the Kosher seal of approval. One of the arsonists, caught by his own arrogant overconfidence, pled the privilege of his race to destroy their enemies, but found that arson, even with such noble motives, was still technically illegal in Britain, and he received, from an apologetic magistrate, the minimum sentence. He was found to be an old hand in Yahweh's service, having been identified as one of the burglars who, equipped with forged credentials as telephone repairmen, "cased" the apartment of David Irving, the author of *The Destruction of Dresden*, and were later caught red-handed in the burglary, equipped with tools from the British postoffices. The daily press in Britain suppressed mention of the deplorable arrest and trial of the high-minded arsonist.[75]

The masters of Britain naturally have their own corps of terrorists, special police, doubtless Englishmen willing to do anything for a small salary, paid by the bovine taxpayers. On 16 April 1981, these goons raided the apartment of an Anglo-Saxon in Brighton who, they said, was suspected of having in his possession a small booklet that did not show proper reverence for God's Race. Since he was at his place of employment, as they doubtless knew, they smashed open the door of his apartment and turned everything upside down, looking vainly for the horrible booklet. Frustrated in their suspicions, they departed with a large package that doubtless contained his expensive camera, the money he had left in a drawer of his desk, and other fenceable property, leaving the broken door open, so that they could claim that someone must have entered the apartment after them. At latest information,

---

75. The trial was concisely reported in the local *Sussex Express*, 17 April 1981. The newspaper, doubtless hoping to be thrown a bone, interpolated the remark: "To say the publications handed to the judge [to justify the arsonist's pious deed] were 'vile and evil' was a masterly understatement." The incident was also reported in the small weekly publication, *Focal Point* (London), 30 May, which *inter alia* observes that since the trial and sentencing took place hurriedly and without the knowledge of the victims of the arson, the purported specimens of their publications that were exhibited to the judge and newspaper may well have been forgeries. That would be only normal! My knowledge of the incident I next mention comes from a document prepared by the victim's solicitor and letters from friends.

the victim, just an Anglo-Saxon, to be sure, has vainly petitioned for redress.

Britain has indeed been blessed with righteousness. An Englishman's home was once his castle; now it is his kennel.

We must cross the Channel to *la belle France* for the most accurate measure of Europe today. In the historic land of *liberté*, Professor Robert Faurisson of the University of Lyons, maintaining the now antiquated tradition of intellectual integrity in academic circles, stated publicly that the Jews' infamous hoax about the "six million" was a preposterous hoax. [76] Squads of Jews attacked him on the campus and burst into his classrooms to make it impossible for him to conduct classes, while the authorities of the university beamed approval. He and his publishers and even newspapers that had printed his replies to their defamation of him were prosecuted in the French courts for "insulting" the Jewish nation by doubting one of the lies by which it most conspicuously exhibits its racial solidarity as a super-organism. He has been beset by multiple prosecutions in the French courts, and he has thus far been sentenced to a public recantation of his veracity and fines that will amount to one million francs in the new currency (one hundred million in the old). His total savings as a university professor with a family amount, he says, to about two thousand francs. And other prosecutions are still pending. The French system of justice doubtless hopes that it can drive the Aryan dog to suicide, but if that does not work, it will probably be wiser than the Inquisition that permitted Galileo to survive and will have Faurisson doused with gasoline and burned in a public square, while Jews dance merrily about the pyre.

It is a nice irony that Professor Faurisson's only support, so far as is known, comes from a Jew, who has disobeyed his race, and a few French "leftists." He would doubtless have been supported by Professor François Duprat, if the Jews, as they openly boast, had not preferred to punish that man for his

---

76. It is said that the Institute for Historical Review will publish English translations of Professor Faurisson's major articles in an issue of its *Journal*. Presumably it will do so unless the Jews, who have made one attempt to burn down the building in which the Institute is located, succeed in a new attempt.

denial of the Holy Hoax by blowing up the automobile in which he and his wife were riding. The "New Right" in France, of which we once entertained some hopes,[77] has been taught a lesson by the Jews, who broke into one of their conferences and clubbed them, permanently crippling one man, while the French police looked on benevolently. The few French champions of Western science and rationality now slip quietly away from their universities or homes to meet, almost furtively, in secluded parts of the countryside, fearing raids by the Jews or the French police; and they are doing their best to pretend they never heard of Professor Faurisson. It's embarrassing, but *courage, mon ami, le pauvre diable n'est pas encore mort, mais il le sera bientôt.*

It is easy to foresee the future. The simplest way out of the disconcerting fact that so many of the "six million" whom the Germans exterminated are alive and conspicuous in such capacities as that of the President of the "European Parliament" will be to claim that the Germans did indeed kill them, but they, being Yahweh's pets, naturally arose from the dead after three days or some other appropriate period of time.

The next step is easy. As Douglas Reed observed in *The Controversy of Zion*, to the Jews "the world is still flat and Judah, its inheritant, is the center of the universe."[78] Surely,

---

77. It even excited alarm in this country. The *National Educator,* a "conservative" periodical that espouses the kind of economics that would have made sense in 1954 and the kind of "education" that is to be based on ramming the Jews' creation-myth into the minds of schoolchildren, gave a page of its issue for May 1981 to a "guest editorial" under a screaming headline: "Europe's 'New Right' turns toward anti-Judaic, anti-Christian paganism," pointing out that the French *Nouvelle Droit* actually believed in scientific research and such wicked things. The editorial made it clear that in this more righteous nation the term 'New Right' must be reserved for the howling dervishes and other shysters who are working the "Moral Majority" racket. A subsequent issue of the journal advertised that ragged old hoax, the Holy Shroud of Turin.

78. See above, note 4. The passage I have quoted occurs on p. 105 and continues, "The ruling sect has been able, in great measure, to impose this theory of life on the great nations of the West, as it originally inflicted The Law on the Judahites themselves." Reed goes on to point out that Jews' mission in this world is based on the promise Yahweh made to Israël: "I will destroy all the people to whom thou shalt come." (*Exod.* 23.27). Reed's is, on the whole, an excellent book, marred only by some

there can be no greater insult to the Jewish nation than to doubt the word of its god, who made the world a flat cake of mud and placed above it the sun and moon, balls of fire floating in the upper atmosphere, so that he could stop them whenever he wanted to help his Holy People massacre the inhabitants of a country they wanted to steal. French courts of justice will surely repress the vile "racists" who cast doubt on Yahweh's words, and a few million-franc fines, supplemented by burning a few incorrigibly sane Frenchmen at the stake, will establish righteousness throughout the beautiful land *où l'oui résonne.*

And then one more step. Yahweh told Moses, "I have made thee a god to Pharaoh [i.e., the unnamed king of the Egyptian *goyim*]." Now it is only proper that the "Sons of the Living God" should be the gods of the lower races and be worshipped by them. It requires no great effort of the imagination to picture thousands of French men and women assembled in Notre Dame, in obedience to the orders of their courts and government, to worship bare-footed rabbis seated on the altars.[79] And the choir will sing the inspired words of the prophecy: "And Israël shall rule the world forever."

Fantastic? Less so than what has now actually happened in Germany, Britain, and France would have seemed before the Suicide of Europe.

Such is a hurried bird's-eye view of the continent that was, for Yockey, "the sacred soil of Europe," the homeland of our civilization. He was young when he was hounded to death, and

charitable efforts to temper the wind for Jesus's lambs. Incidentally, he makes the interesting suggestion (p. 207) that Herzl, the founder of modern Zionism (see note 51 *supra*), whom Samuel Roth described as "probably the first honest Jew in the public life of the world in two thousand years," may have been eliminated by Jews who wanted to take over and pervert his Zionist movement.

79. Ralph Perier in *Liberty Bell*, November 1980, p. 22, has called attention to the extraordinary emotional fixation of the Jews, as shown in passages he cites from both the "Old Testament" and the Dead Sea Scrolls, which demands not only that other races, and especially Aryans, shall become their abject slaves, but shall demonstrate their submission by using their tongues to lick the dirt from the Jews' bare feet. No other race, so far as I know, has ever shown that bizarre lust. Perier also quotes, "Israel shall rule the world forever," from Gaster's translation of the *Dead Sea Scriptures,* where it is the climax of an imagined war in which the Greeks and Romans (i.e., Aryans) are *totally* exterminated, but also survive to do the desired licking.

he did not live to see the Europe of today. Perhaps we should say of him, as Tacitus said of Agricola, *felix opportunitate mortis.*

THE EPITAPH

Yockey's hopes and his striving seem vain and futile in the desolation of today. He appealed to a manhood and an intelligence that had died on a thousand battlefields and have become bodiless wraiths, drifting on the shifting mists of time. But he will be remembered—if there are any to remember us—as a man who sought to resurrect Europe and, in the end, gave his life for the dead. His memory will be honored in the future—if we have a future—as that of a man whose lucid mind enabled him to see the vapidity of the verbiage about "world peace," "brotherhood," "human rights," and the rest of the hallucinatory fictions that are used by evangelists, politicians, and other swindlers to benumb the minds of their victims. He was a man who had the courage to state the grim truth that a nation's survival depends on its spiritual cohesion and its will to power—to naked, undisguised, unmitigated power, power over others.

A nation, a civilization, a race that has lost the will to conquer and dominate has lost its will to live—has lost the vitality that makes it fit to live in a world in which the inexorable laws of nature provide that only the strong and resolute shall survive. Yockey summoned our race to put down its opium-pipes and look outside its den of dreams to the real world, in which it will soon have no choice but to fight belatedly or perish ignominiously. It was not his fault that the drugged minds could not respond, could not comprehend.

After *Imperium* was republished by *The Truth Seeker* (New York) in 1962, Yockey's work, which had been almost completely suppressed and was known only to the few individuals who had the luck to find, and the means to purchase, copies of books that had become extremely rare, became more widely known and accessible to those who wished to know it. It inspired untrammeled minds.

In the late 1960s, some youthful enthusiasts formed the Francis Parker Yockey Society, and, since it was not kept

126

secret, they, few as they were, alarmed the boobherds of more than one local newspaper, ever on the watch for an outbreak of common sense. It was the young men's intention to erect a monument to Yockey, and, after much deliberation, they decided it should bear these words:

TO THE MEMORY OF
FRANCIS PARKER YOCKEY
AUTHOR OF *IMPERIUM*
WHO FOUGHT THE GOOD FIGHT TO THE BITTER END.
Ço sent Rodlanz que la mort l'entreprent, . . .
Sour l'erbe vert si s'est colchiez adenz,
Dessoz lui met s'espede e l'olifant.

The lines from the great *Chanson* may be translated thus:
And then, when Roland felt death coming upon him, he lay down on the green grass, placing his sword and his horn beneath his body, and with his face against the earth.

EPILOGUE, THE ERINYES

In 1945, in the devastated and desolate land of a nation of heroes, the American Army forced a German physician to save the life of a captive who had tried to commit suicide. The wretched man, who had surrendered in the mistaken belief that he was surrendering to civilized human beings, had contrived to find a piece of wire and twist it tightly about his throat in the hope of escaping the long, lingering, and exquisite tortures for which the self-righteous sadists reserved him.

The German physician grimly did what he was compelled to do, but he was a man. He looked the commanding officer in the eye and said calmly: "You Americans have done more than violate the law of nations. You have committed hybris. God will punish you, and if there is no god, Nature will."
Yes, Nature will.

To Americans who do not enjoy leading a precarious and degraded existence in the filth and stench of a multi-racial society, it will seem that Nature has already done so. But, in the vernacular phrase, they haven't seen anything yet.

When the syndicate of organized crime that governs the witless and spineless Americans began to tax the serfs for "aid" to "underdeveloped nations," rushing American food and medical skill to accelerate the savages' already prodigious rate of breeding, giving them American equipment and American engineers to industrialize their jungles, and naturally inciting them to rape and murder the Aryans caught in the newly independent "nations," the ineluctable consequences of that policy were obvious to every man who could perform simple arithmetical calculations.

I did no more than state a patent fact, long known to thoughtful observers, when, in an article published in 1963,[80] I wrote: "At the present rate, the globe, sometime between A.D. 2000 and 2005—that is to say, *within forty years*—will be infested by 5,000,000,000 anatomically human creatures, the maximum number for which food can be supplied by even the most intensive cultivation. And *then*, to keep the globe inhabitable at that bare subsistence level, it will be necessary to kill *every year* more people than now live in the United States—kill them with atomic bombs or clubs, as may be most convenient."

It will be less than twenty years now.

Meanwhile, the Americans, eager to show they have

---

80. *American Opinion*, December 1963, p. 23. The fact was obvious from the "exponential" increase in the world's population of non-Aryans and the geographic determination of the amount of arable land on the planet. But the ineluctable process of nature could have been, and was, foreseen long before the "population explosion" actually occurred. Sixty-seven years ago, before the First World War and while our race's absolute superiority and dominion over the planet seemed assured forever, the great and forgotten American philosopher, Correa Moylan Walsh, wrote in the first volume of his *Climax of Civilization:* "A return will set in of the re-active pressure of nature upon mankind. . . . The struggle for existence will again become sharp and bitter. . . . But woe to the people which has not men that will stand up and fight without flinching. Those countries where the moral decay shall have gone deepest, where the proved stock shall have died out and given way to poor stock, where the greatest effeminization of men shall have taken place (for the masculinization of women will be no compensation), where the strong and the wise and the shrewd shall gain no more of wealth, power, and influence than the weak, silly, and incompetent, all being equal,—those will go to the wall. And when this fate shall have overtaken most of our western white men's countries, our cycle of civilization will be completed."

elephant-sized hearts and canary-sized brains, are importing into their already overpopulated and befouled country hordes of racial enemies who quite frankly boast that they will take over for themselves entire states and groups of states, expelling or killing the stupid Aryans, for whose idiotic generosity they have a supreme and justified contempt. For the details, I must again refer you to James Farrell's *The Judas Syndrome*. [81]

And now the promoters of "aid" to "underdeveloped nations" have discovered what they knew all along, that they hastened a catastrophe from which the opium of superstition and maudlin sentimentality will provide no refuge. The Club of Rome, which had been busy fostering international "understanding" and international looting, hired experts from the Massachusetts Institute of Technology to report on "the predicament of mankind," and published the results in *The Limits to Growth* (London, 1972). What emerges from the report is a desperate hope that catastrophe can be postponed by de-industrializing the "emergent nations" and finding ways to kill off a large part of the prolific anthropoids, so that global starvation will not begin in 2000. There are many graphs to show the possible effects of miracles: if, for example, the yield of food by arable land were *doubled* by some inconceivable means, the starvation crisis could be postponed to 2024. The shock to tender minds is cushioned by speculations about the invention of "perfect" means of birth control, which will be made "available" to everyone—"available" being an euphemism for making the use of such means compulsory, which, being impossible, in turn means mandatory abortions, which are equally impossible of application to the most prolific races—and that makes nonsense of the bland assumption that all races are

---

81. See above, note 74. Since savages are constantly pouring into Florida *from* Haiti, I cannot forbear to notice a little-known historical fact. Abraham Lincoln, who was not a man without foresight and conscience, although he presided over the fratricidal war of aggression that ended the American Republic, actually began to put into practice his determination to export all Blacks from this country. On 31 December 1862, he approved contracts with *entrepeneurs,* chiefly from financial circles in New York City, to export 5000 Negroes *to* Haiti and resettle them there, at a cost to the government of fifty dollars a head. The contracts were carried out, but many of the Blacks wère subsequently brought back to this country by "do-gooders" eager to afflict the white population.

equal and are to be equally reduced. Talk about reducing the birth rate globally is mere verbiage: everyone who knows anything about the non-white races (except Jews) knows that the only practical means of control requires an enormous increase in the death-rate.

The Club of Rome's report also made projections that simply ignored the crucial question of food, and these showed that even if manna showered from the skies, essentially the same crisis and struggle for life would occur at approximately the same time from the exhaustion of the natural resources of our insanely exploited and ravaged earth, and also that if that factor be disregarded, the planet is being so polluted by its anthropoid parasites that, at no distant date, it will cease to sustain their life.

Some glimmering of reality penetrated even the fog in Washington and produced the Global 2000 report which, officially endorsed by the Secretary of State, calls for the elimination of two billion (2,000,000,000) human beings by the year 2000 to avert the otherwise inevitable chaos. The report is naturally evoking screams from the holy men, who like to orate about the day when Jesus will pop out of the clouds and raise Hell, but naturally cannot bear to think about reality, and from a wide variety of others, who find such ideas bad for their businesses.[82] There is much that can be criticized adversely in the report, but not the statistics, and it is the statistics that excite hysterical denials on the grounds that they are unpleasant. The gang in Washington is, of course, trying to use the report for its own purposes, but that is quite another matter.

One thing is quite certain: the population of the globe is going to be drastically reduced within the next twenty years as the struggle for life begins in earnest. Christians will, no doubt, go on bleating about "the sanctity of human life," especially the lowest forms of it, but they might as well expound that silly notion, which only our race has ever taken seriously,[83] to

82. A particularly odd yell of blind indignation is the booklet, *Global 2000*, published by the "National Democratic Policy Committee" = the "U.S. Labor Party" = the mysteriously financed operations of one Lyndon LaRouche. The booklet is well worth reading for its sophistries.

83. The even more absolute doctrine of the "sanctity of all life" appeared in the "Orthodox" religions of India and Buddhism while the

a typhoon or an erupting volcano. The forces of nature do not listen to idle talk. Neither do mammals who must kill or be killed—unless they are degenerate and have lost the will to live.

The population of the globe is going to be drastically reduced, and in the course of that reduction, it is virtually certain that the inferior races will become extinct, as Darwin foresaw, although not in the way he anticipated.[84] The only question is which races will not survive the inevitable war for survival.

Every species of mammal capable of conscious thought thinks of itself as in some way superior, but a claim to racial superiority is particularly congenial to our race, which for long had proof of it in the mastery of the whole world which it suicidally discarded. Aryans still pride themselves on the superiority of their civilization, and it is undoubtedly superior, aesthetically, morally, intellectually, i.e., in terms of its own values, so that 'superiority' is merely a tautology. We must face the brutal fact that the only real superiority is biological, and is shown by a species' ability to survive and increase at the expense of others.

The colored races naturally multiply as do rabbits. In the coming struggle for survival they may eat each other, if they run out of white meat, but they will breed so rapidly that they will survive, unless a superior power makes an intensive effort to exterminate them.

The Jews, whose racial cohesion has made them a super-organism, are undoubtedly a superior species. Beginning as a wretched gang of marauders, they, in only 2500 years, scattered throughout the world while retaining with undeviating concentration the super-organic unity of their purpose, and achieved virtual mastery of the globe. That you may disapprove of their

Aryans were still dominant. In polyphyletic India of today, individuals who humanely avoid injuring the lice they remove from their hair associate with individuals who are votaries of Kali and believe that the highest religious merit is obtained by treacherously murdering a man whose confidence they have cleverly won. Such is the charming diversity of a multi-racial society.

84. See above, note 3.

methods or their character is irrelevant. They have given proof of biological superiority. One wonders whether that superiority will enable them to consummate their total triumph or whether the super-organism is too inflexible, its instincts too fixed and rigid to cope with an entirely novel situation, so that the multiplex organism will perish in the chaos it has created, exulting, perhaps, in the total destruction in which it will also be destroyed.

So far as one can extrapolate from the present, disregarding our pathetic hopes for a psychological and biological miracle, there is one race which, by its own fatuity and degeneracy, seems likely to become extinct less than a century after it was master of the world.

APPENDIX I

A NOTE ON YOCKEY'S CAREER
By Thomas Francis

Francis Parker Yockey (*nom de guerre:* Ulick Varange) was born in Chicago on September 18th, 1917, of European-Spanish and Irish-American parentage. As a youth, he evinced the rare combination of fine reasoning power and bold imagination, and every characteristic of his genius (as that combination is usually called) is evident in his earliest writings, the treatise "On the Philosophy of Constitutional Law" (unpublished MS; 1938) and the article "The Tragedy of Youth" (*Social Justice*, August 21st, 1939). Yockey decided upon his politics early in life. "The fact is that my doctrine, whose principles are entirely superpersonal, is called 'Imperialism,' and that I arrived at its fundamentals in the year 1938, before I had ever visited Europe."

Yockey received his B.A. from the Georgetown University School of Foreign Service (1938) and his degree in law *cum laude* from the Notre Dame University School of Law (1941). Although, in the words of his wife, he was "opposed to the United States fighting Germany" and "felt that Communism was the big danger," Yockey enlisted in the U.S. Army shortly after Roosevelt & Co. provoked the Japanese attack on Pearl Harbor, and served in Army G-2 (intelligence), receiving an honourable discharge in 1943. He then was appointed Assistant Prosecuting Attorney for Wayne County, Michigan, and later worked in the Detroit bureau of the Office of Price Administration. When the War ended, Yockey accepted a position with the "American War Crimes Group" at Wiesbaden, Germany, as an opportunity of finding out whether there remained "any signs of life in the body of fallen Europe." His assigned task was to knit legalistic nooses for the Jews' cowardly lynchings of defeated European soldiers. "Had Yockey been willing to become an accomplice in those crimes," Dr Revilo P. Oliver once remarked, "he could probably have risen to membership in the Warren Gang. But instead of being a good 'Liberal,' he resigned."

Having researched the plight of conquered Europe first-hand, Yockey set down his conclusion that the West could rise again, if it willed, in IMPERIUM: *The Philosophy of History and Politics*, a two-volume work of nearly 700 pages (London: The

Westropa Press, 1948). Only 200 sets of IMPERIUM were printed, but they were read by some of the foremost thinkers and men of action in Europe; Dr Julius Evola, for one, wrote a laudatory review of the book for the first number of the Italian journal *Europa Nazione*. Since its republication in 1962, IMPERIUM has contributed mightily to the development of the "new," militant American Right, indeed, was its single greatest intellectual stimulus. Although based on the teachings of the historian Oswald Spengler and the political scientist Carl Schmitt, IMPERIUM is brilliantly original in its synthesis and application of them. Its treatment of "Culture-Health" and "Culture-Pathology," in particular, is full of concepts and insights that escaped Spengler but which are logically unavoidable extrapolations of his leading ideas. "Yockey's major conclusion," to quote Dr Oliver again, "is substantially that which emerges from every honest and discerning attempt to construct a philosophy of history, although it is sometimes stated less clearly and with more reservations. And that conclusion is the fundamental unity of the West today. As against the rest of the world, the West is a political unity, since the differences between Germany, Italy, France, Britain, and ourselves are, like the differences between Maine, Virginia, Wyoming, and California, relatively negligible—and *necessarily* negligible when the survival of the whole is at stake."

Joining the revived Union Movement of Sir Oswald Mosley, he tried to convince Mosley to adopt the policy he thought most favoured the survival of the West: political pan-Europeanism, a flexible neutralism, and an unyielding anti-Zionism. But Mosley, with four years in prison behind him and the memory of William Joyce fresh in his mind, was wary of this "young man of some ability" who was possessed of an indiscreet "obsession" with the Jewish Question. Of his relations with Mosley he later wrote: "I was interested in his possibilities because of his pre-war orientation as Hitler's voice on the Island. When I discovered that he was pro-Churchill and pro-American, and anti-Russian *à outrance*, even to the extent of mobilizing Europe to fight for American-Jewish victory over Russia, I left him." Marshalling the support of the politically most advanced and militant veterans of the Union Movement, Yockey founded, in 1949, the European Liberation Front, for which he composed a manifesto entitled "The Proclamation of London." Because of conflict of personalities and want of finances—the usual burdens of Rightist undertakings— the Front never got off the ground, though it survived as a "letter slot" organisation and continued publication of its newsletter *Frontfighter* until the mid 1950's.

By that time, continental Europe had become Yockey's principal field of action. From about 1951, he was associated with the group around the *Sozialistische Reichspartei*, a promising electoral-political effort founded in 1949 by Maj. Gen. Otto Ernst Remer, and served as their liaison to American sympathisers. Apparently for the instruction of the SRP leadership, Yockey tried to bring out a German translation of the third volume of IMPERIUM, which he had been unable to publish in London for lack of funds. Again, only 200 copies were printed, for "only the élite" were to receive the book. *Der Feind Europas*, as the book is called, was promptly suppressed by the *Bundesnachrichtendienst, Abteilung K-16*, i.e., the Red/Brown squad of the German precinct of the C.I.A. A few copies that were sent to America before the suppression and deposited in libraries there survive. *Der Feind Europas* is basically a statement of the "Weder Morgenthau noch Moskau!" thesis that was implicit in the programme of the SRP, an echo of which can be heard in pronouncements of the contemporary European Right, Left, and even Centre. Its main points are: (1) that Europe should unite to oppose Bolshevist Russia in its own political interest; (2) failing that, it should remain neutral in the coming war between Jewish-dominated America and barbarian Russia, perhaps favouring the latter for strictly political reasons, but also be prepared to assist America in exchange for its independence, unification, and autonomy. (Yockey, unfortunately, does not make it clear whether the precondition for a European-American alliance would be the overthrow of the Jewish-Banksters régime in America, but it is unlikely that régime would grant the concessions he demands, under any circumstances, so that precondition is implicit); (3) the continuance of American-Jewish domination is more deleterious to Europe than a Russian domination would be; (4) should Russia invade the West, Europeans could survive the Russian occupation and either wear down Russia in a war of attrition or conquer the conqueror "spiritually" and through infiltration of his seat of origin.

Because of his advocacy of this "Third Force" policy, Yockey was attacked by certain elements on the Right in Europe as "pro-Russian" and by the Establishment press in the United States as "anti-American." But as Willis Carto has noted, while "some of his later writing could have been misinterpreted as being pro-Russian, just as IMPERIUM indicates an anti-Russian attitude . . ., Yockey was neither pro- nor anti-Russian; he was concerned with the health and continuity of the West, and his view of the rest of the world was at all times subjective to what he considered the best interests of the

West *at that time.*"

Yockey and his associates were, of course, more interested in the European homeland than the American colony, but that is not to say they were anti-America in the sense our precious "minorities" are. Rather, it followed naturally from their political and historical views that the Liberation of Europe is a necessary precondition for the Liberation of America (though not *vice versa*). They simply did not, unlike many people on the American Right, underestimate the power of Jewry and the extent of the national disintegration it has caused in America nor overestimate the integrity of character of Americans.

Late in November 1952, Yockey went to Prague to observe the show-trials of Rudolf Slánský and ten other prominent Jewish Bolshevists who had been expelled on charges of treason from Russia's post-war puppet-régime in "Czechoslovakia." He believed that the Prague trials signified a "Russian break with Jewry which is becoming deeper and more complete every day" and that "this development, arising as it did from the absolute identity of American and Jewish policy, is favourable to our fight for the liberation of Europe from its outer enemies, America-Jewry and Russia." The U.S. State Department used the trip to "Czechoslovakia" as a pretext for revoking Yockey's passport. But that did not stop him from travelling.

Little definite can be said about his subsequent transcontinental peregrinations, but one may be sure they were far from aimless. A revolutionary in search of a revolution, Yockey was more than once on the scene when a *coup d'état* occurred, and some of the leading political figures of our time granted him interviews. For a while, he collaborated with Anwar El-Sadat in the Information Ministry of Egypt, where he was engaged in recruiting European refugees who, "when the time is right," were to return home and "participate directly in politics." While Yockey considered Gamal Abdul Nasser "a great and vigorous man," Egypt proved a disappointment: "The climate here is so torrid that it takes everything out of a man. There are 20,000 Germans here, and they're all slowly growing oblivious. They are all going black. If I stay here, I will, too—I'm rather sensitive— ; I hate the sun, always have." Now and then, he would return to the United States to visit family and friends. During one such interlude, he may have toyed with the notion of becoming active in American politics, though, as his sometime associate H. Keith Thompson put it, "he had grown to detest the American Right and its mentality."

All this time, Yockey was pursued by a network of foreign

and domestic gumshoes, official and unofficial, and may have been in danger of assassination. His life became a succession of aliases, disguises, hideouts, hasty departures, and all the desperate resorts of a fugitive. The persecution was rendered more distressing by Yockey's belief that he was a man whose "writings and actions are valued only by his enemies."

The manhunt ended on June 6th, 1960, when the F.B.I. arrested Yockey in Oakland, California, after a suitcase of his that had gone astray was opened at the airport and found to contain three doctored passports. As if by the throwing of a main switch, the machinery of injustice began to roll. The Yellow Press, supplied with sinisterly vague leaks by "government spokesmen" and nasty fantasies by "Jewish leaders," painted a lurid picture of the "Passport Mystery Man" as a traitor, a lunatic, or both, implying that to such a desperado the simple protection of law accorded thieves and murderers did not apply, and no matter how unfair the treatment, he somehow deserved it. In a blatant violation of Article VIII of the Bill of Rights, Rabbi Joseph Karesh, the U.S. Commissioner, set Yockey's bail at $50,000—at least ten times the usual surety for one accused of passport fraud. Unable to raise that sum, Yockey was detained in the malodorous San Francisco lock-up, where, of course, he was given "special treatment." "When I visited him in jail," Yockey's sister told an interviewer at the time, "I couldn't see him through the mesh screens that separated us, but the first thing he told me was 'My constitutional rights have been violated eight times to date.' That was like him—not viewing himself personally, but looking at the broader picture." To top all this, Yockey had for his "defence counsel" a person who frankly admitted: "I'm a patent lawyer without any experience in this matter at all," and he inexplicably gave his "enthusiastic support" to a judicial order that Yockey submit to a "mental examination," indeed, "consistently sought a mental test for his client ever since he was arrested." Although Yockey conducted himself with extraordinary presence of mind throughout his ordeal, despite the physical and psychological torments to which he was subjected, and there could be no doubt of his sanity, some observers of the events in San Francisco believe that our enemies might have succeeded in railroading him to one of the Washington régime's psycho-political prisons, where his brains could be chemically picked and surgically scrambled, perhaps with the menticidal techniques developed by the C.I.A. under the codename "MKULTRA," and that would be the end of Yockey—the man, the myth, the menace to America's alien overlords. Yockey was fully aware of the grisly fate planned for him. "They want to make me into an animal," he told another prisoner. On the morning of June 17th, he was found dead in his cell, killed by a minute dose of potassium cyanide.

APPENDIX II

WHAT IS BEHIND THE
HANGING OF THE ELEVEN JEWS IN PRAGUE?
By Francis Parker Yockey
From a mimeographed bulletin
issued anonymously in December, 1952

On Friday, November 27, there burst upon the world an event which, though small in itself, will have gigantic repercussions in the happenings to come. It will have these repercussions because it will force a political reorientation in the minds of the European elite.

That event was the conclusion of the treason trial of the Jews in Prague, and their condemnation to death. During the years 1945 and 1946 the coalition Jewry-Washington-Moscow functioned quite perfectly and frictionlessly. When the Israel "State" was established as the result of armed Jewish aggression, the entire world, dominated by Moscow and Washington, sang hymns of praise and congratulation. Washington recognized the new "State" *de facto* within a few hours of its proclaimed existence. Moscow outbid Washington in pro-Jewishness by giving *de jure* recognition. Both Washington and Moscow vied with one another in seeking to please the Israel operetta-state and aided it by all means moral and material. Russian diplomats boasted that at last, in Haifa, they had a warm-water port.

And now, after a few short years, Israel is recalling its "ambassadors" from Russian vassal-states, and intensifying its anti-Russian policy from its American citadel. Volatile Jews in Israel and America cry out that Stalin is following in the footsteps of Hitler. The entire American press boils with fury at anti-Semitism in Russia. Anti-Semitism, warns the *New York Times*, is the one thing America will not tolerate in the world.

Why this bouleversement?
It began early in 1947 with the Russian refusal to surrender a part of its sovereignty to the so-called "United Nations" for purposes of "control" of the atomic weapon industry. Jewish statesmen, being materialistic in their metaphysics, believe strongly in the "absolute" military power of atomic weapons, and considered it thus indispensable for the success of their policy that they control these weapons unconditionally. This control they already possessed in America through the Atomic

139

Energy Commission, specially created and constituted so that it is beyond the reach of Congress, and responsible only to the President, who is, by the practical rules of American inner-politics, an appointee of the Culture-State-Nation-People-Race of the Jew. They sought the same degree of control of atomic weapons in Russia, and used the device of the "United Nations" to submit an ultimatum to the Russian leadership on this question.

This was in the latter part of 1946, when the tide of atom-worship was at its height, and the minds of nearly all of the poor crop of statesmen who today conduct the political affairs of the world were fantastically dominated by a mere explosive bomb. A similar mania reigned for a short time after the invention of dynamite, after the invention of the machine-gun. The Russian régime also believed in atoms with the same religious faith, and thus regarded the abdication of its "atomic" sovereignty as equivalent to the abdication of its entire sovereignty. Thus the Jewish-American ultimatum in late 1946 was rejected, and in early 1947 the preparation for the Third World War began.

This Russian refusal stymied the plans of the Jewish leadership, which aimed at a surrender of both Russian and American sovereignty to the "United Nations," an instrumentality dominated by the Jewish Culture-State-Nation-People-Race. Even supine, politically-unconscious America could hardly be expected to give up its sovereignty when the only other world-power unconditionally refused, and the entire policy had to be scrapped.

The next policy of the Jewish leadership was to persuade the Stalin régime by the encirclement and pressure of the "Cold War" that it was hopeless to resist. The same tactic was used against the régime of Adolf Hitler from 1933 until 1936, when war was decided upon at the earliest feasible moment.

Because of the Russian rejection of the atomic weapon ultimatum, Russia now found its policy opposed everywhere, in Austria, in Germany, in Korea, in Finland. Those same American publicists who had become so deft at explaining Russia's need for "security" as Russia seized one landscape after another, suddenly turned against Russia the accusation of "aggressor." The faithful Russian servants in the West, like Truman, Acheson, Churchill, Attlee, de Gaulle and the rest, became suddenly—almost—anti-Russian. Naturally they did not use the same sort of language against Russia, the peace-loving democratic people of yesterday, that they had used against Germany, and —naturally again— they did not yet use the language of "Unconditional Surrender" when it came to a military test, in Korea. Although they had eagerly sought Russian aid against Germany, they did not now seek German aid against Russia. That would be going too far, and it is one of the political weaknesses of the Jew that he is the victim of *idées fixes*. The leading obsession of the Jew is his unreasoning hatred of Germany, which, at this present stage of Europe's cultural evolution means: unreasoning hatred of Europe.

For several years there have been grumblings and undertones in the American press against "anti-Semitism" in Russia. These dark mutterings began after the Russian rejection in late 1946 of the Jewish-American ultimatum on the atomic weapon question. It was then that the Stalin régime began its inner-policy of dropping its numerous Jews from the highest positions, then working on down to the lower positions. Elastically, the Stalin régime tried all approaches to the Jewish leadership: it offered aid to Israel; it withdrew the offer and shut off emigration to Israel; it tried every policy, but still the Jewish-American encirclement policy continued. Wooing the Arabs did not change the mood of the Jewish-American leadership, nor did spurning the Arabs. The press campaign against Russia continued in America and all its European vassal-states. "Russia is anti-Semitic"—thus thundered the American press, and, as political initiates know, this is the worst epithet in the American arsenal of political invective. As Eisenhower said, when accused by Truman of being an anti-Semite: "How low can you get? "

* * * * *

The treason trials in Bohemia are neither the beginning nor the end of an historical process, they are merely an *unmistakable* turning point. Henceforth, all must *perforce* reorient their policy in view of the undeniable reshaping of the world-situation. The ostrich-policy is suicide. The talk of "defense against Bolshevism" belongs now to yesterday, as does the nonsense of talking of "the defense of Europe" at a period when every inch of European soil is dominated by the deadly enemies of Europe, those who seek its political-cultural-historical extinction at all costs.

That same barbaric despotism called the Russian empire and presided over by the fat peasant Stalin-Djugashvili, who rules by his cunning a Khanate greater than all those gathered together by the mighty Genghis, is today the only obstacle to the domination of the entire earth by the instrumentality called "United Nations." This vast Russian empire was created by the Jewish-American hatred of Europe-Germany. During the Second World War, in order to prevent Stalin and his pan-Slav nationalist-religious entourage from concluding peace with Europe-Germany, the Jewish-American leadership gave Russian military equipment in unheard-of masses, and political promises, gifts and advantages with unheard-of largesse. With the 14,795 airplanes; 375,883 trucks; and 7,056 tanks given it by America, Russia occupied all Eastern Europe for itself, and advanced into Magdeburg, Weimar and Vienna. The American Secretary of State Marshall acted consciously and openly as a Russian agent in undermining the Chiang régime in China and delivering quietly to Russian vassaldom a quarter of the world's population. It was only later that this conduct of Marshall's seemed reprehensible; at the time, he was regarded as a distinguished diplomat, like Churchill and Roosevelt at Teheran, and was decorated for his service to Russia.

Gradually the picture changed, there was more talk of "anti-Semitism" in Russia, and American public opinion, in prompt and unconditional obedience to the American press, switched over from being anti-German and pro-Russian to being anti-German and anti-Russian.

The epoch marked by the trials in Prague is not absolute; Russian papers still explain that the Jews condemned to death for sacrificing the interests of Bohemia to the interests of Jewry were "enemies of the Jewish people." The American Jewish Committee takes the same line, so that people elsewhere in the world, in places like America and its English appanage, will not develop the idea that it would even be possible for a Jew holding office in a host-country to behave like a Jew, and not like a loyal member of the host-country. The American Jewish Committee, however, gives no explanation whatever, not even in mere words, of what possible reason Russia would have for charging loyal Russian subjects with sacrificing Russian interests to Israel interests. They give us no clue. Apparently they would have the world believe that the canny peasant régime of Stalin is embarking on entirely unmotivated adventures in the same realm of world-politics which destroyed the political power of National Socialist Europe; the power of the Jewish Culture-State-Nation-People-Race.

The question of "guilt" or "innocence" in these, or any other political trials, like the stinking horror of Nürnberg, is historically meaningless. The Jewish victims in Prague, like the Rosenbergs in America, merely did not understand how late it was in the development of the "cold war." The fashion of yesterday, of being pro-Russian in word and act, has changed. The Rosenbergs were not *au courant*. The Jewish officials in Prague also were living in yesterday and felt far more secure than they were. In 1952 they behaved as though they were in 1945.

Anyone who knows the simple meaning of the word "politics" knows that these trials were not spontaneous outbreaks of "race prejudice" on the part of politically wide-awake Stalin and his power-hungry entourage. These men want *power* and they will not attack on a front where, in the event of victory, no power could possibly be gained. For 35 years, Stalin has been pro-Jewish in his inner- and outer-policy, and if he now changes, it is for well-considered reasons of state-necessity.

The same Jewish press which says Stalin is "anti-Semitic" says that his Jewish victims are "enemies of the Jews." If they really believed this of his victims, the trials show that Stalin is pro-Jewish, not that he is anti-Jewish.

However, nothing is easier than to catch the Jewish leaders in contradictions during these times when they are frantically realizing that perhaps their atomic ultimatim, their "United Nations" front against Russia, their "cold war" encirclement of Russia and their Korean war were gigantic blunders.

Up to now, their objective within Russia has been to replace the Stalin régime, which the Jews consider as a traitor to the fundamental principle of Bolshevism, by a new Trotsky. Just as they constantly hoped for an internal revolution in Germany, so they have hoped for a revolution against Stalin, a revolution to return to Trotskyism and the fundamental principle of *international* Bolshevism, a revolution which would embrace the "United Nations" and bring about a Jewish millenium, the reunion of Baruch and Kaganovich, of Lippman and Ehrenburg, of Buttenwieser and Eisner, of Ana Pauker and Ana Rosenberg. But now, this hope has vanished. There is no way of bringing about the millenium by peaceful means, through coercion of Russia by "cold wars" and "United Nations."

It is possible now to record the developments which have been rendered *inevitable* by the clear break signified by the Prague trials.

First, the most important of all to those of us who believe in the Liberation of Europe and the Imperium of Europe: this is the beginning of the end of the American hegemony of Europe. The shoddy structure of Morgenthau Plan and Marshall Plan, of Schuman Plan and Strassburg Plan, of the American flag flying over European capitals, of NATO, of the systematic subjugation and spoilation of Germany, of the Satanic project of constructing a German Army to fight Russia on behalf of the occupying Jewish-American enemy, an Army without a General Staff, officered by democrats and armed with the weapons of 1870, the whole prolonged democratic holiday of churchills, gaulles, spaaks, gasperis, adenauers and schumanns. For Europe, the Prague trials will act as an historical cathartic to flush out the historical waste-matter of churchills and their liberal-democratic-communist dirt.

The American hegemony is doomed because all Europe realizes with a start—what *Imperium, The Proclamation of London,* and the *Frontfighter* have preached for years—that the power on whose behalf Europe is asked to fight "Bolshevism" is none other than the Jewish State-Nation-People-Race, that entity which itself is the historical creator and leader of political Bolshevism.

It is obvious that events which were strong enough to force Stalin to reorient his entire world-policy and to become openly anti-Jewish will have the same effect on the elite of Europe. For the American hegemony to endure, it is necessary that the European elite be quite passive—it is, of course, quite impossible that the European elite would ever actively cooperate with primitive human material like McCloy, Truman, Acheson or Eisenhower—and the Prague trials have gone off with an explosive roar to waken this elite to active resistance against the death plans being hatched for the European organism in Washington by the Jewish-American leadership.

America cannot undo the Prague trials any more than Russia can. From these trials there is now no going back. They are a war-declaration by Russia on the Jewish-American leadership, no matter whether or not the Russian press still wraps its explanations in wooly words disclaiming "anti-Semitism." What matters, in politics above all, is not what one *says,* but what one *does.* The fact is: the Russian leadership is killing Jews for treason to Russia, for services to the Jewish entity. Nothing can gainsay, or reverse this fact. The European elite will *perforce* note this fact and be governed accordingly. Russia has publicly before the world named its power-enemy, and has thus removed all controversy on the question of who is the real power-beneficiary of the American hegemony of Europe.

In the dark days of 1945, many Europeans embraced the American occupation as the lesser of two evils. During the past 7 years the comparative destructiveness of Russian barbarism and American-Jewish Bolshevism has appeared in its true proportions, the proportions set forth in *Imperium*, Volume II: a Russian occupation would be far less dangerous to Europe because of the abysmal cultural gulf between the Russian and the West. This gulf would render impossible the erection of a vassal-state system, because there are no religious pan-Slavs in Europe, and the Russian barbarian leadership trusts no one else. The notion—fostered by wild American propaganda—that Russia could kill off the 250,000,000 people of Europe need not be taken seriously. It is a vile insult to European spiritual resources and masculinity, as well as being an historical nightmare and originated no doubt in the brain of some American writer of science-fantasy stories.

For political purposes, and increasingly for total cultural purposes, America is dominated absolutely by the Culture-State-Nation-People-Race of the Jew. America in Europe appeals to all the forces of Culture-Retardation and reaction, the forces of laziness and degeneracy, of inferiority and bad instincts. From the spiritual sewers of Europe, America can siphon up an endless number of churchills to do its dirty work of dividing, despoiling and destroying Europe in a suicidal war.

Henceforth, the European elite can emerge more and more into affairs, and will force the Jewish-American leadership to render back, step by step, the custody of European Destiny to Europe, its best forces, its natural, organic leadership. If the Jewish-American leaders refuse, the new leaders of Europe will threaten them with the Russian bogey. By thus playing off Russia against the Jewish-American leadership, Europe can bring about its Liberation, possibly even before the Third World War.

* * * * *

A second inevitable development from the turning-point of the Prague trials is the intensification of the American diplomatic offensive against Russia, the "cold war." The press campaign will intensify in America and in Europe; Russia will become morally blacker and blacker; the American armament will be accelerated; all potential Soviet agents will be liquidated by the "United Nations." Russia will naturally retaliate: today *Pravda* says "Zionism is a tool of American imperialism." Tomorrow it will say: "American imperialism is the tool of Zionism."

A third inevitable development: the collapse of the American-Jewish position in the Near East and throughout Islam. Since Russia will be unable to retreat from its anti-Jewish policy and the Jewish State-Nation-People-Race from its anti-Russian policy, since for each one there is no other power-occupant in the world, Russia will *perforce* ally itself with Islam, and Islam will *perforce* ally itself with Russia. Dark clouds of tragedy are gathering over the operetta-State of Israel, with its 1,000,000 population surrounded by a sea of 300,000,000 Mohamedans in whose face it has just spat, emboldened by the brawn of its big American lackey. The lackey is still big, still stupid, still willing—but he is 5,000 miles away, and the concern will grow graver in Israel, and in secret places there, evacuation plans are being re-examined . . . . .

A fourth inevitable development is the weakening of the American position in Japan, and within a few years it is quite possible we will see the final expulsion of the American occupation troops from Japan. Even today these troops are ordered to wear mufti on the Japanese streets, and it is unavoidable that the coming intensification of Russian policy against the Jewish-American régime of Washington will automatically heighten the nationalist activity of the politically-conscious Japanese elite.

Many other developments *must* follow, developments which no head in the Kremlin is now contemplating. Some are regular, and foreseeable, others are Imponderables and cannot even be imagined: one thing is sure—whoever declares war on the Jew will soon be engaged in a fight of world-wide dimensions and increasing viciousness, for the power of the Jewish State-Nation-People-Race is widespread, and the leadership of this State-Nation-People-Race conducts its policy with its emotions rather than intellectually, subject as it is to obsessions and *idées fixes.*

To us in Europe, the trials are welcome; they clear the air. The opponents have now defined themselves. America recedes now to its proper position, that of the armorer and the technician, the world's assembly line, the supplier of biological units called G.I.'s to whoever is situated to pull the appropriate strings—in the First World War, it was England, in the Second it was Jewry.

146

As far as Europe is concerned, the Jewish leaders may as well pull down the Stars and Stripes and run up the Star of David.

It was fatuous enough to ask Europe to fight for America, it was silly enough to ask it to "defend itself against Bolshevism" —under the leadership of Frankfurter, Lehmann, and Morgenthau!—but now it is too absurd to ask Europe to fight to wipe out "anti-Semitism" in Russia. Is there *one* European—just *one*—who would respond to this war-aim? But today, openly, without any possible disguise, this is the *raison d'être* of the coalition against Russia, for Russia has named its chief enemy, its sole enemy, and the sly peasant leadership of pan-Slavs in the Kremlin is not given to frivolity in its foreign policy.

The trials have made easier the task of the European Liberation Front. This Front was the first organ to warn Europe of the extinction in slavery, promised for it by an alliance, supposedly with America, but actually the Culture-State-Nation-People-Race of the Jew.

We repeat our message to Europe: no European must ever fight except for sovereign Europe; no European must ever fight one enemy of Europe on behalf of another enemy.

Europe has one aim: to actualize its Destiny. This means, to reconquer its sovereignty, to reassert its mission, to establish its Imperium, to give to the world an era of order and European peace. In the actualization of this mighty, irresistible Destiny, all extraneous events are mere material to be utilized. Inwardly, therefore, the words of the *Proclamation of London* are as true today as they were in 1948, as they will be in 1960: "No, Europe is no more interested in this projected war than in a struggle between to negro tribes in the Sudan."

CPSIA information can be obtained at www.ICGtesting.com
Printed in the USA
BVOW01s1428300816

460628BV00001B/5/P